ENTER AND DIE!

Tu Dia Tu Dia Tu Dia

ENTER AND DIE!

James W. Milliken

James W. Milliken

" *Melkman* "

To order additional copies of this book, contact:
Xlibris Corporation
1-888-795-4274
www.Xlibris.com
Orders@Xlibris.com
59532

CONTENTS

DEDICATION

This book is dedicated to the members of the Third Platoon, Delta Company, Second Battalion, Sixtieth Infantry Regiment of the Ninth Infantry Division. The Third Platoon epitomizes the outstanding army units that served their country with honor. The men distinguished themselves in battle, especially during a time when the platoon experienced combat for more than sixty consecutive days. Despite enduring many hardships and continual stress, the men performed their duties extremely well, gaining a reputation as one of the best platoons in the battalion.

We bonded as a platoon and were proud of our accomplishments, devotion to duty, and willingness to make the supreme sacrifice to save another man's life. When we returned home, each of us had to forget our life-changing experiences in order to blend into a divided nation. We were not honored for service to our country and accomplishments but were scorned for being veterans who were labeled as misfits and baby killers.

I wrote this book thirty-eight years after serving in Vietnam to give recognition to the men of the Third Platoon and Delta Company, whom I have admired with an enduring brotherly love. Today I proudly boast about the Third Platoon as *brothers forever*. God bless those men in this book that made the supreme sacrifice in Vietnam and those brothers who have since departed our ranks.

ACKNOWLEDGMENTS

Many years after my tour in Vietnam, I have realized a dream of writing about my life with the Third Platoon. Most of the men were recent high school and college graduates who took on responsibilities and performed feats that they could never imagine doing. The hardships were many, courage a daily necessity, and unselfishness for one's life shown often. I had to write this book because of the pride, respect, and love I have for each member of the Third Platoon. These men helped shape my life forever by giving me values and skills to deal with continual changes through life.

First, I must thank my wife, Linda, for encouraging me to write the book. She was my editor and has done an excellent job correcting my grammar and sentence structure, while maintaining a meaningful flow in the book without changing my thought process. Thank you, Linda, for always supporting me as a Vietnam veteran, especially when it was not popular. I love you very much!

The detail and chronology of events are extracted from seventy-five letters I wrote to my parents, William and Violet Milliken, and my best friend, James Giancola. These letters kept my memory fresh about major events and the time period in which they occurred. All the events are true, but the time frame is uncertain for some minor events. The book was written from my perspective as accurately as possible. It is intended to be a historical document of the time. This is my story of the Third Platoon as I experienced as a combat soldier. Each man in the Third Platoon could write a similar book from his point of view of how the war affected him. It would be impossible for one soldier to write about everything that happened in conflict.

The following members of the Third Platoon were helpful in providing detail of events that involved them: Peter Wood, Ralph Senical, Thomas Gabig, John Sassian, Bruce Falkum, Larry Boneck, and Don Sarault.

The cover of the book with the *Tu Dia* sign was a photograph given to me by Dwight Whitlatch, a member of the Third Platoon. I received the combat photographs as a gift from Larry Sandage, who made the Third Platoon one of the most publicized units in Vietnam through his photography. During my Instamatic camera breaks, I took the other photographs. I cherish these pictures because they capture the moment and keep them alive in my memory.

Thank you to William Cass, author of *The Last Flight of Liberator 41-1133,* and my niece Jennifer Davis, an award-winning Pennsylvania Newspaper Publishers' Association writer. Their reviewing skills and suggestions made *Enter and Die!* a better book.

My final acknowledgement is of James Longnecker, who was my cross-country coach at Grove City College. Jim was the best coach and teacher I ever had and was an outstanding role model who inspired me to be a better athlete and person. I always have felt I am not an amputee because of the training methods he used to develop my strong legs that sustained such an injury.

So much negativity has been printed about Vietnam veterans portraying the soldiers as losers in society unable to adjust to the civilian environment. The Third Platoon sacrificed during the Vietnam War by postponing careers, suffering financially, and putting relationships on hold to serve their country. When others ridiculed them, they honored the right to protest. The Third Platoon adapted to society; and its members successfully entered new occupations, married, and raised families. I hope this book will shed light on the sacrifices and hardships endured by the Vietnam veterans and thus change perceptions of them.

1

May 12, 1969

"Saddle up, Third Platoon!" came the command from Staff Sergeant Gary Abrams. The men of the Third Platoon put on their gear and check their weapons before heading out to the main road in front of Camp Scott, to board Huey slicks for daily operations in the field. This is normal routine for the Third Platoon, preparing for insertion into enemy territory. I walk on the road to the choppers and hear someone call out my nickname, "Hey, Milkman!" I recognize the voice immediately. The person shouting is Clyde Poland, who christened me with the nickname. Clyde is eighteen years old, has a rugged-looking face, and is missing his front teeth, which makes him appear much older than his teenage years. He was raised in Round Pond, Maine, and has a distinctive New England accent. I believe he gave me that nickname because of his inability to pronounce my last name, Milliken. In Vietnam, GIs are usually addressed by a nickname or last name, rather than their given first name.

Clyde asks me if I heard anything about today's mission. I reply, "No, nothing really important." Pete Wood, our platoon leader, whom we refer to as Delta 3-6, told us that two platoons of the company are going to act as a support element to any friendly forces that might require our help. Pete said the platoons will catch some "blade time" in the morning while we wait for a radio response from friendly forces that need our assistance. If our support backup unit doesn't receive an emergency assistance call within an hour, the two airborne platoons of Delta Company will change their mission to search-and-destroy insertions.

Clyde grins with a toothless smile and says, "Milkman, that's my favorite thing to do in the field, just fly in the choppers and enjoy the scenery below." I agree with him and just hope the day will turn out to be a pleasant one. Unfortunately, it seems every time we go out to the field, our platoon is in a combat situation. To date, according to my records, our Delta Company has incurred sixty-seven casualties since December 1, 1968. The casualties include twelve men killed in action, plus fifty-five men wounded, mostly by booby traps. Delta Company consists of three platoons, and it is my luck that I serve in the Third Platoon, which has sustained fewer casualties than the First and Second platoons.

Clyde and I part each other's company, and get on different choppers because of our assignments in the platoon. I board the last Huey for our platoon because I was recently assigned the position of squad leader in charge of rear security for the platoon. I notice that the Second Platoon will accompany us on our mission for the day. We have eight Hueys loaded with troops and have an escort of two Cobra helicopters. To most people, this would be an impressive sight, but to the troops of Delta Company, this is how we are transported to do our job.

The choppers fly to our objective for the day. Once we arrive at the assigned area, we fly over the countryside, awaiting a distress call. Clyde is right. The checkered pattern of the rice paddies below between the woodlines and waterways are a breathtaking natural spectacle. I sit on the floor of the Huey with my feet dangling outside the chopper and enjoy the gentle, refreshing breeze rushing by. My mind has blocked out the distinctive sound of the helicopter rotors at work and the pilot's conversation over the radio. I imagine I'm in heaven in a suspended state of euphoria, enjoying a moment of total relaxation and calm.

Quickly I come back to the reality of war when an emergency call comes over the radio. The transmission is garbled and difficult to understand, but it's apparent from the sender that a group of soldiers are in danger of being overrun. Terry Terhune, a rifleman in the Third Platoon, is close to the radio and clearly overhears the message. Terry says, "A squad of men from Alpha Company has been hit by a large force of North Vietnamese Army soldiers. The squad leader says his men are completely surrounded by an enemy force and already have three wounded men." The squad leader is told to hold the position, and the rescue force will be there within ten minutes.

Everyone in the chopper tries to listen to the frantic messages that are sent. The guys talk in a feverish pitch, psyching themselves for the rescue and the imminent confrontation with the NVA. Adrenaline pumps throughout my body. It feels like shocks of electricity bouncing off the insides of my chest. My body and mind are hyped to the highest state of readiness that I can attain. In the last six months I have developed a tremendous capacity to handle stress. I can adjust from a completely relaxed state to a heightened, stressed state within seconds during the excitement and intensity created by combat and fear of death. It takes many months of training and combat experience to achieve this response. I believe it will take even more time to readjust to an everyday environment back in the States. Because of my high tolerance for stress, my system craves a certain amount of danger and fear to get through the day.

The choppers approach the insertion point. The Hueys are in a line formation. The Cobra gunships follow on both sides of the formation. As we approach the rice paddies to land, the Cobra assault helicopters begin strafing and rocketing the enemy positions to provide protection for our landing. The Huey machine gunners open up on enemy woodline positions. Usually soldiers aren't permitted to fire out of the transporting helicopters, but this situation is an exception because there is a large enemy force on the ground. The landing zone is extremely hot and enemy soldiers run everywhere. I begin to fire at some NVA soldiers who run parallel to the paddy dike system the choppers are approaching for landing. There is little chance of my hitting them because of the speed, altitude, and angle of flight on our descent. The goal is to obtain firepower over the enemy for a safe insertion.

The squad pops yellow smoke in order for us to locate their position. The pilots spot the identifying smoke and deploy troops without actually landing on the ground. This is a tactic used on hot LZs to protect the helicopters and the troops. The Hueys fly into the landing zone and hover several feet off the ground for a few seconds, which allows us to exit so they can depart immediately from the landing zone.

Our leaders begin to assemble the men to fight and defend positions. Lieutenant Wood gives orders to me and two other men to approach the ambushed squad's location and provide cover for their safe exit. Sergeant Larry Field, Terry Terhune, and I begin to low crawl beside a paddy dike in the direction of the men. As we low crawl in the mud and water toward the squad, we keep our bodies next to the paddy dike because there is intense enemy fire on our position. We hear the bullets whistling a few inches over our heads. An inch in combat can mean the difference between experiencing life's many opportunities and being denied what many people take for granted. I find it amazing how the mind reacts to conflict when you think about your future knowing death could be only a moment away. We low crawl for approximately seventy-five feet before we meet the men, who are low crawling in our direction and using the same dike system for protection.

The men look completely exhausted from their escape and evasion tactics needed to survive the ambush. Field, Terhune, and I open up fire on the enemy positions in order to provide cover for the squad's safe return to our lines. Three of the men are wounded. They strip down to only necessary gear because the men are suffering from extreme heat fatigue. The temperature is over one hundred degrees, and I begin to feel sick from low crawling and firing at the enemy. My M16 is scorching hot from the many magazines of ammunition I expended. The three of us wait until the squad is near our lines before we begin our hasty low-crawl retreat. I trail the other two because I carry an M60 machine gun, which the squad's gunner gave me. The gunner is too exhausted to carry the twenty-pound weapon. While low crawling with the machine gun, I quickly understand how fatigued he must have been. When we return to our platoon's defensive position, Field, Terhune, and I strip off our gear and camouflage shirts and lie in paddy water to revive ourselves. We suffer from heat exhaustion, so we relax in the water and cool down our bodies while the fighting continues. I get out my Instamatic camera and shoot a few pictures of the MEDEVAC helicopter picking up the wounded. Then I take some pictures of Field and Terhune cooling off in the water. Finally, I take shots of jets on bombing runs. Fighting is going on all around me, and as in many other similar situations, I took an Instamatic break to shoot a few pictures. I begin to feel better and recover, so I stow the camera inside my helmet to protect it from the elements.

Alpha Company soldiers leave the battlefield after being
rescued by Delta Company Troops.

Dustoff helicopter picks up wounded from Alpha Company,
2nd/60th, Ninth Infantry Division.

Terry Terhune recovers from heat exhaustion.

Lieutenant Wood comes over to my position and says, "Milkman, did you bring your binoculars?" I tell him I left them in base camp. Pete replies, "Damn it! We could really use them." Pete immediately turns around and goes back to the command position. Pete is right; this is a perfect situation for using binoculars. The enemy flees into the rice paddies to get away from the bombing runs, and if Pete had binoculars, command would be able to pinpoint targets for the gunships and jets. When I became a pointman for the platoon, I requested a set of field binoculars. I was disappointed to learn that binoculars were not an item stocked for combat use. That didn't surprise me because only a few guys in the platoon had bayonets issued with their M16s. When I went on R&R, I purchased binoculars in Tokyo. I found them very useful in the field and carried them every day when I walked point. In the last few weeks I left the binoculars in base camp because my duties changed.

A jet on a strafing run flies over the rice paddies in front of us. Three NVA soldiers stand up and fire their AK-47s at the jet in hopes of hitting the aircraft. I watch in amusement, thinking these soldiers have to be out of their minds if they imagine small arms fire will bring down a jet. I believe the jet killed one of the three. After the jet finishes the run, enemy heads begin to pop up behind paddy dikes about seventy-five meters away. Our platoon opens up with M79 grenade launchers firing at the enemy behind the dikes. The M79 rounds flush out the NVA; then the platoon opens up with our M16s and record a few enemy hits. We keep on firing even though we see no additional movement. Probably the NVA are low crawling out of the area by using the dikes as shields like we did on our earlier rescue.

I think it will be easy to kill the NVA soldiers if there are only a few of them behind the dikes. A squad of men can move up a paddy dike perpendicular to the one the NVA are hiding behind. The other men in our platoon can return suppressive fire to protect the squad's movement. When the squad reaches the dike, if the enemy is behind it, they can rise up and catch the soldiers in a cross fire ambush. The situation always looks easy from afar, but inevitably complications arise to make the mission more difficult than it first appears. Besides, I refuse to be an Audie Murphy, and why take the risk when our element has air and artillery support?

All of a sudden, the sky darkens, winds cool the temperature dramatically, and a deluge of rain descends on the battle scene. Everyone starts to bitch because the troops had a perfect situation with the enemy pinned down. This storm provides cover for some of the enemy to escape. I remove my camera from under my helmet and shoot a few pictures of the monsoon storm. Within half an hour, the storm passes by and the sky is a clear brilliant blue again. In fifteen or twenty minutes our fatigues will dry out and the men will have to contend only with the muddy paddies. This is my first monsoon rain, and I dread the thought of the coming rainy season in Vietnam. Veterans who have been through the monsoon season say soldiers are always wet and dirty. Mosquitoes thrive in the wet paddies, and ringworm becomes a nuisance requiring daily attention to keep the contagious skin disease under control. Living conditions in base camp become deplorable.

Sergeant Lonnie Ritter passes the word that the platoon is going to move out and try to penetrate the woodline facing us. No one is thrilled about this order, but we spread out and keep a substantial distance between each other, moving in a crouching stance as we approach the woodline. In the rear of our advancing element, I act as a squad leader to our new replacements. Firing commences from enemy positions when we reach an area of tall grass adjacent to the woodline. We hit the ground and let the NVA fire without returning fire in order not to disclose our exact position. I notice the new replacements are uneasy about being fired upon.

Possibly this is the first time the men have experienced combat. I crack a couple of funny remarks and assure them the platoon is in no immediate threat because the NVA is just using probing fire to get us to reveal our positions. Ritter gives us the word to return to our original positions. I see a sense of relief on the faces of the new men as we retrace our trail back to our lines. We accomplish our objective of learning the NVA are still firmly entrenched in the woodline. The infantry remains in a blocking position while reinforcements from the Ninth Division arrive to encircle the NVA. Our job is to contain the enemy force while the aircraft and artillery hammer them throughout the night.

Dusk settles, and within half an hour, it will be dark. The jets make bombing runs while the artillery pounds the wooded area with a barrage of 155 mm howitzer rounds. I make preparations for a nighttime position with Bruce "Whitey" Falkum and Jim Hughes. Our location is at the extreme left flank of our column, only fifty meters or less from enemy lines. We position ourselves behind a paddy dike in a rice paddy that is full of water. I say to Whitey and Jim, "Guys, I'm exhausted. I can't keep my eyes open. If it's okay with you, I'm going to take the first sleep at this position." Whitey says, "That's okay with us. We'll wake you if all hell breaks loose."

I put my head on the edge of the rice paddy dike and use it for a pillow. My helmet protects my head while my body is immersed in water below my chest. The water is shallow, but I lie in a prone position for protection from enemy fire. Thus the water is near my chest. I feel guilty about wanting a rest because I never go to sleep during conflict or threat of enemy nearby. However, I am safe next to Whitey and Jim. The guys are outstanding soldiers and can be counted on at any time. I think to myself before I close my eyes that the only way I could get injured would be to get shot by aircraft. Since the NVA doesn't have air support, there is nothing to worry about. I drift off to sleep with the sound of gunfire and explosions all around me.

Suddenly, something hits me with great force. I'm in an exhausted, confused state and find it difficult to make sense about what is happening. It seems miles away that someone is yelling, "Is anyone hit? Is anyone hit? Is anyone hit?" I have trouble distinguishing between reality and a possible nightmare. For some reason I scream, "I'm hit! I'm hit!" Instinctively I believe I'm in serious trouble, not realizing what has occurred. Whitey screams out, "Milliken's hit! Milliken's hit!" I hear other screams for help. "Need a medic! Get Doc! Get Doc!" I wonder what the hell is going on!

Within seconds I sense a great deal of pain in my left thigh. I reach down with my hand and feel blood pumping out of my thigh through a wound that is bigger than my hand. I try to stop the bleeding by holding my hand over the wound. While holding the palm of my hand over the wound, I feel compressions in my leg moving up and down, creating a blood flow that spurts around my hand. The pain increases, and I lose control and begin to scream. The pain is so intense I imagine a road paver sitting on my legs. My lower body feels like it's crushed and is being twisted like a pretzel. I realize my body is going into shock, which scares the hell out of me because I can remember how Twiggy died from shock. I begin to talk to myself, "Calm down! Calm down, Jim! Get control of yourself! Relax! Relax!"

I can clearly hear Pete screaming, "Cease fire! Cease fire! Cease fire! Cease fire! Damn it, you hit friendly positions! Cease fire! Cease fire!" Pete goes on a tirade giving hell to someone. Only a few minutes pass before a medic appears. I hope the medic is Doc Brothers, but instead it's Doc Burry, a new medic whom I never met. He asks, "Where are you hit?" Before I have a chance to respond, light flashes from an explosion to reveal my left-thigh wound. Doc, with the help of others, tries to move me up on the paddy dike so he can work on my leg. When they move me, I begin to scream because the pain is unbearable. Then I realize the femur bone in my leg is blown apart. I can feel bone splitters jagging tissue throughout my leg. Doc senses my intense pain and says, "Would you like a shot of morphine?" Without hesitation I respond, "Give it to me!"

Another medic arrives and helps Doc Burry move me to a better position to administer aid. The other medic says, "He is shot in his right thigh too." That frightens me because I feel no pain in my right leg. I wonder if I have more bullet wounds. The medics begin to tear apart my fatigues and bandage the wounds. As they patch me up, Pete comes over to check on my status. I overhear Pete cursing on the radio to someone that a Cobra helicopter shot up one of his positions and there is a casualty. He requests an immediate dust-off. Pete asks the medic the status of my wounds. Someone says to him that I am really in bad shape. Pete gasps, "My god! I can see through his leg!"

While Pete talks to the medics, I hear a distant yell. "Milkman, I'm here! It's Doobie!" My spirits are lifted when Platoon Sergeant Stancill appears and wishes me well. I calm down a little until Pete Wood informs me the MEDEVAC dust-off will be here shortly. I tell Pete I don't want to get extracted at night. The MEDEVAC chopper lands at night with its headlights on. This routine situation has been performed many times before when the enemy waits until the wounded are near the chopper for loading before they open up with intense fire. They aim at the lights in hopes of disabling the helicopter and inflicting additional casualties on the crew and litter carriers. I would rather stay in the paddy the remainder of the night than further risk my life and the lives of others. I can't shed the thought out of my mind that Twiggy died under similar circumstances when he was shot and went into shock. Pete says, "Milkman, shut up! You have no choice about remaining here. You can't lie in this dirty paddy water all night with those wounds."

While the medics prepare me for extraction, I keep on passing out and waking every few minutes. I become disoriented by the extreme pain and periods of blackening out. I ask Doc, "Can I have another shot of morphine?" Doc replies, "Another shot so soon will kill you. Give the morphine a few minutes and you will be in la-la land."

Pete takes charge of the dust-off. Four guys appear to carry me on a litter. I black out and regain consciousness when I feel my body thrown about on a litter when the four men run toward the MEDEVAC. Again I black out until I awaken to a thud. I have been thrown on the dust-off helicopter. I look around for the medics and no one is visible. Then I notice bodies with their hands over their heads lying on the floor of the helicopter next to me. I hear the chopper taking hits from enemy rounds and begin to say a prayer as the chopper gains altitude. I can tell by the sound of the rotors and the time elapsed that the chopper is at a safe altitude from enemy fire. My hell in Vietnam has just ended in a manner I anticipated—getting seriously wounded in a situation in which I had no control. This was my destiny. I feel relieved to be alive, but sadness overcomes me with the realization of leaving my friends, whom I consider my brothers in Vietnam.

I awake lying on a table with bright lights hanging overhead. I'm in a large bunker field hospital room. The hospital staff is overwhelmed with the casualties to whom they attend. Directly in front of me is a Vietnamese woman with her two children. The woman is soaked in blood and screams uncontrollably. Her children seem to be uninjured but are crying in sympathy, reacting to the mother's screams. To my right are two soldiers who are being treated for gunshot wounds. The GI to my left is

---

lying on a table and is waiting for a doctor. The room is full of activity with doctors and staff running around and attending to the wounded amid the screaming and crying. The bloody mess looks more like the remains in a butcher shop than a hospital room.

A doctor notices my regaining consciousness and comes over to my table. He says, "Soldier, how do you feel?" I say, "Doc, I feel fine." He replies, "Let's take a look at your wounds." He proceeds to take the bandages off my right thigh. He says, "You seem to have a clean flesh wound in this thigh. The bullet appears to have entered and exited the leg without causing too much damage." I can see the two openings in my leg, and to me it seems repairable, even though my leg is swollen to close the wounds. The doc looks into my face. He knew my left thigh would be another story because of the amount of bandaging around my leg. When he finishes undressing the bandage on my left thigh, he remains silent. I look at my thigh and immediately realize it will be difficult to save my leg. It appears the insides of the leg have been blown out and are hanging by tissue and bone to what is left of my outer-thigh area. I look at Doc and say, "When you amputate my leg, try to leave as much of the leg nearest to the hip so I'll be able to walk with a prosthesis." Doc looks at me in disbelief at what I just said and replies, "That might not be necessary. Let's perform a few tests to determine the extent of your injuries." I guess the doctor thinks I'm being brave about the possibility of amputation. In actuality the morphine is talking for me. Pain has left my body, and if I had support for my left leg, I feel as though I would be able to walk.

Doc examines me for nerve damage in both legs. To our surprise, I can feel the instrument touching my calves and toes on both legs. Doc says, "That is a good sign that you have feeling in both legs." I fall asleep with the comforting news that there are positive aspects about my injuries. I awake in a hospital ward with other soldiers. The first thing I notice is that my left leg is in traction. Tears come to my eyes because I expected to wake up as an amputee. What a relief to know my leg is saved! Two guys from our Second Platoon come over to my bed to wish me the best when they realize I woke up. Sergeant Dan Driscoll says to me, "You are really fucked up." I laugh and say, "You have no idea how good I feel at this moment." Sheridan Schwark tells me I was shot by a Cobra helicopter. Both of them were shot in the left arm. Dan was shot through the left elbow, and his wounds are the worst of the two.

—

The guys leave after a short visit, and I drift into a deep sleep, thinking of all the hell I experienced in half a year. Before falling asleep, I give thanks to God for sparing my life. I realize the only place in my body that I could survive a twenty-millimeter cannon fire from a Cobra would be gunshot wounds to my thighs. Five years of running cross-country at West Chester High School and Grove City College have paid dividends. My thigh muscles became the strongest part of my body from the many years of training and running. I feel as though a lifetime has passed by me in six months of combat, and I know I'll have trouble dealing with a new life on such a short notice. I want to be home in a safe environment, but I fear the unknown of dealing with people and my new set of values.

I wake up in extreme pain and notice a team of men working on my left leg. My leg is supported only at the buttock and heel by metal devices. The thigh and calf of my leg are suspended with no support between these two devices. I scream in pain, questioning them about their intentions. I explain that the femur bone has been blown apart, causing the ends of the damaged bone to penetrate into the muscle tissue. One man answers that he is quite aware of my wounds, but they must do this procedure to place me in a full-body cast for transporting. I cuss at them until I pass out.

The next time I gain consciousness, someone is at my bedside trying to wake me. I'm totally confused about what is going on. I feel very sick and find it difficult to comprehend his questions because of the drugs in my body. Finally, what the attendant says makes sense after I take a few moments to focus and clear my head. The man states that I can notify my parents of my condition in twenty-five words or less. In military slang I give him the following message: "Mom and Dad, I was hit by a gunship. Both legs are wounded. I will be okay. Love, Jim." He leaves just as another individual approaches my bedside. This man is a lt. colonel who awards me a Purple Heart. I get very upset being awarded this medal while I'm in such a sick and confused state that I throw the medal at him. My response to him is, "Leave me alone!" The officer says nothing and leaves my bedside. I quickly drift off into a deep sleep.

I wake up to the sound of many voices around me. Two people are moving me through an airport corridor on a litter carrier. The attendants are taking me to a staging location to wait my turn to be loaded on a plane. I have no idea where I'm going. A woman approaches me and wishes me a speedy recovery. She says her companion is Mrs. Ellsworth Bunker, the wife of the ambassador to Vietnam. She asks me, "Would you like to meet Mrs. Bunker?" I rudely say, "No!" When she hears my response, she gets the message and leaves me alone. When soldiers are seriously wounded, what possesses people to bother them with their goodwill public relations bullshit?

Finally, the attendants load me on a large military transport. I lie on the lowest cot, which is attached to a makeshift wall support in the plane. The cots are three tiers high and extend the length of the cargo plane. I look down the aisle of the plane and notice a number of intravenous bottles and tubes attached to each patient. It's overwhelming to see all these wounded men in such a deplorable state. If people could see this terrible aftermath resulting from war and the thousands of wounded and dead who are transported home, maybe they would resolve to find a better solution to world crises.

Near the end of the loading, a few ambulatory amputee soldiers walk on the plane. I ask one soldier where he lost his foot. He replies, "In Korea from a booby trap." I say, "Korea? Most people are completely unaware there is fighting going on in that country." He laughs, "They don't publish casualties because the Korean War is supposed to be over."

Many doctors and nurses make last-minute checks on their patients before the plane takes off for Japan. My nurse checks my intravenous drips and shows me where my barf bag is located. The staff prepares for takeoff by going to their seats in the front of the plane. When the plane leaves the runway and climbs into the sky, almost every patient on the plane begins to vomit. What a sight! I throw up in my barf bag while others miss their bags. I pity the staff whose responsibility is to clean these patients and try to make their trip as pleasant as possible. I imagine the medical personnel are experts at handling so many sick people at once.

When the plane arrives in Japan, the attendants transport me to a temporary staging area to await a further transfer to another hospital. The nurse takes my temperature and pulse. My temperature registers 104 degrees. She asks me, "Can I do something to make you more comfortable?" I respond, "I would like to have a bottle of Coke." She says, "There are no soda machines in this area." I reply, "I would pay a million dollars for a Coke if I had the money." The nurse says nothing and leaves the area. About fifteen minutes later, she returns with a Coca-Cola. I tell her she is a true angel for being so considerate of my request. The cold soda is very refreshing and is a much-needed treat. The nurse says soon they expect to transport me to my final destination, Camp Zama,

Japan. Ironically, I return to Camp Zama as a patient. I was there only a few weeks ago on R&R to visit Larry Boneck, a good friend of mine from the Third Platoon.

The next time I wake up, I'm in a bed at Camp Zama. Surgeons have operated on me again, and now my left leg is in traction stabilized at a forty-five-degree angle. I can see large metal sutures in both thighs with a quarter-inch pin inserted in my left calf bone to hold my leg in traction. There are twenty pounds of weight hanging over the end of my bed that support the pulley system, which is attached to the pin in my leg. My body cast has been removed, and I feel much better. There was a handle on the stomach area of the body cast that enabled staff to easily pick me up when I was transported. I felt like a piece of luggage with the handle on the body cast.

I quietly look over my new surroundings. There are six men on my side of the hallway, which is sectioned off by curtains used as wall barriers. I can also see six beds on the other side of the hallway, but my only view is curtains. The man next to me is talking to his family in the States. When he takes a break from his conversation, I ask him where in the States he is calling. He replies, "Ellwood City, Pennsylvania." I can't believe what he just said. I ask him to hold the line because my parents live in Ellwood City. When he finishes his conversation, I take the phone and give the operator my parents' number.

Shortly thereafter, my mother answers the phone and begins to cry when she hears my voice. She is so upset that she calls for my father to get on an extension phone. They explain to me that they were notified last night by a ham radio operator from Sharon, Pennsylvania, that I was wounded. I tell them I was shot in both thighs and that I would have a long recovery period. I assure them about my condition, even though a doctor hasn't briefed me of my prognosis. We say our good-byes and I promise to write immediately with all the details.

After I get off the phone, I introduce myself to DeWayne Edinger, of Ellwood City. He says his parents live in Wiley Hill while my parents live close by in an area called Knox Plan. DeWayne is also shot in the left femur. He was shot on Hamburger Hill. He says Camp Zama is crowded with casualties from Hamburger Hill. The staff has run out of beds and is administering to patients who are temporarily located in the hallways. DeWayne introduces me to the other two men who are bedridden. To the left of DeWayne is Tony Payne, who has also been shot in the left femur. Tony says we will be on our backs for at least six months. In front of us is First Lieutenant Jim Fitzgerald, who was injured by a rocket that penetrated the building where he was working. Jim had two fingers amputated and suffered from serious shrapnel wounds. The other man is a Green Beret captain, waiting for surgery. We expect a new arrival for the last bed.

Now that I know I will be spending months in bed recuperating from my wounds, I begin to reflect on my tour in Vietnam. The multitude of combat experiences and the comradeship of the Third Platoon are embedded in my mind. I must tell my story before time erases my memory. The end of my tour of duty in Vietnam is an appropriate introduction to my story.

3d Bde, Viets Kill 91 in joint effort

Colonel Gray killed during intense battle

TAN AN — The enemy was routed and the operation had to be termed a success when Go Devil infantrymen and Vietnamese soldiers killed 91 NVA near Thu Thua, but the price was high.

Colonel Asa Gray Jr., the Long An province senior advisor, was mortally wounded while directing his forces on the ground.

Americans and Vietnamese paid tribute to him during memorial services here May 16 at Gray's Rural Popular Force troops of Long An Province constantly work closely with the Division's 3d Brigade and played a major role in the battle in which Gray lost his life.

Lieutenant Colonel Dale J. Clitenberger, 3d Brigade commander, said "Colonel Gray's contributions to the success of Vietnamese and American efforts in Long An Province were numerous. As a senior province advisor, he gave his life in aid of our Vietnamese allies.

"The success of allied activities in the 3d Brigade area reflect Colonel Gray's accomplishments. His loss will be long felt by both Americans and Vietnamese in Long An Province."

TAN AN — Go Devil infantrymen of the 3d Brigade teamed with ARVN, Regional and Popular Forces and supporting elements to kill 91 NVA soldiers in two days of intensive fighting May 12-13 around the village of Thu Thua, four miles northwest of here.

Action began when an artillery aerial observer received heavy ground fire as he flew over the area just before sun-up May 12. Stogie gunships of the 3d Squadron, 17th Cavalry scrambled to the area where they also received heavy ground fire.

U.S. ground elements were inserted by helicopters and Navy assault craft north of the Kinh Moi Canal while Regional Forces and ARVN troops pushed towards the area.

During the two-day battle, a single reconnaissance platoon of the 2d Battalion (Mechanized), 47th Infantry killed 22 of the enemy while other ground units of the 2d Battalion, 60th Infantry and 5th Battalion, 60th Infantry,

air strikes, artillery and gunships accounted for the remaining 41 dead.

ARVN, Regional Force and Popular Force companies killed 18 NVA and captured eight individual weapons and two crew served weapons.

Sergeant Richard Jenkins, a squad leader from Eugene, Ore., was with Company B, 2/60th when they were inserted by helicopters into the area of contact late in the afternoon of the first day of the operation.

"As soon as the choppers put us on the ground, we were pinned down by 30 caliber machinegun fire," Jenkins said. "Stogie gunships put a stop to that right away, and we were able to move right into the woodline.

"Early the next morning, Company B swept the area at first light.

DIRECTING TRAFFIC—Captain Alan G. Anderson of Palm Beach, Fla., company commander of Company A, 5th Battalion, 60th Infantry, spreads his men out while on an operation in the Mekong Delta.
(Photo by SP5 Thom Niece)

Battle of May 12, 1969 with North Vietnamese Army.

2

Arrival and First Two Weeks

It's 9:30 a.m. on November 20, 1968, when the pilot announces over the intercom, "Gentlemen, Vietnam can now be viewed from the right side of the aircraft. The flight plan requires us to maintain a high altitude over mainland Vietnam due to the war zone below. Our approach to Bien Hoa Air Base will require a more rapid descent because of the altitude restrictions. Be prepared for a quick departure after our landing." The pilot continues with instructions, but everyone is moving to the right side of the DC8 to view the destination, Vietnam. Tim Firestone, a good friend of mine since 1963, says to me, "Let's take a look." I reply, "Okay," expecting to see a devastated, war-torn land. I move to the window with Tim, and we share a view for a few minutes with some other GIs. Vietnam looks beautiful from our vantage point. The country looks like a picture postcard with its lush vegetation, waterways, and highlands. We can see no signs of any developed areas. After a brief exchange of words, everyone returns to his seat and a dead silence fills the plane. Tim and I have been friends for five years but we have nothing to say to each other.

Small talk ceases with the stewardesses and other GIs. An air of fear permeates the plane as each man thinks only of himself at this time. I quickly realize all the soldiers aboard the plane are in deep thought about their fate and are feeling the same pain of loneliness and despair that transcends throughout my body. To me it seems to be a personal and private war that I'll be able to share only with myself. I try to psych myself by repeating in my mind, *I'm as prepared to fight as I'll ever be.* I know additional training would give me no more confidence, courage, skills, or knowledge to endure the physical and mental suffering that awaits me. Then I experience numbing fear when I finally realize Vietnam is no longer an imaginary dream but a reality. There is no turning back. I'm well aware that my ego can get me in trouble. I make a final pledge to myself: *I promise I'll not get emotionally entangled with the war to the extent of jeopardizing my own life. My only goal will be to DEROS from Vietnam in one piece. Lord, give me the faith to endure this challenge and give me guidance to make the right decisions as a civilized human being in war. In the name of Jesus Christ I pray. Amen.*

The plane begins its approach to land at the Bien Hoa Air Base. When the plane descends, we observe firefights in different sectors of the land. The sight of fires, smoke, and helicopter rocket flames reinforces the thought in my mind that this is going to be a grueling, incredible challenge and that only the strong will survive. I wonder how many of the men on this plane will return as a noncasualty—probably none.

Soon the plane lands while a jeep approaches the tarmac with a lieutenant shouting orders. He orders a quick departure from the plane to nearby waiting buses. Apparently, urgency is a safety measure because the previous night there was a mortar attack on the air base and the fighting continues around the base. As we move hastily toward the buses, the new troops pass veterans going to board the plane we just departed. I expect to see joy and relief in their faces upon leaving Vietnam and maybe a little kidding about our greenness, but that isn't the case. Instead, they're very quiet, sullen, and seem to be emotionally destroyed from what they've experienced. They appear unsure about returning to the States.

The bus ride to the Ninth Division, Ninetieth Replacement Station is my first venture in Vietnam. My training buddies and I are seated together. Tim and I try to keep our spirits up by making wise remarks about the condition of the bus and the deplorable surroundings. Lasting impressions are formed in my mind as I'm transported in the drab, olive green bus. The bus windows are broken, and the steel bars in front of the windows don't afford proper protection from bullets and items thrown at the bus. We pass through populated areas that are completely destroyed by bombs. The Vietnamese people give us a cold stare when we pass, as if we're responsible for their plight. The children either beg or scream obscenities at those on the bus. Others throw rocks or trash at the bus. Tim looks at me and laughs while saying, "Welcome to Vietnam!" The trip is depressing and I feel afraid. I begin to wonder if I can really handle this war. My manhood is challenged. I've been in Vietnam only an hour, yet I feel as though I've aged a year. I can't imagine how I'll change after a year here when I have such strong feelings after one hour.

At the Ninetieth Replacement Station I'm shocked to see the level of trust the American command gives the Vietnamese civilians. The Vietnamese are everywhere in the base complex, doing almost any kind of job. I'm especially fearful of their working in the mess hall where they prepare and serve food to military personnel. In combat training, soldiers are indoctrinated not to trust any Vietnamese. They're told, "The only good gook is a dead gook." What the hell is going on here? What am I to believe? The army teaches one doctrine while soldiers practice another.

Even the plane flight to Vietnam indicates this is a strange war. In what other war did troops go to the front in commercial jet aircraft and were served meals every four hours by hostesses in miniskirts? In what other war did combat troops wear their dress uniforms to the front because they weren't issued combat gear or weapons? In what other war were combat troops shown an orientation movie portraying the American soldiers as guests in the country in which they'd come to fight? The movie is designed like a vacation brochure describing the country and how we should respect the Vietnamese people and their land. The propaganda movie begins:

> Discover the Pacific nation of Vietnam, a country with a blend of the Orient and the West.
>
> The people are friendly and hospitable.
>
> It's a land of beautiful scenery, mountain retreats, and secluded beaches.
>
> Visit the charm of ancient imperial cities.
>
> Experience the thrills of big game hunting . . .

My initial impression of Vietnam gives me a feeling of fear and great distrust. I begin to view the army and Vietnamese government in the same manner. Their intentions are to appease each other, and these agendas aren't beneficial to the American soldier. My fellow soldiers and I conclude that there are more political and economical factors behind the scenes, and they'll determine the outcome of the war, regardless of who wins the fighting. After our informal introduction at the Ninetieth Replacement Station, we move to another area to get our new orders for unit assignment in Vietnam. When we're processed as replacements, we cross paths with another group of veterans who are leaving Vietnam. Astonishingly there's little joy in their faces. Most of them have expressions that show a sense of duty. They appear indifferent, but they pity those who are replacing them. There is little conversation between veteran and replacement; each apparently is trying to prepare himself for the next experience life has to offer. The veteran contemplates how society will accept him, while the replacement fears the outcome of battle with the enemy.

I'm assigned to Delta Company, Second Battalion, Sixtieth Infantry Regiment, Ninth Infantry Division. I leave the Quonset hut after receiving my assignment and wait outside to find out where my buddies are assigned. Tim appears and says, "Where are you assigned?" I answer, "Second and Sixtieth of the Ninth Infantry Division." He asks, "Delta Company?" I say, "Yes, and I bet you have the same orders." Tim laughs and jokes, "I will never get away from you!"

Tim and I seem to be joined at the hip. Maybe that is why we're referred to as the Bobbsey Twins. Our educational and military backgrounds are almost identical. We both graduated in 1967 from Grove City College, a Christian liberal arts college located north of Pittsburgh, Pennsylvania. We met early in our freshman year and took similar classes in business administration. Tim was a business administration major while accounting was my field. In our freshman year we studied and did homework together. Tim owned fancier cars than I did in college. He usually drove a custom Volkswagen with a Porsche engine. In good weather he preferred his 850 cc Norton motorcycle. He loved fast vehicles and had a special talent for restoring cars and building engines.

Ironically, nine months after graduating from Grove City College, we crossed paths at the Fort Dix Army Basic Training Camp. Both of us joined the army approximately the same time and had most of our military training together at Fort Dix, New Jersey. Each of us signed up for the Officer Candidate Program at Fort Benning, Georgia, in hopes

—
20

that we could get a branch transfer from infantry to transportation or finance school. However, because the war escalated and infantry officers were needed, branch transfers from the infantry school were terminated. The army changed an enlistee's service period by allowing veterans of Vietnam the option of leaving the military after a year's assignment. Tim and I knew we would eventually be assigned to Vietnam, so we decided to quit Officer Candidate School and transfer to a casualty company. The casualty company at Fort Benning is a temporary holding company that consists mostly of dropouts from NCO and Officer Candidate Schools. Infantry personnel who transfer to casualty companies usually receive orders to Vietnam within a month. The earlier we receive orders to Vietnam, the better. We calculated that we could be out of the service in seventeen months and could get on with our lives. To date, all of our orders have been the same. Possibly the army thinks we enlisted under the Buddy Plan.

We check with Tom Moreno, Lee Blank, John Failes, and David Golwitzer about their assignments. They're each assigned to different units within the Ninth Infantry Division. We decide to celebrate for a few hours since this will probably be our last time together. I'll miss these guys, especially Tom Moreno with whom I roomed in basic training. The socializing takes place in the nearest bar. This bar is unique because almost everyone is high on drugs, not booze. I feel animosity toward General Westmoreland's command when I witness these men using drugs. During army training, drugs and even alcohol were prohibited. Why are drugs and the excessive use of alcohol tolerated in a combat zone when so many lives are at stake? The leaders ignore their sense of duty by compromising the safety of the soldiers in this unjust war. Whatever the reason for this behavior, I know drugs aren't the answer. I have just as much fear as anyone else and have no intention of taking drugs while I'm in a combat situation.

On my first night in Vietnam I'm selected for guard duty in a huge warehouse at the processing station. I'm relieved to be on duty because I'm afraid of the Vietnamese, the army, and the environment. I know sleeping my first night in the country is out of the question. In the morning we're transferred to Camp Bearcat for five days of in-country training. Upon completion of training, we report to our unit assignments. Finally, we're issued M16 automatic rifles. My rifle looks as though it has been through hell. The stock is scratched and cut up with green stains embedded

---

in the plastic. The outside of the barrel is a little rusty and has a crack in the plastic stock handgrip. Of course, the M16 is complete minus the bayonet. For some reason, I thought we would be issued new weapons. What a joke! I just hope I can depend on this weapon for survival. After having been issued the M16, I'm beginning to feel like a soldier. It's a wonder how a weapon will bolster one's confidence in a war zone.

The five days of training were a farce. Veterans supposedly administer the training. They might have been veterans of base camps but I doubt they were combat veterans. All the instructors did was instill fear in the GIs about the Vietcong and how good Charlie is in his unorthodox methods of fighting. There weren't constructive methods given to the GIs to instill confidence in their ability to fight the enemy.

Camp Bearcat is being phased out as the Ninth Division Headquarters and will be replaced by Dong Tam, a base south of Saigon in the Mekong Delta. Camp Bearcat has the luxuries of a Dairy Queen, hot dog stand, library, bars, massage parlor, and a PX that sells everything from toothpaste to televisions. I ask myself, "Is this a war or a dream I'm experiencing?"

Our five days of training turn into two weeks of waiting before being transferred to our units. During these two weeks, we become active patrons of the Thai bars located in the camp. The US Army is turning the base over to the armies of Thailand and Korea for their military operations in Vietnam. Rumors circulate in base camp that the Thais and ROKs are fierce fighters. Yesterday some ROKs returned to Bearcat with several decapitated Vietcong heads attached to the ends of bayonets. My observations reveal their fierceness as fighters to be more of a myth than reality. After trying for three days to fly the remaining Camp Bearcat infantry trainees into Dong Tam, the army cancelled the airlift because of the monsoon weather. One time we were airborne and halfway to Dong Tam and had to be flown back to Bearcat. The cargo plane flew into a monsoon storm so violent that wind shear pounding the plane caused the outer skin to flex back and forth. Due to time constraints, a truck convoy becomes our transportation south.

The convoy consists of about fifteen army deuce-and-a-half trucks. Tim and I are on the lead truck jammed in the back with twenty other GIs. A lt. colonel riding in the cab of our truck is in charge of the convoy. The journey is uneventful until we arrive in Saigon's city limits. As the convoy moves through the narrow city streets, we approach a particular section of the city that isn't secure. The trucks stop momentarily. The lt. colonel gives the order to lock and load and fire at anything that seems threatening. He gives further orders to the truckers to drive at maximum speed and not to stop for any reason. He says convoys are frequently ambushed on this section of highway. The convoy starts moving quickly through the city with horns blasting to clear the highway of pedestrians and small motorized vehicles. The troops are jostled and thrown about in the back of the trucks. Out of nowhere appears a jeep carrying two MPs who are trying to stop the convoy. The lead truck doesn't stop until we reach a more secure area of the road. The lt. colonel motions for the driver to pull over, and as soon as the truck stops, a verbal altercation ensues between the officer and the MPs. The MPs proceed to write a speeding citation to the convoy. Imagine the stupidity of getting a speeding ticket in Nam! The lt. colonel goes into a tirade, screaming obscenities, and takes the MPs' identification, promising them a demotion for their actions. It appears to Tim and me that both parties are exerting a power play to not lose face.

Late in the afternoon we arrive at Dong Tam. This base is the size of a small town. The roads are especially wide for military vehicles and elevated for protection against monsoon rains. The buildings are newly constructed and look essentially the same as most military complexes. In the evening, Tim and I ask the location of the enlisted men's beer hall. The beer hall is huge; it seems like it could hold a battalion of men. The bar is the longest I've ever seen and has a wide variety of beer to choose from. Probably a hundred men could stand at the bar drinking beer. Tim and I stand at the bar drinking Budweiser and strike up conversations with GIs who might have some knowledge of the Second and Sixtieth. One GI shares a story that, just a few days ago, one of the companies in the battalion got their asses kicked by a sniper in the field. He says nine men were wounded or killed by the sniper. Tim asks him if he knows what company took the casualties. He can't remember. Another GI informs us the battalion is waterborne, operating out of boats on daily missions. I mention to Tim that I've heard enough bullshit for the evening because it's not doing anything for my confidence since I can't swim. I say to Tim, "Everything we hear about the unit is negative, so I guess when we arrive tomorrow, our spirits can only go up." Tim toasts me, "One more beer to chase the Vietcong away." I make a toast, "Here's to you, Charlie! May you never meet up with the Bobbseys."

The next day Tim and I load up with our duffel bags, M16s, and ammunition. We walk to the edge of the base camp and arrive at the entrance around 1000 hours and wait half an hour. No vehicles pass by. I ask Tim, "Do you think we're in the correct location for pickup?" Tim replies, "The directions were simple, but there are no markings indicating this is a pickup point. Eventually someone will come by and we can find out if this is the correct location for hitching a ride to Camp Scott."

The procedure for getting to our final destination, Camp Scott, in Tan Tru, Vietnam, is quite loose by military standards. Replacements wait at the entrance of the Ninth Division base camp for a motorized ride to their battalion base camp. Vehicles travel back and forth daily from division headquarters to battalion base camps on a variety of missions transporting supplies and equipment. The drivers like the idea of picking up infantrymen for added security when driving between bases. To them the more firepower they have, the less likelihood they will be ambushed.

At 1100 hours a jeep approaches us, and the soldier riding shotgun asks us if we're going to Tan Tru. Tim says, "Yes, we're replacements for Delta Company of the Second and Sixtieth." Both guys say in unison, "Get in." Tim and I load our gear and jump in the back of the jeep. We hold on to our M16s as if they were newborn babies. The guys in the jeep introduce themselves and comment how fortunate they are to pick up two infantrymen for security. Usually they're lucky to have one additional GI traveling with them. Tim and I ask questions about our new base camp, but the two guys keep changing the topic about our trip to Camp Scott. I feel as though we're getting a briefing every mile of the trip about the possible dangers ahead of us. The driver tells us there is typically not any military traffic on the road to Tan Tru until after 1100 hours due to the morning mine clearing. That explains why we had to wait at the entrance of Dong Tam.

The driver explains that we're approaching the location where a jeep was ambushed the previous day. According to him, both men on the jeep were killed. He continues, saying the area is a heavily populated town with a very narrow main street surrounded by two-story buildings. The main street has been renamed Thunder Alley by the GIs. Tim and I stop talking and concentrate on the congested, narrow road ahead. I watch the second-floor windows and balconies of the buildings while Tim and the others concentrate on the activity at ground level. We prepare to shoot at anything that looks threatening. Within a few minutes we successfully drive through Thunder Alley without incident.

After an uneventful journey, we arrive at Camp Scott. We thank the guys for the ride, and they express appreciation to us for the added fire support. Delta Company is the first company headquarters on the left as we enter the gates to Camp Scott. Tim says, "Welcome to your new home." I reply, "What a slum. I never imagined our living conditions would be this poor." The slums of the United States are an improvement compared to these conditions. The monsoon rains are over, but the ground is covered with mud and pools of filthy water. Garbage and debris litter the barracks area, and the buildings are filthy and look like temporary shelters. Tim and I look inside one of the barracks, which is littered with military cots, equipment, and trash. I can't believe there are grenades and ammunition lying everywhere on the floor. It's obvious these troops have adopted a different lifestyle. The area is almost impassable to walk through. I say to Tim, "My initial impression makes me believe it's going to take all the energy we can muster to survive a year here." He says, "No shit! We will make it. After all, we are Grove City grads." We both begin to laugh. If the Grovers could see us now—their successful grads!

Tim and I check into company headquarters and are assigned to the Third Platoon of Delta Company by the company clerk, Sergeant Barry Timm. Barry is a nice guy and says Delta Company is a new company being formed by members of the battalion's other companies and new recruits. Most of the veterans in the Third Platoon were former members of Charlie Company. Barry reviews our orders and says since we're such good friends with similar backgrounds, we will be assigned to the same platoon. He explains to us that most of the men are in the field, so he will take a little time to show us around. Barry takes us to the Third Platoon barracks and instructs us to find an empty cot under which to store our gear. He says the platoon won't be coming in until tomorrow. Barry shows us the company shower and gives us directions to the mess hall. After supper, he tells us to stop by headquarters and that he will treat us to a few beers at the Mortar Platoon Bar. Tim and I thank him for his help and assigning us to the Third Platoon.

After eating at the mess hall, Tim and I feel we need some alcohol to hopefully kill whatever we ate. Darkness approaches, and we head back to Delta Company after a short walk through the battalion area. Sergeant Timm is in the headquarters area by himself just as when we reported for duty. Timm says, "You guys look a little dry." We nod in approval of his intentions.

As we walk to the Mortar Platoon Bar, Timm tells us, "Usually around nightfall artillery fire opens up outside the bar." The bar is merely a place to socialize and have a cold beer. The beers are cheap, and the best part about it is Timm's treating. Timm gives us some insight about Delta Company, its operations, and the leaders in the company and platoons. He mentions the battalion is an air mobile unit and predominantly travels to the field by helicopter. I'm relieved to hear this news. We enjoy each other's company when a loud blast shakes the building. The artillery begins to fire 155 mm howitzer shells. The sound is deafening. We decide to head back to Delta Company.

3

Base Camp Life

The next morning Ray Cartigiano, from Brooklyn, New York, introduces himself to Tim and me. Ray says the Third Platoon is formed from a group of veterans who will act as mentors giving advice and training to the new replacements. Ray emphasizes we're lucky to be in a platoon with exceptional leaders. He praises Lieutenant Tom Deutschlander and SSG Bo Senical as soldiers whose main concern is for the welfare of the men under them. This is encouraging news to our ears because Tim and I learned the opposite about leadership in Officer Candidate School. According to the school, the mission is paramount and orders should be followed without question. Soldiers can always be replaced. I once questioned a classroom OCS officer instructor about obeying stupid orders when an officer knows his platoon is going to be wiped out in a futile mission. He recited the mission statement to me and said new men would replace those lost on the mission. I couldn't believe how he accepted that injustice for fellow soldiers. That is a main reason why I left OCS. I have a conscience that wouldn't tolerate such inhumane behavior to those who count on my leadership.

Ray says he will introduce us to the other guys when they return from the field later in the day. Ray tells us he got a day off from the field but is still obligated to complete a few assigned duties around the company area. Then he asks us, "How does a tour around base camp fit in with your plans?" Tim replies, "Do you have time?" "No sweat," says Ray.

"You can call me the Kid. Everyone has a nickname in our platoon or goes by their last name. Within a week someone will baptize you with a name that will stick for the duration of your tour." Ray's nickname surely fits because he's a very small Italian guy who looks too young to be in Vietnam.

On our tour Ray points out battalion headquarters, a Vietnamese school located inside the compound, and New Life Village located outside the base camp perimeter. He also gives us the general positioning of the four listening posts that are manned each night for early warning of ground attacks. Ray says our battalion engages in two types of daily missions: the Bush Master and the Eagle flights. The Bush Master is an extended stay in the field for three days or more, setting up night ambushes, while Eagle flights are daily search-and-destroy missions to the field utilizing Huey helicopters for transportation. The Eagle flights are the preferred mission because the enemy can't easily pinpoint our location due to the unit's constant movement. If the enemy isn't engaged within a reasonable time frame for a particular insertion, the troops are pulled out of that location for insertion into the next target area. The platoon has the advantage of surprise on Eagle flights, whereas the enemy has the advantage of setting up ambushes and booby traps while they're observing our movements on a longer stay in the field.

The Kid states, "Next on the tour will be the barbershop and laundry." A Vietnamese woman referred to as Ms. Ahn runs the laundry with a small number of Vietnamese boys who help her. She charges fifty cents to wash and press a set of fatigues. The laundry is taken to an off-site location where it's cleaned and pressed. Ms. Ahn acts as an agent between the Vietnamese laundry and the soldiers. I watch Ms. Ahn carefully. She seems to be very friendly to all the GIs in need of her service. I think she has the perfect situation of getting information from GIs and helping the Vietcong. I distrust all the Vietnamese at this point. Before leaving the laundry, the Kid recommends we get our fatigues tapered by Ms. Ahn's laundry. He explains the tapering cuts down on the amount of mud and water that adheres to your fatigues, which allows your clothes to dry more quickly. An additional benefit is that it is easier to maneuver through heavy vegetation. I expect to get my uniforms tapered later because of these reasons, plus my emotional state will be uplifted when I look like a professional soldier.

Ms. Ahn—Manager of Vietnamese laundry in Camp Scott.

The barbershop is next to the laundry. It's an open-air shop with a Vietnamese barber. The barber charges forty cents for a haircut and fifteen cents for a head massage. A haircut, a shave, and a complete massage costs $2.20. I ask Tim, "Would you let that Vietnamese barber put a razor next to your neck?" Tim laughs, saying, "Of course, I would." The Kid says, "No sweat." I look at him and say, "No sweat my ass!"

Ray proceeds to take us to the Enlisted Men's Club. We pass by the mess hall and many other shacklike buildings. He points out where Charlie Company is located. The EM club is closed, but Ray promises to bring us back after dinner. He says the guys frequent the place after dinner for a few beers, music, and slot machine entertainment. The only other nightly entertainment is a movie shown outside under the stars near battalion headquarters. The Kid says GIs usually bring their beer and sit in the bleachers to watch the movie, like being at a drive-in theater. Our tour took about an hour. We thank the Kid and proceed back to Delta Company. On our tour I notice the battalion is very lax about attire worn around base camp. The Kid told us you can wear anything as long as it's military. Most everyone wore cutoff military fatigues for shorts and cut the sleeves off their old shirts.

Command allows the GIs to wear sandals inside the base camp. As we approach Delta Company, Ray notices the water truck departing from the company shower building. The truck has just filled the water storage tank utilized for taking showers. He advises us to get a shower before the platoons come back from the field. When they arrive, getting a shower, a cold beer, and the mail are a must. Ray also warns us to not take showers at night because the mosquitoes will eat us alive. He says they really like to attack your balls, and if you're not a dancer, you will learn quickly with them chomping at your nuts. Tim and I take the Kid's advice and decide to get a shower.

We go back to the Third Platoon's barracks and get clean fatigues, towel, and a wash cloth for our shower adventure. It seems as though everyday tasks become adventures because we're in a strange environment. Other guys are already taking showers when we arrive. The shower system is a disaster. The showers are located in a small building that has screens above the men's shoulders. While taking a shower, one can watch the traffic going by on the dirt road next to the building. The lower part of the building is constructed of cheap wood siding. The floor consists of wood slats that allow the soapy water to drain into the soil underneath the building. One must pull a cord attached to a shower head that releases the water from the storage tank on the roof of the building. To save water, we're told by one of the other men to first get wet, then lather up with soap, and follow by rinsing. I can understand why showers must be taken in the daytime because we're getting seriously bitten by mosquitoes right now. The water falls on their breeding grounds beneath the shower building, causing them to rise between the slats to make a meal of us.

While we shower, a moped taxi cart with women passengers stops beside the shower building. The driver is having mechanical problems with the vehicle. The Vietnamese women are watching us take a shower and begin to laugh at our antics. Tim and I look on as the other guys begin to cheer and tease the women. The guys grab some new bars of soap and offer the soap to the women. Soap is a luxury for Vietnamese peasants. The women motion for us to come out and visit. We don't need any encouragement. We grab our towels to cover our asses and hasten out to the girls. We distribute cakes of soap to the girls and try to converse with them. Some of the guys moon the girls, to their delight. The taxi driver fixes the moped and it starts. However, some of the guys get on the back of the taxi, and the extra weight raises the front of the moped

---

off the ground. The taxi driver begins to scream at us because his moped is running but going nowhere when the front wheel is off the ground. This scene should be in a movie. Our mischievous fun causes a lot of screaming and laughing. After a few minutes of sheer bedlam, the guys get off the back of the moped cart and allow the driver to speed away. We return to finish our showers.

Around 1600 hours the Third Platoon returns from their Bush Master in the field. Everyone seems upbeat. Tim and I give the veterans some space so they can shower, read mail, clean their gear, and just take time to relax. The guys' fatigues, boots, and gear are filthy. The men joke with each other, displaying affection by using nicknames. A few guys make positive comments about seeing new replacements. The main reason the new guys are welcomed so readily into the platoon is because the workload is overwhelming. The replacements are immediately viewed as extra bodies that will relieve the veterans of some of their duties. As I understand it, the replacements get all the "shit" details such as guard duty, listening post, road duty, and general cleanup in the company area. After a short time performing these duties, the replacements are assigned specific responsibilities within the platoon. A full platoon has thirty-six men, but the norm is usually less due to casualties, sickness, or special assignments.

I notice one of the men reading a newspaper. I walk by to get a closer look and see the paper titled *The Herald*. I couldn't believe it! The paper is from Sharon, Pennsylvania, a town located near Grove City where Tim and I graduated from college. My mother and father live in Ellwood City, which isn't far away. I approach him and introduce myself, telling him I went to Grove City College. He introduces himself as Tom Gabig, of Sharpsville, Pennsylvania. Tom says, "Everyone here calls me Gabe. Believe it or not, I graduated from Grove City High School. Sure is a small world." Gabe and I talk for about ten minutes, and he tells me how to order my hometown newspaper. Gabe comments, "I'll give you the Sharon paper after I'm finished with it." I reply, "Thanks, Gabe, I really appreciate the gesture. I'll be able to keep up on local sports." "No sweat," he replies with a laugh. I notice Gabe laughs a lot when he talks with someone. He seems to be a happy person. Gabe says, "Let me introduce you to some of the platoon." We walk around the outside of the billet area, and he introduces me to the following men: Delbert Stancill, of

Dalton, Georgia; Cleveland Roberts, of Catawba, Ohio; Clyde Poland, of Round Pond, Maine; Earl Henderson, of Olive Hill, Kentucky; Bill Bentley, of Burlington, Vermont; Ballard Curtis, of Wendall, North Carolina; and Leroy Wolfe, of Moorefield, West Virginia.

Staff Sergeant Senical calls for the platoon to meet outside for the night's assignments. Senical introduces himself to the new recruits and says everyone calls him Bo or Delta 3-5. The latter nickname is his call sign on the radio. Delta 3-5 stands for Delta Company, Third Platoon, and platoon sergeant. Bo gives nightly assignments to almost all of the men. I'm assigned to berm guard with Doug Taylor and Jim Talarico.

Berm guard duty consists of watching a portion of our company's sector of the base camp perimeter. Usually there are three men on duty at a position, and these men alternate with one hour on watch and two hours of sleep. Therefore, if guard duty begins at 2100 hours, the first man in rotation has watch from 2100 to 2200 hours; then he will have two hours off until 2400 hours. The cycle continues until 0600 hours the next morning. Officers check the berm guard positions at night to see if the guard on duty is awake. If someone is caught sleeping, the guard will be reprimanded, possibly with an Article 15. Sometimes it's very difficult to stay awake, especially if an infantryman has had constant day and night duty over a prolonged period of time. I hear this is the rule rather than the exception. We are told it's a soldier's duty to seek relief in pulling guard if one feels he might fall asleep. It's better to take extra duty for someone than to fall asleep, which might cause someone's death. I volunteer for first guard because Taylor and Talarico were on the Bush Master.

After guard duty, we have a few hours to eat, clean up, and attend to personal needs. Last night while on guard duty, I wrote three letters. I wrote to my mother, father, and sister in Ellwood City. I usually tell them all the good and funny things that happen. In the letter I mentioned Gabe and that he is giving me his copies of the Sharon newspaper called *The Herald*. I ask for a subscription to the *Daily Local News*, the local newspaper of West Chester, Pennsylvania, where I grew up. I also ask my mother to make some shorts out of old fatigues I left at home. The other two letters were written to my best friends from West Chester. John Baumhauer is getting his master's degree at Rensselaer Polytechnic Institute in New York, and Jim Giancola is studying for his master's degree at Purdue University in

Indiana. I inform them I arrived at my final destination in Vietnam. When something exciting happens, I promise to write them with all the gory details. They will have to keep the war stories to themselves because I don't want the truth filtering back to my family.

The next day Bob Bukoski, the company armorer, asks me if I want to see something that will leave a lasting impression on me. I say, "Yes." Bob instructs, "Meet me in front of the Delta Headquarters sign in fifteen minutes." I reply, "Okay, I'll be there." When I arrive, Bob is standing in front of a truckload of garbage, which consists mostly of spoiled food.

Bukoski says, "We're going to the garbage dump on the riverside of the base camp. Be prepared for an emotional experience." I tell Bob, "I bet you conned me into helping unload the garbage." He retorts, "No, you won't have to unload the truck. When we get near our dumping site, the truck will be charged by children, who will jump on the truck and look for food while the garbage is unloaded." Bob stops at the mess hall on the way to the dump. He goes inside and returns with some milk, bread, and other food. He puts the food inside the cab and continues on his way to the road leading to the dump site. I ask Bob to hurry up because the stench from the spoiled food and curdled milk he's hauling is making me sick.

Approximately one hundred feet from our dumping destination, children appear from nowhere and run toward the truck. Within seconds, five or six kids jump onto the bed of the moving truck and begin throwing garbage off the truck while sifting through the mess for something to eat. Many grab half-filled cartons of curdled milk and drink the milk while others eat spoiled food. I am sick from the smell and the sight of these children acting like wild animals. Bob slows down the truck because he fears one of them might get injured. Now we're completely surrounded by twenty to twenty-five children. The older ones continue to throw garbage off the truck to the younger children. The ages of the kids probably range from three to twelve, but ages are difficult to determine because they're so undernourished. All the kids have a crazed look on their faces. They stare at us with fear in their eyes and make hissing sounds to us as though they can't speak. When Bob stops the truck, half of the contents are gone before we reach the dumping site. Bukoski yells at the kids to get away from the truck and asks me to help unload the remaining contents.

It's difficult to force starving people away from the only food they have for survival. But Bukoski has performed this ritual many times, and he seems to be able to be firm enough to handle the situation. Bukoski says other GIs who dump food use their M16s to keep the kids at a reasonable distance. The kids move back as we throw the remaining garbage off the truck. Then they run to the unloading area as if someone hit a pinata that distributes candy and gifts.

Bob and I observe the spectacle with feelings of sadness and helplessness. I'm amazed at the savage animal characteristics of these children. They grab the garbage food and sometimes take it from each other, like a pack of wolves fighting over a kill. The kids always maintain a safe distance from us. Maybe they fear our M16s, but I feel they would stay away even if we didn't have our weapons because they behave like wild animals. Bukoski takes fresh food from the truck cab and tries to get the kids to come to us. They act as though we're trying to poison them, and they seem satisfied eating garbage. After the older ones are fed, some kids who look to be about six years old start feeding the younger ones. Imagine a six-year-old being responsible for a younger sibling. Bob places the food he has on flat rocks and we leave.

I say to Bob, "You are right. I'll never forget this experience." One has to ask why people on earth have to be so insensitive to human life. Bob and I return to Delta Company in dead silence. I thank Bob for sharing this experience of human tragedy with me. He repeats this experience over and over, but he never gets used to it.

Tonight I'm assigned to the second listening post with three other guys: Doug Taylor, Leroy Sherfinski, and Eddie Foster, the team leader. Eddie has been my adopted mom the last few days. He has given me survival tips and has kept an eye on me to make sure I don't screw up. Eddie is a really likeable guy whom everybody in the platoon respects. I'm lucky to have such a person to take me under his wing and show me the ropes. As Eddie says, there is no room for mistakes and one must learn fast.

The four of us depart to battalion headquarters for our briefing on LP-2. A first lieutenant gives us our assignment and instructs Eddie to set up the LP next to the Vam Co River, which flows parallel to the base camp. After the briefing, we walk toward the road that leads to the dump site where I'd been earlier in the day. It's now dark, and we're about to leave the perimeter of the base camp and follow the road to the river. I ask Eddie, "Are we really going to the river's edge?" Eddie looks at us and says, "I'm not crazy. We're going only fifty meters outside the base perimeter next to the road berm. That way, if the VC appear, we'll have plenty of time to get back inside base camp."

We move approximately fifty meters and position ourselves for the night. Eddie waits about fifteen minutes before he calls in our first sit rep (situation reported) to say our LP is set up as instructed for the night. Every hour we call in our status. We identify ourselves and give our report, which is sit rep—negative (situation reported—no activity).

We all stay awake for the first hour; then Taylor and Sherfinski take turns sleeping while Eddie and I remain on guard. Eddie says, "I find it difficult to sleep on these four-man LPs because it's easy for the guy on guard to fall asleep. I usually stay awake until 0200 hours when the enemy movement curtails for the night." He continues, "These listening posts are positioned in the same areas every night outside base camp. I'm sure the VC is aware of the general vicinity of all the LP locations. The advantage we have over the enemy at night is the ability to see their movement while looking into the starlight scope. The scope uses the light from the stars and moon to illuminate the darkness as if it were daytime." Eddie tells us, "When you requisition a starlight scope, make sure the battery is well charged. A weak battery or poor light from the heavens is a disadvantage."

As Eddie and I talk, we observe two AC-47 gunships fire on an enemy position. It's like being entertained by a Fourth of July fireworks display. Eddie tries to pick up the fighting transmissions on our radio. By changing frequencies and fooling around with the radio, sometimes other combat activity can be located in our area.

Finally my one-hour watch is over and Eddie takes the next watch. The night is uneventful, and we report back to battalion headquarters in the morning. The four of us go to breakfast together. The mess hall is a sight to see. The men serving food wear army green tee-shirts that are soaked with sweat from preparing and cooking food for hours in the hot kitchen. During lunchtime when the temperature is usually in the high nineties, the servers sweat so much that the perspiration rolls off their bodies into the food. Nobody seems concerned. The men are delighted to have a hot meal. After getting some eggs, bacon, and toast, we find an empty table strewn with half-filled milk cartons. I try drinking milk, but it has already begun to spoil. What a shame there are four to five cartons of milk on each table that are unfit to drink. I decide to have Kool-Aid instead.

After breakfast we go back to our quarters. Our platoon gets its gear ready for the day's operations. Eddie is going to field operations while Taylor, Sherfinski, and I have duty working on building a new bunker. Taylor is in charge of the Vietnamese women who are hired by battalion headquarters to collect the trash left by the soldiers going to the field. Cases of C rations are distributed to each platoon assigned to field operations for the day. The men open the cases and look through the different kinds of C ration meals, taking only the meals they like. Ham is a favorite meat selection while peaches are the best fruit. I notice the boxes of C rations have a packaging date of 1946. The rations were made over twenty years ago and still suffice for a quick meal. Taylor allows the women to take rations left behind by the troops. He is becoming a favorite with the women.

The bunker we work on is made of heavy wooden beams. It has wood interior sides and a layer of 105 mm howitzer boxes filled with mud and reinforced with two layers of sandbags. The bottom section is set up as a machine gun nest with an M60 machine gun, and the top section serves as a lookout post and an area for the guards to sleep. The left side of Delta Company's perimeter has a similar bunker.

My assignment tonight is berm guard. Tim and I have been informed that tomorrow will be our first day in the field with the Third Platoon. I'm excited and terrified about the thought of being in combat operations. In a few weeks I'll probably develop a routine of preparing myself like the other men in the platoon. I've noticed that everyone has his way and style of putting on a combat face. The highlight of berm guard is watching the women come out of their hootches in New Life Village to defecate in the rice paddy. New Life Village is adjacent to our base camp on Delta Company's sector of the perimeter. It seems the women turn their asses toward the guards to show disrespect to them when they do their business. After they come out of the paddies, they always wash their bodies and their muddy clothing.

Aerial View of Camp Scott, Tan Tru, Vietnam.

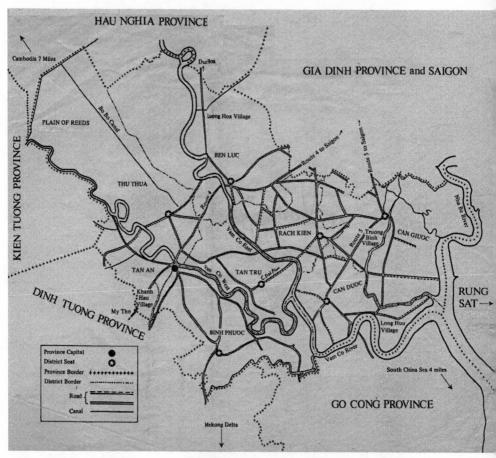

Map of Long An Province

4

First Day in Field December 8

Eddie Foster comes over to me and says, "Jim, I will walk with you to the choppers and will give you an idea of what to expect today." I feel relieved to have a veteran take interest in my welfare. I ask him, "Will it be okay if I ride on the same chopper with you?" He says, "No, I'll be riding on the lead Huey since I'm walking point today. Sergeant Dinsmore is your team leader, and you're to board the same chopper with him and a few other new grunts." Foster says, "Listen to Dinsmore who'll receive orders from others in the platoon according to the situation at hand. Depend on the veterans to make the right decisions and give proper leadership in the field. Enough said. The day will go quickly, and this will probably be a good training exercise for you."

We reach the road outside the base camp and see the troops in position for the choppers to arrive. I thank Eddie for his advice and walk over to the group forming by Dinsmore. Tim is already there standing with Leroy Wolfe. Dinsmore says, "I'll wait until all six of us are here before I give instructions on boarding and departing from the choppers." Shortly Doug Taylor and Bobby Holman show up, and in the distance the choppers appear. Dinsmore demonstrates how we're to carefully approach the chopper, running perpendicular toward the Huey in a low-crouching position and staying clear of the rotor blades. Dinsmore emphasizes, "As soon as the Huey lands, you should board immediately and allow plenty of space for others to follow. When we land in the field, disembark the chopper immediately so the Huey won't be in danger of being shot down. Speed and safety entering and exiting is paramount."

The choppers land, and we board immediately and are in flight within seconds. The new recruits sit on the seats inside the chopper while the veterans sit on the chopper floor with their feet dangling outside the Huey just above the skids. As the Huey gains altitude, I feel insecure because of the helicopter's openness. Both sides of the chopper are wide open, which creates a nice breeze inside the chopper. I think Dinsmore and the guys sitting on the floor are nuts. Of course, my good buddy Tim is sitting on the floor with a big grin on his face. Tim says, "There is room by me." I reply, "Fuck you!" Tim laughs and says, "Fuck you too!"

Third Platoon on Eagle flights fly to thier next LZ in the Mekong Delta.

Dinsmore yells over the thumping sound of the rotor blades, "Prepare for landing." I survey the landing site, which is a dry rice paddy near some hootches that border a woodline. The landing site is picturesque. It has dry and wet paddies. The perimeter consists of lush tropical vegetation in the woodlines. The Hueys swoop down for their landing, and we quickly exit the choppers as instructed. Dinsmore directs his squad to the outside of the woodline in sight of some nearby hootches. The point team and the veterans proceed to search the hootches and check the inhabitants for proper identification. All civilians are required to have proper government identification at all times. Our platoon searches for military-age men who look suspicious or lack proper identification. Military-age men in the country should be in the Vietnamese Armed Forces. If not, they're most likely the enemy, the local Vietcong. The only exception is if a civilian has a disability.

About fifteen minutes later, we hear a lot of automatic gunfire. I can tell by the sound of the weapons fire that it's both enemy and friendly fire. The squad leaders give orders, and Dinsmore tells our group to hold our positions until further notice. The weapons fire is intense for a few moments; then the firing becomes more sporadic. Those of us in the rear are at wits' end trying to figure out what is going on. Shortly after the initial burst of gunfire, we hear guys yelling for Doc. When cries for the medic are heard, that usually means the platoon has incurred a casualty. Everyone intensely waits for information to filter back on what is happening.

Nearly half an hour later, the word comes back that Eddie Foster was killed. A dead silence hangs in the air after we learn of Eddie's death. Minutes before, the situation was chaotic, noisy, and tense because of the uncertainty of the outcome. Now a quiet, calm, and serene atmosphere pervades as the platoon gives final respect to Eddie. My heart sank in my chest when I learned the horrible news. It's almost impossible for me to comprehend what I heard. Only a short time earlier, Eddie was full of life; and if anybody deserved to survive this war, it was he. I take time to pray for Eddie and ask God to welcome this fine young man into his kingdom. God bless Eddie Foster.

While we wait for further information on what has happened, I try to find some consolation in his death. Why Eddie? Why Eddie? I guess there is truth in the statement the Lord takes the good people first. Hopefully, his death will set an example for me to have the strength, fortitude, and knowledge to survive. I want his death to mean something.

The word comes back that Eddie was killed by a Vietcong who shot him at close range with an AK-47 rifle. Bo Senical witnessed Eddie's death, and neither Eddie nor Bo could react fast enough to save Eddie. Bo killed the Vietcong who shot Eddie. It kind of made me feel better knowing the VC is dead, but I know in my heart this is all insanity. War is definitely hell and nobody gains from it. Everyone in the Third Platoon is a casualty today. I am definitely one of the mental casualties because I lost my mentor, Eddie Foster.

Orders come from higher command that we'll remain in the area overnight. Lieutenant D and Bo Senical keep the platoon moving until dark. At dusk, the platoon sets up an L-shaped ambush in a rice paddy. I settle down in one of the three-man positions next to a paddy dike. On one side of the dike is water, and on the other side is a dry paddy. I have never been in a combat situation before and don't know what is really expected of me. I'm mentally exhausted trying to block Eddie's death out of my mind. I tell myself this will happen again and again, and I'll go crazy if I let war become my personal tragedy. I realize this is only the beginning of a challenging year when I'll have to deal with trauma on a routine basis.

I'm cold from the chilly air and the damp fatigues, which are a result of humping through the wet rice paddies. My socks are soaked and rub against my sore ankles. We learned in stateside training it's a good idea to attend to one's feet. I try to block the day's events from my mind. I take off my boots and begin to wring out my wet socks when Sergeant Billy West appears. West sees me with my boots off and goes into a tirade, yelling, "What the hell are you doing?" I say, "I'm drying out my socks." West looks at me, befuddled, and says, "What are you going to do if we're to move out or a firefight starts?" I say to Billy, "I'll move out barefooted." With that response, West shakes his head in disbelief and leaves.

I put my boots on when Billy returns with Sergeant Senical. Bill goes into another tirade telling Senical that I'm a dumb ass. Bo looks at me in disgust, says nothing, and leaves. I feel like whale shit at the bottom of the ocean. I let my superiors down on my first day in the field. I respect these veterans, and I'm ashamed of my actions. Hopefully, I'll be able to regain their respect after giving them a bad first impression.

After pulling my guard on our position, I find a place to sleep on the rice paddy dike. Gunfire erupts late at night, and I roll over into the wet rice paddy in the direction of the firing. Quickly I jump out of the line of fire to the other side of the dike. The probing fire stops, and I learn another lesson about being ready at all times. Lieutenant D gives orders for the platoon to move to a new position to avoid a possible mortar attack. Activity for the night ceases.

The night is long, and everyone is mentally exhausted from losing our most admired buddy. The choppers pick us up later in the day, and we arrive back in base camp to perform mundane personal chores of showering, shaving, cleaning laundry, and writing letters. First Sergeant Robert Laughead welcomes us back to the company area by patting us on the back and giving words of encouragement. He is like a father figure to the men. Sergeant Laughead tries to welcome the troops home especially when he knows we've had a rough time in the field.

At mail call I receive Christmas cards from Aunt Jean and Uncle Johnny Long, Uncle Tom and Aunt Virginia Milliken, and John and Hilma Hackman. I write a letter to Mom, giving her some ideas of what to include in a Christmas package for me.

In the evening Bo Senical announces the Third Platoon is going to have an inspection the following afternoon. The inspection includes our billet area, rifle, ammunition, and field gear. We spend most of the morning preparing for the inspection. We fieldstrip our weapons and use kerosene to brush and clean all the parts. I disassemble my M16, clean the parts, and reassemble the rifle. The receiver mechanism is lubricated with a special creamy rifle gel to prevent the inner workings from rusting and jamming during operation. In Vietnam an M16 can rust overnight. It's a major problem keeping one's weapon clean and functional. Another important step is to clean the magazines and ammunition. The magazine clips are removed in order to dump the bullets out of the magazine. The magazines are cleaned in kerosene and laid out to dry. The clips are reinserted and the ammunition is put into the magazine. I'm surprised to see that my ammunition is very dirty and definitely could have been a problem in combat. It's customary to insert only eighteen rounds in a twenty-round magazine. I've been told that filling a magazine might cause the rifle to jam. Another lesson learned is to keep the ammunition clean. Lieutenant Deutschlander's inspection is a good idea because each of us then takes precautions so that our equipment doesn't become dysfunctional in a short period of time. Lieutenant D and Bo inspect the billet area but overlook the weapon inspection because they observed our cleaning methods while preparing for inspection. The vets of the Third Platoon help the newcomers with the fieldstripping of the weapons. Lieutenant D and Bo don't make a big deal about the inspection. Basically it's to impress upon us the first requirement when coming out of the field is to properly clean the weapons, ammunition, and field gear before taking care of personal hygiene. A soldier has to be prepared to fight at a moment's notice, and the proper functioning of one's weapon could mean life or death to the soldier or his buddies.

Lieutenant D gives orders to saddle up and meet at the front gate of the base camp. He says we're going outside the base camp perimeter to practice setting up night ambushes. We're out for about an hour and are shown the proper way to form an L-shaped ambush by utilizing firing zones and Claymore mines. I appreciate the instruction because I know I'm weak in the tactics of assembling and positioning Claymore mines. The instruction made everyone aware of his duties and what is expected of each of us in an ambush. After the training exercise, we're informed that we'll be leaving on a Bush Master tomorrow for three days.

I decide to take two sets of my fatigues to Ms. Ahn's laundry to have the pant legs tapered and the shirts altered in the midsection. When we come back from the Bush Master, the fatigues should be ready to wear. It's best to arrange one's laundry drop-off according to how long he'll be out in the field.

We're back from the Bush Master, which was uneventful as far as having contact with the enemy. Believe me I'm not complaining! However, some unusual incidents did occur. When Tim followed the platoon, he brushed up against a branch on a beautiful tree with bright red leaves. He began to scream, "Red ants! Red ants! Help, they're all over me!" I ran over with two other men, and we helped Tim strip off his gear and clothes while we brushed at the ants covering his body. The red ants managed to severely sting him, causing his skin to swell and redden. We took our time freeing his gear and clothes of these ants that had swarmed over Tim. The tree was completely covered with red ants so that it looked like a beautiful red tree from a distance. We should have known better because Vietnam has no such vegetation in our area of operation.

While taking a break in a Vietnamese hootch, I noticed a mama-san picking something out of a child's hair and sticking it in her mouth like a monkey grooming her young. I asked Sergeant Dinsmore what she's doing. Dinsmore laughed and says, "You do not want to know. She is picking lice out of her daughter's hair and eating them." An old lady, who is probably the grandma, fingered a pink paste in a small bowl and applied the paste to her gums and rotten teeth. Dinsmore informed us they make powdered paste out of strong opiumlike drug, which they use as a painkiller. The old lady had the biggest smile on her face and revealed she was completely under the influence of the ingredients in the paste. I saw enough in this hootch and decided to go to another hootch to observe the Vietnamese locals.

In the next hootch I met a cute little girl. I wanted to give her a gift, but I thought it best to make her work for her treat. I didn't encourage Vietnamese children to be beggars. In more populated areas where the platoon travels, the children rate gifts from one to ten, with ten as the worst gift. Usually when they rate a gift that low, they throw it back in disgust. This happened to me when I offered a certain type of C ration. I asked the child to fill my canteen with rainwater that was in a large covered piece of pottery next to the hootch. Of course, I used hand gestures to express my wish. She smiled and seemed happy about doing me a favor. I gave her a package of life savers for her chore, and the expression on her face showed me this was probably one of the first gifts she had ever received. We both smiled instinctively, and I felt satisfied because I brought joy into her life by giving her a pack of candy.

When we return to Camp Scott from the Bush Master, First Sergeant Laughead greets the men as they enter the company area. We call our first sergeant Top, the name referred to most company first sergeants held in high esteem. Sergeant Laughead is liked by all the men in the company. He realizes his number one priority is to administer to the troops' needs, and he does a wonderful job of attending to our welfare. He announces shower water is available and SP packages will be disbursed to the platoons. The SP packages contain sundries for our personal hygiene, a large assortment of candy and gum, writing materials, and decks of cards for amusement. Sometimes we receive a carton of cigarettes per soldier with the SP packages.

Tim and I finish our showers and walk back to the temporary housing, which is a large green tent we share with other members of the platoon. The tent is better accommodations than the billet area because it's open to the air. The billet area is too small and is very hot inside. Tim and I lie on our cots to write letters back home. Tim says, "Who are you writing to?" I say, "My girlfriend, Violet Milliken." Tim laughs because he knows I'm referring to my mother. He says, "What are you writing about?" I reply, "I am telling my family that being an infantryman is a twenty-five-hour job." Believe it or not I've been on duty day and night for the last eighteen days. Time sure passes quickly when one is having fun!

Tim says he's writing to his wife, Gail. I ask him what he's saying in his letter. Tim responds, "I tell her Vietnam is made up of mud, mosquitoes, and red ants, and I can't bear the thought of fighting for any one of those damn things!" Tim and I laugh. Tim quips, "We should write a letter to Grove City College expressing how our education has helped us in a combat zone." I agree with him, "Yeah, great idea! We can enclose a picture of us humping in the rice paddies." What a success story for the *GCC Alumni News*. We both laugh again until the pain of laughter hurts, forcing us to curtail our funny comments. I can feel a special bond developing between Tim and me in these trying circumstances.

A Huey circles our company area to land. The left side of our tent is blown loose. As I jump up to hold down that section of the tent, my hat blows off into a pool of water next to our tent. I run after the hat and fall into the water and get completely soaked. Tim laughs uncontrollably at me sitting in the water after I'd just put on a clean set of fatigues. I begin to laugh because Tim is really enjoying the sight of me floundering in the dirty paddy water. I yell to him over the roar of the helicopter engine and rotor blades, "Take a picture for GCC!"

After dusk, all hell breaks loose at Delta Company's berm. I'm in the billet area playing cards when gunfire erupts in Delta Company's sector of the base camp perimeter. Everyone grabs his weapon and charges to the berm to defend the perimeter. I run in a low-crouching position to protect my body from enemy fire. Within a few minutes, the entire company, including support personnel, is in fighting position returning fire to enemy locations. I'm next to Billy West, who shouts out orders. The veterans take charge, repositioning men and their weapons while screaming orders to gain firepower over the attacking NVA troops. Bill spots an NVA soldier on the roof of one of the hootches in New Life Village and yells, "Shoot the son of a bitch on top of the hootch!" West and the men around Billy open up on the gook. He disappears from sight, and the hootch is set on fire from the barrage of M16 fire. Now most of the fire is directed at the village where the enemy seeks refuge.

The scene is breathtaking. Imagine one hundred men on the berm firing automatic weapons, such as M16 rifles, M60, or .50 machine guns. Men also fire M79 grenade launchers and await word to set off Claymore mines. Visibility becomes very poor due to the dense smoke from fires and the expended ammunition. The air hangs heavy, smelling of sulfur and burning debris. No one can really tell how close the enemy is or how many there are because of the high level of noise and poor visibility. The steady stream of bullets from the automatic weapons is awesome. I can't envision trying to penetrate that field of fire. Bo Senical comes down the line and gives orders for the Third Platoon to field dress and meet at the rear of the barracks.

I want to pretend I didn't hear that order, but I don't have it in me to be a coward. The Third Platoon rushes back to the barracks to saddle up for the field. In a few minutes, we meet at the rear of the barracks and quickly move down the main road in a westerly direction. When we arrive at the gate, which crosses the road leading to Tan Tru, we stop for a short briefing by Bo. We're told that a small LP group or reconnaissance team is trapped outside of the base camp, and it's our mission to provide cover for their safe return to the base camp. The platoon is to remain outside the base camp to sweep for enemy casualties and weapons.

The Third Platoon moves out, and inadvertently I end up in the front of the column with Senical. I wonder how I managed to make such a bad move. This is definitely not where I want to be. Senical keeps in touch with the base camp while we move toward the trapped men. Within a short time, a squad of men moves by us to the secure base camp. Senical receives additional orders to check a woodline where gunships spotted an enemy mortar tube that fired on the base. It takes the platoon an hour to reach the location. The area was rocketed by gunships, but we don't find any bodies, weapons, or enemy supplies indicating where a mortar tube emplacement could be found.

Senical has us move out of the woodline with Sam, who is our tiger scout and pointman. The pointman's job is to find and avoid booby traps, prevent ambushes, and locate the target area while searching for the enemy at all times. Usually the pointman is the first individual in a platoon to engage in combat with the VC or NVA troops. Sam leads us through dense vegetation before we reach a clearing of rice paddies. The sky is still pitch-black when Sam yells out, "Booby trap!" Everyone freezes in his footsteps. I'm amazed he found a booby trap at night. How could he do this? Is this dumb luck or is he that good? My confidence level in his ability is questioned. I make it a priority to find out more about him as an individual and a soldier. He was a Vietcong before becoming a tiger scout. After we destroy the booby trap, we proceed to sweep back to the base camp.

Sam—Vietnamese Tiger Scout walks point.

The platoon goes straight to the mess hall for an early breakfast after spending most of the night outside of the base camp sweeping the perimeter. During breakfast I question many of the men in the platoon about Sam's qualifications as a tiger scout. Everyone speaks highly of Sam, especially Bo Senical and Billy West. The men are in agreement that Sam is definitely the best scout in the battalion. He is trustworthy and excels in the field at gathering intelligence, finding booby traps, and fighting the VC and NVA. Bo told me that Sam has a large bounty placed on him by the enemy for his capture or death. Since the men praise Sam and the enemy recognizes his accomplishments as a scout, I have no further doubts about him.

When we return to our barracks, the platoon is told to prepare for another Bush Master in two hours. The army sure has a way of playing with one's mind. I guess it's good not to have enough time to reflect on what happened the previous day. The battalion commander sends a word of praise to our company commander, saying he never saw such an amazing force of firepower coming from Delta Company during a ground attack. He was definitely impressed. Apparently the battalion incurred a few casualties, but kept the NVA troops from penetrating our base perimeter. We heard nothing about enemy casualties because they are difficult to determine since they usually hide or carry away their dead.

The Bush Master proves to be a waste of time. The enemy activity in the Delta seems to be curtailed for now. Maybe they're regrouping for the Tet New Year. The last two times on Bush Masters, we experienced no major enemy confrontations, only sniper fire, which is very unusual on that type of operation.

When we come in from the field, the first item on the agenda is to enjoy a cold beer. To our surprise, there is no beer or soda. All our beer and soda were stolen while we're in the field. The platoon is really pissed off. Tim and I had three cases of beer and one case of soda taken. As a group we decide to have a platoon member who is not going to the field designated as the individual to keep guard on our valuables. Another result of the theft is our bonding together as a platoon to buy beer and soda. A group of guys in the platoon who refer to themselves as the Begoni Clan take the initiative to build large coolers that we can lock when we're out in the field. The clan requisitions 155 mm howitzer shell casing boxes from the mortar platoon area. These boxes are lined with insulation to protect the rounds and, with modifications, make great beer and soda coolers.

The Begoni Clan's inspirational leader is Dave Johnson, of Waukeska, Wisconsin, whom we call Big Lou Begoni. The clan was formed to act as a coping mechanism against the daily rigors of combat. Each member is given a fictitious Bigoni name. When in the platoon area, the members assume their Bigoni name as though they are someone else not in Vietnam. Other charter members of the clan are Leroy Sherfinski, of Waukeska, Wisconsin; Bruce Falkum, of Minneapolis, Minnesota; Ralph Groshen, of Stillwater, Minnesota; Jim Hughes, of Lacrosse, Wisconsin; Gary Reitan, of Hinckley, Minnesota; and Tim Firestone, of Camp Hill, Pennsylvania. Most of these men come from the same general area of the United States, which makes for a natural bonding element in the clan.

The group decides to go to the PX base store that is open for a short time on Wednesdays. The store has only three items for sale: beer, soda, and cigarettes. On the first trip to the PX, the group purchases thirty-six cases of beer and soda. While standing in line, the men are amused by another soldier's pet monkey. The monkey is drinking a beer while trying to smoke a cigarette at the same time. When the drunken monkey gets nasty, the GI is asked to leave with his pet. Whoever is on stand-down has the responsibility of getting ice and keeping the coolers full of beer and soda for the troops arriving from the field.

Later in the day, I spend time with John Sassian, of Buffalo, New York; Joe Simmons, of Jacksonville, Florida; Dave Pickering, of Hemlock, Michigan; and John Price, of Flint, Michigan, taking photographs of each other to send home for Christmas. Bo Senical stops by for picture taking and informs us we have a cake mission tomorrow: pulling security at the Bo Bo Canal on the border of Vietnam and Cambodia.

It took a week before I got in the groove riding on the choppers. I now sit on the floor of the Huey and dangle my legs out of the chopper over the skids. There is a certain exhilaration and freedom one experiences in an open helicopter when transported at high altitudes. Sometimes I feel like a bird, surveying the beautiful countryside for a place to land.

We can view the Bo Bo Canal separating the Vietnamese and Cambodian borders. The helicopters land on the Vietnamese side of the waterway since Cambodia is off-limits to American intervention. The landing is in a rice paddy near the canal, and we immediately move out in the direction of the canal. Larry Sandage, a Ninth Division combat photographer, joins us in the field today. Larry is busy shooting photographs of the men approaching the canal.

The location on the canal we are to secure is free of vegetation on both sides. The canal water has a brown color from a lot of silt in the water. The canal has the appearance of a river with sampan traffic. Our side of the canal has a wide footpath, which the Vietnamese use as a makeshift road. Hootches are near the waterway on the other side of the canal. Women work outside of the homes with their children playing nearby.

Lieutenant Deutschlander and Bo Senical come by and say it's okay to go swimming and have some fun. Most of the guys like the idea and strip

---

50

down to go in for a dip. I keep my clothes on and stand guard while they frolic around in the nude. Guys swim in the canal and flirt with women going by on the sampans. Everyone is having a good time, including the Cambodian women, who peek out from their homes to watch the spectacle of the nude soldiers at play. A few other nonswimmers and I keep guard over those in the water, their weapons, and equipment on shore.

Bo and Larry Sandage come by and ask if anyone has any money for beer. I volunteer twenty dollars in military payment currency (MPC), which I give Bo for the beer. They scout the area and learn about a military outpost that isn't too far down the footpath. Bo says he'll reimburse me when we return to base camp. Bo and Larry hike off on a beer run.

I feel leery about the Vietnamese kids getting too close to us. They're pointing at our private parts and the hair around them. That is unusual for them to see because the Vietnamese have little hair on their bodies. I feel uneasy about so few of us guarding the many men in the water. I make everyone passing by on the footpath keep an appropriate distance between them and us. Periodically I raise my M16 and point to get my message across.

Bo and his foraging partner Larry return with cases of beer. Everyone hears the announcement, "Get your cold beer!" When the men exit the canal, they look like mud men because the silt clings to their skin. What a time they have trying to clean the silt off with dirty brown water! The day is a welcomed treat for the platoon because the vessels that needed our security never showed up. We had an uneventful day in the field with plenty of fun drinking beer and swimming. Larry enjoys himself taking photographs of the Third Platoon in staged poses. He takes one of Ray Cartigiano and me with our backs together silhouetted against the canal and nipa palm. He promises to have copies of the photographs made for us. Larry really enjoys his photography work and likes taking combat pictures of the Third Platoon because of the quality leadership and the high caliber of soldiers in the platoon. I believe Larry feels quite secure with us, even in a combat situation.

5

Christmas 1968 Vietnam Holiday?

Christmas is only four days from now, and it seems the battalion is going to ease up on field assignments until after the twenty-fifth. Mail call was great today. I received many cards. I wrote to my parents telling them who sent me Christmas cards. From Ellwood City, Pennsylvania, I received cards from Bill and Helen Fisher, Bert and Flo Staggers, Dean and Ethel McDonald, Juanita Clutter, Mrs. Graham, and other folks I don't even know. From West Chester, Pennsylvania, I received cards from John and Fran Baumhauer, John and Kathy Dulin, Tony and Betty Saggese, and Jim Giancola. Family members who sent cards include Dick and Jane Milliken, Jim and Louise Milliken, and my grandparents William and Pearl Milliken. I got a chuckle from my grandmother's card wishing me well and enclosing two dollars, which she gives each of her nineteen grandchildren. I tell her I'm too old to receive the two dollars. She says, "I treat all my grandchildren the same, regardless of their ages." I also received a Christmas package loaded with goodies and some items I requested from my parents.

Today we received word that the battalion is instituting a new dress code in base camp. Command says we must wear a full uniform in base camp during the day, unless we're on detail. We can wear military cutoff shorts after 1700 hours. I'm sure these rules will be impossible to enforce. This dress code is asinine because most of the troops in base camp suffer from a skin disease or a foot infection. Ringworm and forms of trench foot are common problems for soldiers in this wet, hot climate. The best treatment for skin problems is sunlight and exposure to the air. Troops usually wear unaltered fatigues at night to protect themselves from mosquito bites. I guess command has nothing better to do than screw around with our minds.

Tim, the Kid, Larry Boneck, and I are assigned to sweep the perimeter of the base camp to look for mortar tubes the enemy sometimes sets up during the day. The Vietcong pretend to be rice farmers, and instead of working their fields, they set up homemade mortar tubes in the paddies. Tim says, "Bring your Instamatic camera and we'll take some shots outside the base camp perimeter." I say, "Good thinking. Most of the pictures we've taken are inside the base camp." We sweep the dry rice paddies outside of Delta Company's berm when the Kid yells out, "I think I see a mortar tube!" Tim, who likes to work with explosives, goes over to Ray and verifies the Kid's find. Sure enough it's a crude tube emplacement with a mortar round aimed at one of the large berm bunkers. Tim is our RTO, so he's awarded the privilege of calling in our discovery to headquarters. They'll send out an ordinance disposal team while we continue our sweep. Now we take our mission more seriously because we didn't expect to find anything. The area is searched more thoroughly, but we don't find any more tubes.

Ray says, "Let's go into New Life Village and finish up our film." Larry leads the way to the village. On our way to the village, Larry and I look for a good background to take a picture. Larry says to me, "Milkman, a shot of you sitting on that grave marker would make a great picture." I state, "Sure!" In a kidding manner I remark to Boneck, "Tell me how you want me to pose." Larry and I tease each other because only a couple of days before, I posed for Larry Sandage on a similar grave marker during a combat photo rest break. It's common to see individual graves in the countryside rice fields because the Vietnamese have a custom of burying their family in the rice paddies where they worked during their lives. This grave marker is impressive in its appearance. It's made out of cement with blue and gold decorative designs that outline the coffinlike structure. Many of the markers have decorative porcelain plates that are attached to the monuments with cement. The marker where I posed two days prior for Larry Sandage was in poor condition, like most of the markers one sees in the countryside. That grave marker was in a state of disintegration because it was torn apart by bullets and explosions.

Jim Milliken poses on a Vietnamese grave burial plot located
in a rice paddy.

The villagers are surprised to see us because the soldiers in
base camp rarely come into the village on a social visit. There is a
listening post on the other side of the village, which is manned by
GIs and ARVNs at night. To get to the post, a squad of men must
travel through the village at dusk. Normally, this is the only daily
contact the GIs have with the villagers. We wander around the small
village, looking for interesting sites to photograph. I take pictures of
village houses and decide I would like to have a picture of a typical
Vietnamese family. I notice children outside a nearby hootch. I walk
over to the children and show them my camera. I ask them to get their
papa-san and mama-san for a picture. The children get their parents,
but they're apprehensive about having a family picture taken next to
their home. I bribe them with cigarettes and candy. What an attitude
change! They are ready to have their picture taken. I yell to Tim, "Get
your ass over here to take this picture of the family and me before
they change their minds." Tim hurries over, grabs my camera, and
begins to act like a fool by trying to get the family to say "cheese"

in unison. I scream at Tim, "Just take the damn picture!" He replies, "This will cost you." The Kid and Boneck come over and announce it's time to return to the company area for an afternoon delight of a beer or two or three.

Typical Vietnamese family in New Life Village. Soldier is Jim Milliken.

While we relax drinking beers and enjoying a game of poker, word circulates that we'll be in the field the next two days. One day the platoon will sweep for enemy activity and the other day will be a Medcap in a nearby village. Medcaps are assignments where troops go into a populated location and render medical assistance to the general population. The health system in Vietnam is terrible. The people suffer from diseases such as malaria, yellow fever, cholera, and bubonic plague. Fortunately, the GIs are given pills for malaria and have been inoculated for the other diseases. In the southern part of Vietnam, the mosquitoes aren't the malaria-carrying type. We are given pills, although no one takes them because the danger of getting malaria is minimal and there is a side effect of loose bowels. Believe me, it would be a hardship if an infantryman had loose bowels. I'm notified I have guard duty again tonight. I should have another beer to improve my eyesight and night vision.

Today is December 24, and our platoon is scheduled for field duty, but I've been selected for stand-down. I'm sure company headquarters will find some jobs for those on stand-down. Even when the infantry is in base camp, we receive little free time to relax and rest. Sergeant Dinsmore stops by and asks for twelve volunteers for a Medcap to Tan Tru village. I never volunteer for details, but I tell him to include me on the list. His detail will be more fun and interesting than the assignments one gets in base camp. Dinsmore says, "We'll form in front of the company headquarters at 1300 hours. A truck will transport us to Tan Tru." I reply, "Okay, I'll be there."

The group of twelve men included guys from all three platoons of Delta Company. The ride to Tan Tru is a short trip. The truck stops in a small village plaza that appears to be a dead end to the main road. There is one main building in the plaza that looks like a store and a community center. We disembark from the truck and walk over to homes that are adjacent to the village town. The medics select a location for a makeshift clinic to examine and treat the villagers. All the men bring gifts to share with the local population. The kids enjoy candy and the adults receive C rations. I brought a fruitcake my parents sent me for Christmas. I think the cake will be a great gift for an entire family to enjoy. Now it's my job to find that perfect family.

The people seem a little cautious about our intentions. They probably think we have ulterior motives other than being goodwill ambassadors. Finally, I meet a young boy who can actually speak and understand a little English. We do our best to converse, and I indicate to him I would be honored to meet his family. He takes me to a nearby hootch and invites me inside to meet his father. The boy speaks Vietnamese to his father, explaining to him my goodwill intention. The father nods his head to me, and I offer my hand to shake. I take C rations out of a sock that is attached to the back of my web gear and offer my gift to him. To my surprise, the papa-san is elated and calls out to other family members in the bunker. The shy mother approaches me, and I offer her a package containing the fruitcake. With a little coaxing, the mama-san opens the package. When she sees the fruitcake, her face begins to glow like a light bulb. I instantly feel gratified. Immediately the family begins to converse in a feverish pitch. I ask the boy what they're saying. He tells me the family wants to celebrate with me and share the cake. I tell him it will be an honor to celebrate with his family.

The mama-san puts a cloth on the dried mud floor inside the hootch, and we all sit down with our legs crossed. She cuts the large cake in very small pieces and offers me the first slice with hot tea. The papa-san gets out his rice whiskey and pours me a taste in a small saucer. He pours the whiskey for himself and offers a toast. I drink the rice whiskey and smile, saying, "Number 1! Number 1!" I think to myself this is a treasured moment in my life that I'll always remember. We finish our cake and I talk with the family. Their son interprets. I learn they have an older son who is in the Vietnamese Army. I give additional gifts of candy and soap to the boy and his two sisters.

The young boy and I go outside his home to talk. He gives me lessons in Vietnamese, and I ask him to write the phrases in a small pink address book that the Salvation Army gave me when I left the States. He tells me he is fourteen years old, and he teaches me how to count to ten and say the days of the week in Vietnamese. I spend about two hours with the family before I make my way back to the clinic. The medic is still treating children and the elders of Tan Tru. The Medcap is definitely a success. On our way back to Camp Scott, I reminisce about the family I just met and wonder if they'll survive the war.

We arrive at base camp around 1600 hours, and I receive an immediate assignment for guard duty on Christmas Eve. I just heard First Lieutenant Patrick Woods of Delta Company was killed in the field today. I don't know the man, but I'll say a prayer for him and his family. I can't imagine my family getting notice of my death during the Christmas holidays. I find it difficult to get in the holiday spirit.

Top, our company's first sergeant, has returned from Saigon on a foraging mission. Apparently, he took a few of the men in a jeep with an attached trailer to Saigon and division headquarters to confiscate steaks, mushrooms, beer, and other goodies for a Christmas Eve barbecue. Top is always trying to brighten our outlook in base camp because he knows of the infantryman's untiring effort to cope with the sadness and depression of field operations. The Begoni Clan promises to bring me barbecued steaks to eat while I am assigned to bunker guard. At 1700 hours, a group of the Begoni boys, including me since I am now a member, go to chow. After dinner, a trip to the EM club is in order for slot machine action and a few Buds. I get lucky and win eight dollars on the nickel slots and treat my platoon members to a round of drinks. I leave the club early to prepare for guard duty. I'm a little apprehensive about guard duty on Christmas Eve. This would be a great night for the enemy to have a ground attack when all the troops are celebrating.

Darkness settles in with the aroma of grilled steaks. I sit on the second floor of the guard bunker, anxiously awaiting my Christmas Eve treat. The smell of barbecued steaks permeates the air for an hour before the Begoni brothers appear with four huge steaks and all the trimmings, but no beer for us on guard duty. The night is quiet except for the chatter around the barracks. Most of the men stay up late because tomorrow is supposed to be a "down day" for the battalion.

"Merry Christmas! Merry Christmas! Merry Christmas to all!" comes the greeting from a loudspeaker on a Huey chopper hovering over Camp Scott at 0600 hours. The Huey circles the base camp blaring Christmas carols from the sound system. "Jingle Bells" is a delight to hear but seems out of place in a tropical climate. Santa Claus smiles and waves to the troops and is assisted by women helpers who are doing the same. The greetings continue for ten minutes. Then the chopper lands on the battalion commander's helicopter pad adjacent to our bunker. Santa Claus and his helpers, who are Donut Dollies dressed up in Christmas costumes, walk toward battalion headquarters. Today begins in a cheerful manner. The troops expect to have a relaxing afternoon with a Christmas dinner and entertainment that is planned behind the EM club.

At 1300 hours our platoon leaves early to get good seats for the floor show. When we arrive, all the seats near the stage are occupied. I select the top of a bunker for my seat. Clyde, Tim, and other members of the Third Platoon join me, while the other men choose to sit together. The troops are really psyched for the entertainment. The act consists of four Korean girls singing '60s and '70s American songs, accompanied by Korean musicians. The girls put on a great show singing their hearts out in one-hundred-degree heat. They change their costumes because perspiring makes their outfits cling to their bodies. Midway through the stage show, one of the girls does a striptease. None of us expected her performance, but we thoroughly enjoy it. I think that takes guts in front of so many horny GIs. As the show ends, the Third Platoon receives word to return immediately to the company area to saddle up for the field. We run back to our billets because when soldiers are on alert, minutes can mean the difference between life and death.

Korean USO performers. December 25, 1968

Half an hour later, the Third Platoon is in the field looking for a Vietcong called the Mad Miner. This man has been responsible for many casualties and disruption of supply services to Camp Scott. Almost daily he sets up mines and booby traps on the road leading into our base camp. Every morning the road is swept for many miles by the engineers with mine detectors. The engineers are supported by a squad of infantrymen searching the paddies on each side of the road. Ordinance is usually found and destroyed every day.

A suspicious person is spotted in the far distance near a woodline. The platoon begins to run toward the suspect through the rice paddies in knee-deep water and mud. The individual disappears in the woodline when we reach a halfway point between the platoon and the Vietcong. We run about one hundred meters, and I begin to get sick from the extreme heat and running in the mud. I approach Tim, who is sitting on a paddy dike trying to recover from exhaustion. In addition to the regular gear each of us carries, Tim has a twenty-pound radio on his back. I look at Tim and ask, "Are you okay?" He replies, "This is crazy!" I say, "Can I carry something to lighten your load?" Tim grins, "Yeah, take this radio." I joke, "I'm not qualified to use the radio." After bitching about all of us chasing one Vietcong who wants to lead us into a booby trap, we're ready to resume the chase. We run up next to a blue, which is at low tide. The sides of the blue are steep and muddy. We slide down one side of the bank to cross the blue and try to negotiate up the other side. The bank is very muddy and is difficult to maneuver. We're exhausted. We look like pigs wallowing in a sty. Sergeant Curtis Dix takes pity on our hopeless ascent of the muddy bank and offers his hand to help us. We follow Sergeant Dix, whom we called Dixie, to a nearby village. Dixie searches two hootches and says the Mad Miner probably lives in this area. We stay for a short time before we head back to the main road to catch trucks for a ride to base camp. From this mission, Tim and I learn we're not in shape to run in muddy rice paddies. I thought I was in great shape, but there is a definite technique to walking and running in knee-deep water and mud.

When we arrive at our company area, we clean our weapons, gear, and, lastly, ourselves. My fatigues are covered with so much dried mud that I wear them in the shower and wash my fatigues on me, then strip to clean my body. Feeling better, I trek off to the mess hall with members of the Third Herd for a Christmas dinner of roast turkey and all the trimmings. This is better than Tim's and my Thanksgiving dinner of spaghetti rations. We enjoy a delicious dinner and decide to pay a visit to the EM club for refreshments and entertainment supplied by a GI band. Today, the day after Christmas, I receive a lot of mail, including cards from my aunt Helen and uncle Kenny Main, in Ohio; Joanne and Gene Shank; and Helen and Amos Hess, of West Chester. Helen wrote an entertaining and funny letter about folks in my old neighborhood. Johnny Baumhauer wrote and said Jimmy Giancola is getting serious about his girlfriend, Toni Galli. At this time, most of the guys in the platoon are writing letters, reading, or playing cards. Recently, Dave Johnson composed a poem titled "An Infantryman's Prayer." I think the poem is special, and I ask him to copy it for me so I can send it home. The poem reads:

As I tread the jungle dense, as I sweat and strain,
Christ, upon my shoulders rest.
Please help to ease the pain.
Lord, I need your mighty hands to guide my tired feet.
The sun's so hot and burning now in brush that I do beat.
Courage give upon this day the enemy I face.
Take the fear that fills my heart.
Put wisdom in its place.
This rifle that I carry never let it cease to function as I mean it as an
instrument of peace.
Jesus, aid me through this year and through this awful fight to help
men, not to hurt them, to know the wrong from right.
If it be your desire to take me to your gate.
Grant that I will be ready that I'll not have to wait.
But if I am to live on, more rivers yet to span, load the pack upon my
back and help me be a man.

It is 0900 hours on December 27 and the platoon is airborne to perform our daily search-and-destroy missions. We catch blade time while Sergeant David Roland points out familiar land formations, such as the Bowling Alley and the Nuts, where we frequently engage in enemy activity. The Nuts, or what some guys call the Testicles, is a land formation surrounded by water that is shaped like a man's balls as seen from the air. It seems every time Delta Company enters this enemy turf, we have contact with the Vietcong. The choppers turn around and descend to a lower level in an area where they previously flew at a higher altitude. This is a tactic used to make the enemy feel safe when we go over their position at a high altitude, then swoop down at treetop level for insertion.

We land near the Nuts, and the First and Third platoons split up to search different areas. There is no firing as we sweep paddies and woodlines for enemy signs, but the Vietcong seem content to avoid contact. Late in the afternoon, we must cross a wide blue that is deep in the center of the waterway. Clyde finds an old sampan that has a small hole in the bottom of the craft. We decide the sampan can do the job of transporting us to the other side of the blue. Only three men can get in the sampan at one time. We have to paddle like hell with our M16s so that the sampan reaches the shallow water on the other side before it sinks. This method works, but we sink the boat about twenty times on both sides of the blue before everyone in the platoon crosses to the other side. The men have a contest about how far their paddling will get them before the sampan sinks.

The time is now 1500 hours, and the helicopters return early for pickup to base camp. Many of the veterans have been invited to division headquarters to see the *Bob Hope Christmas Show*. Bo Senical comes over and gives Tim, Doug Taylor, Jim Talarico, and me some bad news. We must remain in the field tonight with the First Platoon because they're short of men. I don't like this because, recently, the First Platoon has gotten its ass kicked in the field. I feel more confident with the leadership and experience of the men in the Third Platoon.

The four of us are assigned rear security for the platoon, which is a relief to know we're not going to be a lead element. First Platoon sets up around three hootches to have our evening meal of C rations. With dinner over and dusk approaching, the First Platoon moves out to walk on a dike near the woodline. Tim and I bullshit and complain about being with the First Platoon and try to figure out how we got selected for the mission. We know Senical doesn't like to lend his men to other units, so I guess he had no choice in the matter. Bo has a lot of pressure on him since we lost Lieutenant Deutschlander, who was relieved of duty with our unit to be assigned to a long-range reconnaissance unit. Apparently, Lieutenant D was reassigned because he refused to obey a stupid order that would jeopardize his men's safety.

I have a great deal of respect for Lieutenant D, as do the other platoon members. I would follow him in battle anytime and believe he was the best officer in the battalion. I thought his reassignment was a military political maneuver because he set standards other officers would not or could not follow. All of a sudden, gunfire erupts everywhere. I hit the ground in a state of confusion as to where the firing is coming from. I lie in paddy water with only my nose above the water level, looking through the water at tracer rounds crisscrossing inches above my head. The ambush is so intense I can't rise up to defend myself or I'll be shot. I want to get up next to the paddy dike to afford protection to return fire. A number of guys in the platoon panic. I can hear screaming and yelling of orders above the roar of enemy weapons firing. Tim yells to me, "Are you hit?" I respond, "No, but I'm pinned down." Tim continues, "How are Doug and Short Round?" I reply, "I don't see them." Then Doug calls out, "Where are you?" I scream, "Over here. Follow my voice." Doug and Short Round Talarico low crawl to my position. All of us are terrified and believe it could be minutes before the VC kill us. Doug and Short Round flip out, saying they heard five or six men were killed in the initial outburst. We have not returned fire because the enemy fire from many directions is overpowering. I say to Tim, "If you feel they're getting close to us, we should jump up and return fire like madmen."

All four of us lie on our backs with our M16s resting on our chests. I try to keep my M16 out of the mud so it won't jam. There is so much conflicting information filtering back to us about the platoon's status that we expect the worst scenario. Finally, the word reaches us to low crawl forward to create a closer defensive formation. I move over to Tim, and he looks distressed. Tim says, "I think the leaders are moving us closer together because we're in danger of getting overrun. Be prepared for hand-to-hand combat." We both agree to fight like hell and not be taken prisoner. We'll make them kill us. We low crawl forward and meet other guys in the platoon. They say the only casualty reported is the pointman Joe Twigg, who has been shot.

Joe, whom the men call Twiggy, is trapped close to an enemy position. The First Platoon prepares to rescue him. Sergeant Vaughn sets up an M60 machine gun to provide fire support for the rescue. He begins firing like a madman. Others fire while a rescue group pulls Twiggy away from the enemy position. I'm really impressed with Vaughn; he is quite a fighter. The word is that Twiggy is still alive but has been shot three times. They call for a dust-off. We get orders to move even closer together because the platoon sergeant is directing artillery fire close to our position. Jets have been summoned to provide air support. The artillery immediately begins firing all around us, concentrating on the nearby woodline. A MEDEVAC helicopter is on the way to extract Twiggy. The helicopter appears, and orders come down the line to set up a perimeter to cover the chopper's landing and extraction. Four guys have Twiggy in a poncho, waiting for the rescue helicopter. As the MEDEVAC approaches for the landing, its headlights are turned on, and the four men race toward the helicopter with Twiggy. The perimeter element opens up with intense fire to provide the necessary fire support.

My M16 jams, and I start to panic when I realize my means of protection no longer exists. The blasts from the nearby artillery rounds exploding give me enough light to see a bullet lodged at an angle in my receiver. I try to clear the weapon, but the round is wedged in such a way

---

63

that the bullet appears to be bent in the receiver. The enemy opens up with a barrage of fire on the MEDEVAC helicopter. I hear the rounds piercing the metal shell of the chopper. The MEDEVAC tries to land but is taking too many hits from enemy weapons. The helicopter is forced to lift off the ground without Twiggy. The guys drop to the ground with Twiggy, and the word comes back that Twiggy died in the rescue attempt. The jets arrive and start to strafe the paddies in front of us and the hootches to our left flank.

I yell to Tim that my M16 is jammed. Tim crawls over, grabs my rifle and tries to dislodge the bullet. I tried this earlier without any luck. The artillery bombardment going on enables us to see the jam clearly from the flashing light of the explosions. Tim kicks the receiver to dislodge the bullet. I yell at him, "What the fuck are you doing? The bullet will explode!" He looks at me with a pissed expression and says, "This is fucking war, not training camp!" The next kick dislodges the bullet, and I feel immediate relief to have my weapon clear. Tim gives the rifle to me, and I carefully insert another magazine and resume firing. We continue firing until we receive orders to move to another position to protect ourselves from enemy mortar fire.

We low crawl to a position near where the helicopter rescue attempt was made. The jets continue their bombing and strafing runs, while artillery pounds away at enemy positions. The jets dive at night and hit enemy targets directly in front of us. The rounds travel no more than twenty feet over our heads, hitting these targets. I'm sure if the jets are off only a fraction in their firing coordinates, we could kiss our sweet ass good-bye.

We're ordered to move again. I low crawl to my left and come into contact with another GI. I yell, "Time to move out!" There is no response, so I get closer to the head of the individual and holler, "Move out!" Just as I approach closer, a flash of light from an explosion flickers on his face, revealing to me this man is dead. I've just crawled up next to Twiggy. Tim yells, "Come on, he is dead. You can't do anything for him." I low crawl over to Tim and say, "Should we drag him along with us?" Tim replies, "They said to leave him there, we'll be close by. We'll have to move many more times tonight. It is best not to move him from position to position all night long." Somehow it seems dehumanizing to me, leaving that boy lying in a dirty rice paddy by himself. For the first time, I really feel the emptiness and insignificance of life that is an aftermath of battle. After we move to another location, the firing ceases. It appears the artillery and jets performed remarkably in rescuing the platoon. We suffer only one casualty in the ambush, which is a miracle. I will always remember tonight.

The next morning the Third Platoon comes out in the field to relieve the First Platoon. I'm glad to see my unit. A helicopter arrives to pick up our lost comrade, Joe Twigg. I say another prayer for him when the chopper looks as though it's ascending into heaven. Bo Senical tells the four of us to take a break while they search the grounds for signs of last night's battle. I ask around for a cigarette. My cigarettes are ruined from spending most of the night in paddy water. Doug, whom we call Same-Same, says he saw an old papa-san walking by smoking a cigarette. Doug and I catch up to the man and ask him for a smoke. He pulls out a pack of Ruby Queens, which I think is a weird name for a cigarette. I take a puff and realize this cigarette has some unusual qualities, including the smell. The papa-san smiles, displaying his raunchy, decayed stained teeth, and says, "Number 1." When he says that, I figure I'm having my first taste of marijuana. I put the cigarette out and say, "Number 10." The papa-san has given me a joint. That will be my first and last joint.

The Third Platoon finds a woman in a hootch that has been shot. They call in a MEDEVAC to take her to a hospital for treatment. She is probably one of those who ambushed us the night before. There is no way to prove it as she's wearing civilian clothes. The First Platoon loads onto choppers to return to base camp. Tim, Doug, Short Round, and I remain in the field with the Third Platoon.

The platoon expands its search throughout the paddies and woodline, looking for signs of casualties. It's difficult to imagine how intense the fighting was the night before because the enemy left little evidence of their presence. Realistically, I know they had to have incurred greater losses than we sustained because we inflicted massive firepower upon them; however, there are no signs of losses, not even blood trails, which psychologically bothers me.

Senical alerts us, "Get ready! The choppers are on their way." That is the word I want to hear. After last night, being able to return to base camp has a special meaning for me. I realize it is a privilege and not something to take for granted.

6

A New Year 1969

I enjoy having the night off on the evening on December 30. I just wrote to the *Daily Local News* in West Chester to subscribe to my local newspaper. Now I'll be reading the news from both sides of Pennsylvania. Big Lou begins to strum on a new guitar he purchased at Dong Tam. He sings a song he recently composed about the Third Platoon fighting in the Delta. The song is similar to the lyrics of "The Battle of New Orleans," and he plays the guitar to that melody. The tune goes:

> In 1969
> I took a little trip along with Louie 3-6 down a narrow candy strip.
> I took a belt of ammo and a pack of Cs and went out on a journey to meet the enemy.
>
> The point team and minesweeper were movin' kinda slow, when they spotted a *Tu Dia* sign, said, "Please don't make us go!"
> Though concerned for your safety, the mission it comes first.
> And now that you mentioned it for VC I've a thirst.
>
> Chorus:
>
> And they ran through the paddies, and they ran through the nipa, down the Mekong Delta to the muddy China Sea.

So we showed 'em, rock and rolled 'em moved some toward
eternity.
Just to teach 'em not to mess with the boys of Delta Three.

Big Lou sings verse after verse with a soft, mellow voice, which
enhances the character of the song. The Begoni Clan joins in for the
chorus, singing with a loud proud sound of who we are. A bottle of
bourbon is passed around to add more cheer to the bonding that is
occurring. Big Lou has become the central figure in the Third Herd by
providing entertainment and fun times, making us true brothers on and
off the field. Members of the clan give Big Lou requests for more songs.
The singing and drinking continue until we notice one of the guys is
ready to perform his solo, "The Masturbation Song." The guys hoot and
holler and egg him on for an encore. What a great time we had amusing
ourselves. Now it's time to hit the rack, and the Begoni Clan will sleep
well tonight after polishing off the bourbon.

Today I've been assigned to the observation post on the road from
Highway 4 to Tan Tru. Don Sarault, of Crawfordsville, Indiana, and Carl
Williams, of Claremont, Virginia, will be joining me for this duty. After
the roads are cleared of mines and booby traps, we're trucked out to
specific locations with other men to guard the road. I'm surprised to see
the volume of vehicle and foot traffic along this road. Children come up
to our position, which puts me on alert. I fear children as much as I do
adults, so I hold my M16 in an authoritative position to let them know
I'm cautiously watching them. The guys say I'm too uptight. I would
rather be uptight than sorry for not defending myself against a child or a
woman. I've been here for only a short time, but I've heard and read too
many horror stories about soldiers interacting with Vietnamese women
and children. It pays to not be sympathetic to those Vietnamese. We take
our fatigue shirts off and bake in the sun all day. Soon the truck returns to
drive the guards back to Camp Scott. The three of us are happy that the
boring afternoon is over. I managed to get sunburn on my face, shoulders,
chest, and back.

Back in the company area, Delta Headquarters group is preparing
for another steak barbecue. All the company areas are going to have
barbecues for their New Year's Eve dinner. Jim Youhan stops by to say
hello and Happy New Year to his old platoon buddies. Jimmie is off the
line working in battalion headquarters as an S-3 Air NCO. I have guard

duty tonight, which I'm happy about. I would rather be on guard duty New Year's Eve than partying with the guys. I feel much safer being on guard during holidays. At midnight all hell breaks loose in base camp for about five minutes. We expect this because it happened the previous year. Men throughout the base camp shoot their M16s straight into the air to celebrate the moment. The sky is filled with myriad patterns of crisscrossing tracer rounds, making it look like the finale on the Fourth of July. I think I would rather not be here on the Fourth if this is any indication of how crazy it gets.

It's New Year's Day, and I'm happy 1968 is in the past. Last year was the worst year of my life. I'm upbeat about 1969 because I'll DEROS from Vietnam and the army in November. Today we go out in the field for about five hours. Holidays, weekends, and other special days of celebration have become just another day of survival in Vietnam.

Senical informs the platoon to take it easy today. He always cautions us and reiterates that the only successful mission is when all the men return safely to base camp. Everyone is in a good mood when we leave base camp since we're going to have a short day in the field. We are survivors of 1968, and 1969 is our year to go home to the States.

At the first LZ, the choppers drop the platoon off in a desolated area near some abandoned hootches situated close to a woodline. It rained the night before, making the paddies wet and muddy. This is the first time it has rained since I've been in Vietnam. As the platoon moves out in the paddies, an eerie feeling develops among the men. Just from my brief experience in the field, I know trouble is brewing. The hootches, although abandoned, give the impression that people had recently occupied them. There is a lot of wild growth of weedlike plants and bushes around the paddy dikes, indicating the paddies haven't been used recently to plant and harvest rice. One senses these fields were once farmed by the Vietnamese civilians but are now controlled by the Vietcong.

Bentley and Sassian are walking point for the platoon and notice *Tu Dia* signs in the paddies. No one is too keen about searching a possible booby trap environment because the signs reaffirm each individual's apprehension about the possible danger ahead. However, the decision is made to proceed since the area looks suspicious. Another determining factor to continue the search of this location is that the platoon has just been dropped off, and it wouldn't look good requesting a pullout without spending an appropriate period of time

---

in this landing zone. Many times these signs only act as a means of psychological warfare against the US troops.

Bentley and Sassian work their way through the muddy water to a dike near a paddy that is in terrible shape because of inactivity. It's obvious someone is using this dike because it's worn down into a footpath with weeds growing on the side of the dike. The pointmen get on the dike path and follow it parallel to the woodline. They travel the path for only a couple of minutes when a loud explosion occurs. Everyone tenses, awaiting the inevitable screams, "Doc! Doc! Medic! Doc!" Gabig and West shout for Doc Joe Struzik to help at the site of the explosion. Calling for Doc is inevitable when emergencies occur and explosions are heard. Doc Struzik is heading toward the sound of the blast and doesn't have to be summoned because he knows his services will be required. The men of the platoon ready themselves in a defense position in case the enemy opens fire. Doc rushes by me and is out of sight within seconds. The word comes down to close ranks and secure the area. We wait for further instructions and the news of the outcome of the explosion.

It seems like an eternity, but word comes that both Sassian and Bentley are wounded. Shouting commences down the line, "Does anyone have a poncho?" I yell, "I have one." I know the need for the poncho means someone is critically wounded. I don't try to take off the poncho that is tied on the back of my web gear but instead hurry forward. As I move forward, I hear guys shouting, "The poncho is on the way. Milkman has one." When I arrive at the site of the explosion, I'm overwhelmed at what I see. Doc Struzik is frantically working on Sassian, trying to save his life. Sassian's head is covered with blood, which is pumping out of the left side of his neck. Doc applies pressure bandages to try and stop the profuse bleeding, while at the same time he tries to clear Sassian's air passage. The excessive bleeding causes clotting in his throat. I turn my head the other way when Doc makes preparations to perform an emergency tracheotomy to help John breathe. Bentley has shrapnel wounds in his leg from the booby trap grenade explosion. He stands up, leaning to one side, and watches the efforts to save Sassian's life. Senical is on the horn requesting a dust-off. Doc screams to Senical that he has to get Sassian out of here or he is going to die. I think to myself, hoping Sassian is not aware of how badly he is wounded. Senical gets on the radio again but changes his tactics by requesting a gunship overhead to land and evacuate Sassian and Bentley. The pilot tells Senical he has to wait for a MEDEVAC helicopter, explaining his chopper is too valuable to risk a rescue. Doc screams, "We can't wait for the MEDEVAC! Tell him to get his ass down here." Senical orders the gunship to land or we'll be the ones to shoot it out of the air. Finally, Senical's urgency and threat change the pilot's opinion of the emergency. The pilot agrees to come down for a brief moment, but he warns Senical that the wounded better be at the extraction point because he'll leave without them.

Senical asks Bentley if he can walk to the dust-off site at the end of the path where the point team just walked. Bentley says, "I can make it." Senical gives the order, "Leave now while we prepare Sassian for extraction." My poncho is laid on the ground, and Sassian is delicately picked up and placed in the poncho.

I join three men in grabbing a corner of the poncho litter and begin to move at a fast gait down the path, retracing our previous steps. The path of the dike is too narrow to walk on; therefore, we hold the litter over the path and run in mud and water on the sides. It's very awkward carrying Sassian in the poncho. There are two tall guys on one side and two short guys on the other side of the litter, which creates an imbalance while we're running. John is thrown around in the poncho and must be terrified that we'll drop him. The terrain is rough, muddy, and slippery from the recent rain. I am one of the short guys who is constantly tripping and faltering from the strain of the shifting weight. Halfway there I can feel the fatigue settling in my arms and legs. The fatigue is causing pain in my muscles, and I fear my legs may go into spasms and cause me to drop Sassian. We come to a small waterway on my side of the dike, where I have to traverse paddy water and mud that is above my knees. Now I try to hold the poncho at shoulder level while moving through this waterway. The other guys have to move at my slow pace through the deep mud. I begin to strain from the weight of the litter and the ordeal of fighting the muddy conditions. Muscle spasms tense my arms and legs. Billy West sees me faltering and grabs me, supporting my body as I continue to move forward in unbearable pain. If John's life wouldn't have been in peril, I would have given up and collapsed in pain. Finally, we reach the extraction point where the gunship lands. Bentley boards as we approach with Sassian. The crew of the gunship screams for us to hurry. The instant we place Sassian on the chopper, it begins to lift off the ground. I collapse next to a paddy dike, lying there in wretched pain with unbearable muscle spasms. I become nauseous and vomit.

Front to Back: Pointmen John Sassian, Bill Bentley with
medic Joe Struzik.

I rest after collapsing and reflect on what had just happened. I can understand how easy it was for our pointmen to hit the booby trap wire that was rigged with a grenade. Sassian and Bentley walked to an intersection in a path that was difficult to see because of the thick bushes that were next to the intersection. A second path was crumbled, probably from another explosion. The booby trap was set at an intersection to have a better chance of killing someone coming from different avenues of approach. I learned a lesson about walking dikes and paths and avoiding intersections as a means of travel. Doc Struzik did an outstanding job of stabilizing John Sassian's condition of excessive blood loss, shock, and breathing problem. I close my eyes and ask God to spare John's life. The hope of a better year has quickly dissipated. I know that I will be losing more friends in the coming months and that I could be that casualty or death everyone will question.

In the distance I can hear the choppers coming for our pickup and return to base camp. Today seems to be a major waste of time and effort in the field. The platoon accomplishes nothing and loses two good men in the process. Everyone is in a solemn mood as we board the choppers for our return to Delta Company. Usually the guys are upbeat about returning for rest and relaxation.

As soon as we arrive at the company area, I change into a pair of shorts, grab a beer, and jump in a hammock that is partially attached to the ammo bunker. I want to be left alone while I drink beer, get some rays from the sun, and think about what John is going through at the present moment. It's only a short time before my solitude is interrupted by Top, announcing the Red Cross girls are on their way to Delta Company. When the girls come, we should dress properly and be on our good behavior. Presently I'm not too happy about putting on clean fatigues and discontinuing my drinking. The girls mean well, but it's difficult to be in a good mood and hospitable when, only an hour earlier, our platoon lost two buddies in the field.

The Red Cross girls arrive, loaded with goodies for the troops. Mary Ann, Pat, and Sandy distribute packages containing writing paper, pens, cigarette lighters, cards, books, and a multitude of other useful items. They provide an amusing letter that GIs can send home to their families and friends. The girls play games with the guys. I'm not a game player, so I graciously exit the billet area to write letters.

On January 2, the Third Platoon gets ready for another Bush Master in the field. On an extended stay in the boonies, each platoon member carries something extra to the field other than his own gear. Today I'll carry a Claymore mine and two large yellow nylon ropes for stream and canal crossings. I've just been assigned the job as rope man for the platoon. These ropes are colored fluorescent yellow, making them a prime target for a sniper a hundred meters away, so I've encased them in two green fatigue shirts for camouflage. The platoon is given C ration boxes to break down for the Bush Master. The men congregate around the boxes, tearing apart the containers to select their favorite foods. I try to pick out my favorite C rations but have the same problem as other men. We all like the same Cs, and there are not enough of certain favorites to supply the platoon for three days. Many of the guys and I use a green sock to store rations and attach it on the H frame at the back of the web gear. I attach two explosive grenades and two smoke grenades to the front of my web gear. I usually carry red smoke to mark an enemy position and yellow smoke to mark my or a friendly position. I carry one bandoleer of seven magazines of ammunition plus two magazines in each ammo pouch, which are hooked to both sides of my web-gear belt. Usually I take one canteen of water, but on extended stays in the field, I take two canteens that are hooked together with metal clasps behind an ammo pouch. I like to travel light, which provides me with more agility and the ability to move faster without tiring.

The first day we sit in Vietnamese hootches during the day and drink tea, coffee, or hot chocolate to pass the time. Ralph, Whitey, Tim, and I are in a small hootch with a mama-san and her three children. The mama-san gets some dried nipa leaves to prepare a fire inside the hootch to cook rice. She labors to start a fire when Tim approaches her and takes out his C4 explosive and lights it for her. She is amazed at how a fire is created from this white substance and says, "Number 1." Tim shows her how to place the rice pan over the flame and not put pressure on the explosive. C4 is an excellent element for heating food, but if you put the flame out by hitting or tramping on the explosive, you will be a casualty. Many a GI has lost a foot by tramping on the C4. The flame is steady and hot, and in about ten minutes or less, the rice can be served. The Vietnamese rice has a better taste than our store brand rice in the United States. The rice is the family's only dish for dinner, with a small cup of tea to drink. I would have a difficult time living in Vietnam because I hate rice.

In the evening we move out to a nighttime ambush position. The night is uneventful, except for dealing with the usual pests of rats and mosquitoes. Vietnam has an unusual amphibious fish called a snakefish, which comes out of the water at night and crawls on the paddy dikes. The fish is about three to four inches long and feels like a snake. I've been awakened a number of times with them crawling on my arms at night. I reach over and grab one when I'm dozing off. When I feel the round slimy body, I become startled and throw the damn fish in the air, thinking I just grabbed a snake.

The second day is a carbon copy of yesterday. Today the four of us, plus the Kid, have decided to stay in a Buddhist family home. This family isn't very friendly or hospitable, even though we're an occupying force in their home. The mama-san goes berserk when I take bananas from a plate in front of a Buddhist idol. I didn't understand the bananas were an offering and gave her money for them. When I understood the purpose of the bananas, I still take them because of her obnoxious behavior. In English I tell her the Buddha will forgive me because of my hunger, even though she believes that I am a heathen. I ask the guys if they want a banana after her tirade. I have no takers.

At dusk we prepare to move out for a nighttime ambush position when gunfire opens up on us. I jump into a small duck pond adjacent to a hootch. I notice a little friend huddling in the mud next to me. The friend is a white duck, who is shaking from the sound of the automatic gunfire. I can't return fire because most of the Third Platoon is directly in front of me, where the enemy fire is coming from. I reach over and grab the duck and cuddle up to it during the firefight. The duck's face and bill are only a few inches from my face. We look at each other as friends, and I try to console the feathered creature by talking to it in a low, calm voice, assuring the duck we'll get through this together. The duck looks at me in a trustful, attentive way, letting me know we're buddies. I feel genuine responsibility toward the duck's emotional well-being. After about ten minutes, the firefight ceases and the platoon prepares to move out again. I say, "Good-bye, Mr. Duck, I enjoyed your company." Every day in Vietnam is an adventure of learning and a myriad of new experiences.

Today is January 5, and I've been assigned bunker guard tonight. The three of us on bunker number 1 decide to sleep outside the bunker behind the berm because the heat is unbearable inside the bunker. Jim Pearson, from Jackson, Tennessee, is going to take first guard. I decide to go in front of the bunker to take a piss in the wiring around the perimeter. Now I'm ready for my short nap. I return to Jimmy's position and lie down on the ground in a forty-five-degree angle on the berm. I doze off when the enemy opens up on bunker 1. I'm so alarmed that I jump up in the line of fire. I hear bullets hitting the bunker and whizzing by my head. In an instant I collect my senses and hit the ground. We return fire along with bunker 2. The firing stops as soon as we expend a couple of magazines of ammunition. The harassing sniper fire causes no damage, and the rest of the night is quiet. Fortunately, the enemy missed his target, which was probably me in front of the bunker pissing. It's amazing how one never knows who is watching. The next morning I examine the bunker and find bullet holes near the location where I relieved myself.

On January 6 I get assigned to bunker guard again. Tonight Tim and I'll be together on bunker 2. Shortly after dark, the listening post on the other side of New Life Village is attacked by the Vietcong. The listening post is under heavy enemy fire, but we're afraid to give supporting fire because there are friendly forces on that post in the direct line of fire. The firing continues for about five minutes before we receive orders to commence firing around the listening post. Delta Company returns fire for another ten minutes until all enemy fire is suppressed. We receive radio transmission that the LP has been overrun by the Vietcong and has sustained casualties. Immediately the base camp mobilizes a supporting force to access the listening post and to provide aid to the wounded.

The next morning, the base camp learns the gory details of the massacre on the New Life Village listening post. There were three Delta Company men and eight Vietnamese local forces that were killed inside the bunker. The only survivor is a Delta Company GI who fell asleep on top of the bunker while pulling guard duty. Because of his negligence, the Vietcong were able to massacre the troops. The GI woke up when the Vietcong were killing the men below and hid on top of the LP. He told his story to command and is now under mental supervision. I feel sorry for this young soldier, who will live with this tragedy the rest of his life. I empathize with him because he'll be held accountable for dereliction of duty, but the army creates such situations by driving men to exhaustion under great stress. It's inevitable these tragedies will occur in combat. The dead from Delta Company include James Grompone, of Greenvale, New York; Charles Thomas, of Macon, Georgia; and Carl Washington, of Detroit, Michigan.

I knew Jimmy Grompone very well but can't remember the other guys by name. Jimmy was a fun-loving Italian kid whom Tim and I befriended. We met him when we flew to Vietnam from Fort Dix, New Jersey. We spent a lot of time together our first two weeks in country playing cards and drinking at the Korean bar in Camp Bearcat. When we were assigned to different platoons in Delta Company, we tried to stay in contact with each other, even though it's difficult because of our duty assignments. Tim and I lost a good buddy and will attend the services performed by the post chaplain.

New Life Village listening post located in the middle foreground. (Site of massacre)

7

Thu Thua Outpost

Good news arrived today. The *Daily Local News* sent me a letter stating my first copy of the newspaper was mailed on January 3. I should have my first copy in a few days. I also received a letter from my good friend, Joanne Shank. She tells me her children are doing well and her husband, Gene, has almost finished remodeling their home. Johnny Baumhauer, Joanne's brother and my best friend, wrote and told me he got two As and one B in his graduate course studies. Johnny is taking a five-day vacation to New York City. He has tickets for *The Johnny Carson Show* and some plays in the Village. Besides the welcomed letters from friends, I received three packages from my parents and a letter from my grandmother. My mother made short-sleeve shirts and shorts out of my old stateside military clothes. These clothes are the best present I've gotten thus far. I enjoy the letters from family and friends, which inform me of what is happening in their lives. I find that their letters give me hope that a better life will eventually be in my throw of the dice.

Presently, I'm taking a break from KP at the mess hall in the company area. Sergeant Jose Roybal, the communications chief, says the Third Platoon is in heavy combat in the field. I run down to the communications room to get an update on the platoon's engagement with the Vietcong. Sergeant Roybal, some men from the First Platoon, and I listen intently to the conversations of Lieutenant Wood, Bo Senical, and the RTOs directing the men in battle. Lieutenant Wood reports an enemy body and prisoner of war count as the fighting continues. I wait to the last minute before I return to KP. When I arrive at the mess hall, I tell a guy from the recon unit who is on detail with me about the action my platoon is experiencing. I tell him I've mixed emotions about being safe here on KP while my buddies are at risk in a firefight. When I return from KP in the evening, I try to talk with the guys about what happened in the field today. Everyone is quiet and not in the mood to discuss the day's activities. The Third Platoon had no casualties, so I respect their privacy and the need to have some personal time. I know the feeling and keep my mouth shut. The next day, I learn Tim Firestone earned a Bronze Star for Valor during the intense fighting the previous day. As close as Tim and I are, he won't elaborate on the previous day's firefight.

We now live in this huge barracks built for the Third Platoon. The dimensions of the living area are thirty feet by sixty feet. The bunks are attached to the sides of the wall and have a cheap set of springs that we use as our mattress. We sleep on the springs fully clothed, including our boots. We use a large table to write our letters and play cards. When Big Lou plays the guitar, we sit on the floor and drink our troubles away. The building is better ventilated than our previous housing and provides more protection from the elements. The structure will be complete when the roof is sandbagged for protection from enemy mortars. This is definitely a step up in life that we all appreciate. Tonight I'm on bunker guard, and early in the evening a small firefight erupts on the main road leading to the base camp. This road is mined and booby-trapped almost daily by the Mad Miner. Every morning a detail of engineers and infantry soldiers take two hours to clear our sector of the road. In the morning we learn an ambush patrol spotted someone on the road leading to the base camp. The patrol opened fire on the individual and apparently alarmed the Vietcong to the point where he set off his own booby trap and killed himself. Everyone in base camp gets a good laugh about this incident because it would be really ironic if the Mad Miner blew himself up.

Today the platoon is trucked to Thu Thua, a remote small outpost that is manned on a rotation basis by Ninth Division troops. The outpost is near the Plain of Reeds adjacent to the Cambodian border. Bo Senical informs the platoon this outpost was overrun the previous week by NVA troops and just about everyone defending Thu Thua was killed. Needless to say, the Third Platoon isn't too keen about spending time at this outpost.

We approach the small outpost, which is off the main road occupied by a few Vietnamese homes and businesses. We leave the main road and drive on a narrower dirt road flanked by rice paddies. Near the turn is an old Esso gas station of 1940s or 1950s vintage. The station looks as though it has been inoperable for at least ten years. The outpost, which will be our new home for a while, is now in sight. The outpost reminds me of a prison. The walls of the compound are sandbagged four or five feet high and are surrounded by layers of barbed wire.

We unload our gear and select a sleeping location in the main building. I bunk near Tim and the Begoni clan. Tim, Ray, and I decide to check out the rest of the compound, which is no larger than one and a half acres. Tim says, "I hope we don't have a ground attack here." Ray replies, "We will be in deep shit if they come over from Cambodia." We walk up to ISG Austin Hullette and Gabe, who are already setting up a .50 caliber machine gun on sandbags at the rear of the compound. Top remarks, "Let's try this baby out for effect." Top opens up with the .50 and fires about ten rounds. He turns around and looks at us with a big smile on his face. We've been here only a short time and he's accomplished the positioning of the crossing lines' fields of fire for the .50 caliber and M60 machine guns. After our short tour, we realize that our lifestyle will suffer a little while stationed here.

Our mission is mainly to disrupt enemy activity in the Plain of Reeds and provide security for the border area. The North Vietnamese Army uses the Plain of Reeds as a crossing point from Cambodia into South Vietnam's Mekong Delta region. It is rumored that there are large, division-size forces of NVA soldiers across the border. They infiltrate smaller groups to avoid detection and attack US and ARVN units, then return back to Cambodia. The NVA uses the country as a safe haven since the United States honors the borders of Cambodia as a no-fire zone.

Yesterday's honeymoon of getting acclimated to our new base of operations is over. The Hueys are transporting the platoon to the Reeds. From the air the Plain of Reeds gives one the impression of the US Midwest wheat fields. The choppers are in formation, moving in for a landing. The grasslike vegetation begins to swirl in round, matting patterns from the force of the rotor blades. The GIs refer to the vegetation as elephant grass because it is five to six feet high. The Reeds are a difficult terrain in which to operate. The flat surface of high grasses easily conceals the enemy. Because the grass is high, it would be possible to walk by an enemy soldier and never see him. The only protection a soldier has in a firefight is the limited visibility provided by the grass. There are no dikes, trees, or any structures to provide cover in battle. The sun is an enemy because temperatures reach 120 degrees. Today's forecast is 118 degrees. There is no cover under which to seek relief from the heat and wet paddies where we can cool off. Everyone brings extra water because the conditions are harsh.

When we sweep an area in the Reeds, the platoon travels close together in a line formation, whereas in the paddies or jungle terrain, we move in a column formation with a pointman leading the platoon. In midafternoon, the troops on my right flank spot some NVA soldiers and a firefight commences. The men on the left flank where I'm located open up in the direction of the sound of enemy fire. I hit the ground and fire through the high grass at an unseen target. I try to maintain a low, grassing line of fire because there are no paddy dikes for protection. Only a short time passes when the platoon begins to have serious problems with men suffering from varying stages of heat exhaustion. Lieutenant Wood radios for dust-offs. One of the guys near me rises up in the air from his ground fighting position in a delirious state with only the whites of his eyeballs showing. I can't even recognize him because his face looks like something from a horror show. Buddy Roberts grabs him and throws him on the ground. Buddy screams, "Who has water? We need a dust-off!" I hand over an extra canteen of warm water. Buddy applies the water to this guy's head. The water isn't doing much good because his eyes are still rolling back in his head. Thank God the firefight has ended because I'm getting sick. The extreme temperature and the heat radiating off my M16 when I fire have given me an intense, nauseous headache. I think both sides stopped fighting because it's too hot. Now everyone suffering from heat exhaustion is just lying down trying to conserve energy. Fortunately, the fighting set fire to only a few small areas near enemy targets. Choppers arrive to remove three men who are in serious condition. Our choppers are on the way to get us out of the field. One day in the Plain of Reeds is enough for me.

The next day in the field is uneventful, but command devises a crazy idea for a night mission. Our platoon is trucked out of the outpost at dusk to a designated river-crossing location. Our mission is to cross the river at night and at daybreak sweep a village where enemy soldiers are suspected of hiding. We leave Thu Thua as scheduled, and within fifteen minutes, it's dark. We travel down a dirt road in a convoy of three trucks; their headlights glare in the still of the night. Tim and I are standing in the back of the lead truck. All the guys in our truck are scared shitless because we're a perfect ambush candidate with the truck headlights visible a mile away. How can command be so stupid? One RPG round or land mine could wipe out a truckload of GIs. I say to Tim, "I would love to be an enemy soldier and have this opportunity of a lifetime. This is definitely what the army calls an infantryman's dream, just like detonating Claymore mines on approaching enemy soldiers." The trucks move about thirty miles an hour, dodging potholes on the poor excuse for a road. Our truck driver slams on the brakes, but the momentum of the truck forces the vehicle to crash into a waterway. Tim and I are almost thrown out of the truck. Pandemonium erupts as everyone screams about the status of their buddies. I'm dazed from the crash but notice the truck is sinking in the water. I look back, expecting the other trucks to follow us into the blue. Fortunately, the other trucks stop at the embankment with their headlights focused on us. I'm really grateful that the trucks were able to stop because most of us in the lead truck would have been killed if another vehicle had toppled on us.

Ray shouts, "Get out! The fucker is sinking!" I climb on the back side of the truck and meet guys from the second truck, who help me get out of the vehicle. Luckily, everyone is rescued before the truck sinks. We have no serious injuries—just cuts and bruises. My rear end is real sore because an M16 barrel was shoved up my ass in the crash. I guess I should be happy the M16 didn't discharge on automatic.

Apparently at one time, there was a bridge crossing over this blue where we had our accident. The bridge is gone, and I guess this could be called another logistical mistake by the army. It would be nice if higher command would use updated maps on our suicide missions. I thought they might abort the mission because of the accident, but oh no, we must play more war games! I suppose the army has a macho image of completing the mission regardless of the obstacles. The other trucks return to the outpost while the Third Platoon moves to its destination by foot. In a short time we reach a large blue that requires a boat for transport to the other side. Someone in the platoon finds an old papa-san who has a large sampan with a small motor. The papa-san agrees to take us to the other side. The papa-san makes a number of trips across the blue in dense fog. By the time we reach the village, the people are up and moving about, thwarting our surprise visit. On our return trip, we see the partially submerged truck in a canal. Command is making arrangements to retrieve the vehicle. When I observe the truck, I say to Tim, "I wonder how many more of these suicide missions are in our future." Tim replies, "Seems like they're becoming more frequent."

When we returned to base camp, I enjoyed some downtime. I just finished reading seven issues of the *Daily Local News*. All of my high school friends are getting engaged or married. One of those taking marriage vows is a friend, upon whom I had a crush on in sixth grade and again later in high school. We didn't have many classes together, and I never dated her because I was shy, but she and I always were in the same homeroom in high school and enjoyed parties with mutual friends. As a teenager, I preferred hanging out with the guys to dating—all the girls seemed too serious.

Recently, I've drastically changed in appearance, habits, and emotions. I fear that I've changed more than I want to accept. I sport a full black mustache that I'm growing longer into a partial Fu Manchu. The mustache makes me look older and gives me a more masculine appearance. I discovered that my older-looking facial features are an asset in dealing with the Vietnamese. Now I smoke a pack of cigarettes and drink five or six beers a day. I cuss more frequently to express myself. When I'm on military operations, it seems every fifth word out of my mouth is the F-word. I'm definitely becoming hard-core in dealing with the issues of a combat soldier, such as more easily relying on booze and cigarettes than water and good food. The hot weather, mud, and constant wetness from sweeping filthy rice paddies are reducing my stamina. I am tormented daily by the native pests, including mosquitoes, rats, red ants, and leaches. The mosquitoes are terrible. At night the repellant lasts less than twenty minutes before the pests fly in your ears, nose, and mouth. The sound of mosquitoes buzzing in your ears drives one crazy, and somehow they can enter your mouth when you're pursing your lips. Every morning I wake up with swellings on my face from the bloodsuckers. One morning I counted fifteen bites on my small finger, which wasn't covered by my jungle fatigue shirt. My body is covered with infections from cuts incurred in the field. They won't heal because I'm in water each day for hours at a time. The bottoms of my feet are full of small holes, and I develop a mild case of immersion foot. The ringworm around my waist and ankles is unmanageable because my belt and boots remain wet most of the day. I get very little rest and sometimes suffer from battle fatigue when I deal with booby traps, firefights, suicide missions, and the trauma associated with friends getting wounded or killed.

Ralph just brought some young Vietnamese kids into our billet area. Apparently, they're let inside regularly by the outpost command to sell services and goods. Leroy just got a fantastic back massage from a young boy. The boy walks on Lee's back and uses his bare feet to massage the muscles. The Begoni Clan forms a line for back massages. When it's my turn, I take off my fatigue shirt and lie facedown on the wood floor. The boy walks up and down my back for a few minutes before he begins the foot massage. I don't even notice his body weight, and the entire experience is delightful. The kid gives massages for over an hour and then collects his pay. We tease him about receiving payment for his services, but we're generous with the young man. Teasing the Vietnamese is becoming a pastime and a form of entertainment for us.

Bo announces that we're going on Eagle flights in the afternoon. It's unusual to leave so late on choppers. Maybe we'll have a welcomed short day in the field. As usual, the platoon is dropped off in a rice paddy near a woodline where enemy presence is suspected. The first insertion yields small arms ammunition and a cache of 57 mm recoilless rockets. After the find, the choppers waste no time in picking us up for our next insertion. This area is populated with an enemy bunker complex. Members of the platoon use grenades to destroy the bunkers. We find no supplies, and there are no secondary explosions when the bunkers are blown up.

To our dismay, orders have been changed. A Chinook helicopter is bringing in supplies for an extra two days in the field. I guess higher command had a reason for our short day in the field. At dusk, two river patrol gunboats approach to pick us up for a nighttime insertion by water. The river gunboats sport quad .50s mounted on the front of the boats. The rear of the craft has .50 caliber machine guns. We board in the center of the small craft for a quick ride to our landing site. By 2300 hours, we settle in our nighttime position. We're instructed that if we see enemy movement, we should be quiet and only observe the activity. I think this is strange for command to not want the platoon to engage the enemy. The night is quiet, and the only "enemy" activity is fighting mosquitoes. We get wet when we exit the gunboats, and our stinking clothes are magnets for the hungry buggers.

At 0800 hours, we move out for our next nighttime ambush site, which is eight thousand to nine thousand meters away. The platoon is going to be humping all day. We receive sporadic sniper fire but ignore it and don't return fire. We encounter stream after stream and utilize the ropes for crossing. Finally, we reach a blue that is very wide and extremely swift. Lieutenant Wood and Bo tell the platoon to take a break to give them time to figure out the safest method to cross the blue. I'm concerned about an ambush at this blue because we're taking too much time preparing for a crossing. When half of our men are on both sides of the blue, it would be a perfect opportunity for the Vietcong to ambush us. When we walk out in the field for hours at a time, the Vietcong like to harass us with sniper fire, trail us to find supplies we may drop, or set up nighttime ambushes as when Twiggy was killed. Recently, when we forded a canal using the ropes, the last man forgot to retrieve the ropes. He was ordered to go back and retrieve the nylon ropes. He spotted a Vietcong trailing us. The Vietcong was crossing the blue on the ropes when he was shot. Since the enemy has a habit of trailing us, we should set up more traps and use clever tactics to kill them.

Pete and Bo find a high bank protruding on a bend upstream. The blue is too swift to swim, so Bo volunteers to jump off the high bank, and hopefully, the current and his swimming skill will take him to the other side. A long nylon rope is tied to Bo's waist in case we have to retrieve him from the blue. Bo gives thumbs-up, dives from the ledge into the swift water, and strokes like hell. He manages to reach calm water on the other side. I never thought he would succeed in the crossing, but he had the confidence in his ability to perform the task.

As soon as he makes it to the calm water, he wraps the rope around his body and anchors his tall frame in thigh-high mud. Bo screams to me, "Milkman, do the same as I did. Wrap and tie the rope around your body and anchor yourself in the blue." I follow his instructions with the help of Whitey. Bo yells, "Are you ready?" I respond, "No, but let's give it a try." The rope is about two inches underwater and is very taut against the mighty current. The men will have to cross monkey-style, utilizing a hand-to-hand swinging motion when they maneuver on the rope. The consequence of failing to traverse the rope will result in certain death by drowning since we have no safety lifelines to aid in the crossing. About half of the men ford the blue successfully. Doug Taylor is next in line. Doug is the biggest guy in the platoon, and I'm concerned that he may not possess the agility and strength to hold on for the distance. Guys are shouting encouragement to Same-Same because he can't swim. Doug gets next to me and grasps the taut line. He begins his trek over to the other side. Doug probably weighs 230 pounds, and his body with full field gear on is parallel to the top of the blue. He maneuvers across the blue like he's done this many times before. My confidence spirals after Doug completes his journey in great form. Eventually I'm replaced as the river pylon, and I make my way across. The crossing requires little strength because the swift water keeps one's weight buoyant and on top of the water. Skill required is to move hand to hand, keeping your head above the water line. It took almost an hour for the platoon to negotiate this blue.

Crossing a blue. Jim Milliken holding rope, Tom Gabig with machine gun.

We move for half an hour before we reach another blue that is small in size and the water is relatively calm, except in a few places. This time it's decided to tie a rope to a five-gallon empty water container and use it as a raft to pull guys one by one over the narrow, deep blue. The guys clown around and enjoy being towed to the other side. Clyde Poland's turn comes, and he jumps on the container, and they start to pull when Clyde loses his grip and goes under the water. Someone yells, "Clyde is drowning!" Pete and Bo rush over to the bank as the lifeguards tie ropes around themselves. Clyde's body went into a swirling deep pool of water and disappeared. Whitey and Jim Hughes dive into the treacherous water trying to grab Clyde's body, which is held under the water by a swirling current. Both lifeguards frantically search while everyone on shore becomes very quiet. At that moment, each of us realizes Clyde has been submerged too long. The lifeguards come up for quick air a few times before they rise, clutching a limb of Clyde's body. Clyde is grabbed and pulled over to the shore. At the same time, Whitey and Jim are pulled to shore by the attached ropes. The lifeguards begin resuscitating Clyde, and he immediately responds by coughing up water. Bruce "Whitey" Falkum and Jim Hughes did a great job in responding quickly to save Clyde's life. Clyde lost his M16 in the blue and took a lot of chiding about not having a weapon. This is the platoon's way of dealing with the near disaster of losing a good buddy. After our fifth blue crossing of the day, we settle down for the night.

The next day we hitch a ride in a large Vietnamese commercial boat that can hold the entire platoon. I don't like the idea of being transported down these waterways in slow, unarmed craft. It seems I spend most of the day in and on water, which creates issues with me since I can't swim. Amazingly, the Third Platoon has a large contingent of nonswimmers. The boat ride lasts less than an hour before we change to a group of small sampans. I voice my concern about being ambushed in the middle of a blue in the sampans. As usual, my bitching falls on deaf ears. It's an accessible mode of travel, and the likelihood of an enemy ambush during the day is highly improbable. While the platoon navigates in a line of five sampans down the blue, I imagine an ambush from the shore. I know the enemy would need only a few soldiers to wreak havoc on our exposed platoon.

We move at a slow speed in the water as the men converse in a casual manner. I'm pissed off and quiet, keeping to myself until we get out of these damn sampans. All of a sudden, automatic weapons begin firing from the banks of the blue. I say to myself, "I'm history. We're all going to be killed." I wait for the bullets to hit the water or sampan before I bail out of the boat. A few seconds pass and there are no bullets hitting the water or whizzing by my body. Confusion sets in because I'm contemplating whether to jump out of the sampan, return fire, or wait for a spray of bullets. I notice the other guys are in a state of anxiety as I am, trying to determine why we're not being shot up. Then the firing stops abruptly as fast as it began. We hear laughter coming from our right flank in the dense undergrowth along the blue. For a joke it appears an ARVN platoon opened up with their M16s to scare us, and I believe this was meant to teach us a lesson for being so visible. No one yells back at them because I'm sure all of us believe we had "bought the farm." I thought we were going to be massacred. We learn an important lesson about exposing the unit to a possible ambush. I believe this will never happen again.

Later, Bo said he saw some bloated bodies in the water near the banks of the blue. Bo thinks the ARVNs were shooting at the bodies and laughed at their antics of tearing the bodies apart with their "mad minute" of firing. Bo's observation of what happened makes more sense than what I'd envisioned. I'm sure most of the guys had different thoughts about the shooting, but we all feel lucky we weren't in a real ambush. After that incident, we make a hasty departure from the sampans. We collect ourselves emotionally while hoofing to a nearby road to await trucks for transportation back to camp.

Today is January 15. The Third Platoon has just been informed that it will be part of a large circle jerk. In the Mekong Delta we use the term "circle jerk" to refer to cordoning off the enemy into a specific area to annihilate them with heavy weapons fire. Usually, the enemy is chased into a woodline surrounded by rice paddies. The infantry's job is to contain the enemy in the woodline while jets bomb and napalm the area. Shelling artillery supports from a distance.

The Ninth Division has a contingent of soldiers from two battalions who have engaged in daylong fighting with a large force of NVA soldiers. Dusk is closing in as we off-load from the choppers to support the two battalions in combat. Our responsibility is to defend and stop the enemy flight from a certain sector of the woodline. We quickly take our positions in the rice paddies circling the woodline and link up with other units doing the same. We set up fifty to seventy-five meters from the woodline perimeter because the heavy artillery attack is in progress. Orders come down to dig foxholes for protection against the artillery shelling. This is a first for our platoon to dig foxholes. Shovels are passed down the line, with orders to dig the holes twenty-five feet apart.

Tim, the Begoni Clan, and I are positioned together behind a small dike facing the woodline. We break off into groups of three to dig the foxholes for protection against the heavy barrage of metal flying in the air from exploding shells and bombs. Tim starts the digging at our position. He has to lie on his side while scooping earth away into a pile of dirt that forms on the dike. We take turns, and within fifteen minutes, we occupy a foxhole that will accommodate three grunts. While digging, we keep our heads below the paddy-dike height for protection from enemy snipers. A sniper has been firing at our foxhole position for nearly ten minutes. His rounds miss by a large margin. Possibly he's baiting us to look up. Now it's time to set up the Claymore mines. I low crawl out of our foxhole to position two Claymores in front of our perimeter. It's necessary to hug the ground because of the sniper fire and the flying shrapnel whipping by us. The Claymores are placed at a forty-five-degree angle in the ground, and I insert the blasting cap and low crawl back to our position, dragging the wire connected to the mine. Then I grab the other mine and follow the same procedure. I return to the foxhole after setting up the second mine and complete the process by connecting the strikers to both mines. The mines are ready to detonate by squeezing the strikers. An electric charge is created by squeezing the striker, which sends a current through the wire, setting off the blasting cap and causing the mine to explode. A path of small metal balls is sent through the air. For some crazy reason, I imagine myself setting off Claymore mines on charging enemy soldiers.

The artillery fire has become very intense. Flashes from the explosions can be seen, and a few seconds later, we hear the shrapnel from the shells whiz over the foxhole and land with a thud near the hole. I'm one of the few men in the Third Platoon who wears a metal helmet. At this time I wish I could find a way to tuck my whole body inside the helmet. Thud! Thud! Thud! Pieces of artillery shells drop all around us. Tim yells out, "What the hell was that?" He reaches over next to me in the foxhole and grabs a large piece of metal the size of his hand. "Damn it! I just burned my hand!" Tim knows the shrapnel is hot for a few minutes after the explosion, but he's so overjoyed none of us are casualties. He picks up the shrapnel to show us. The barrage continues, and we have a few small pieces of dead shrapnel hit us, causing superficial burns.

At about 0100 hours, the NVA try to exit the woodline using our defensive position as their avenue for escape. An intense firefight begins and lasts about fifteen minutes. As much as the North Vietnamese soldiers wanted to elude the artillery shelling, they soon realize it would be certain death to exit in our direction. The enemy retreat into the woodline and try another escape route. During the firefight, a sniper concentrated his efforts on our position. After the firefight, we decide to have a little fun with the sniper. We know he is a terrible shot, so we decide to tease him by putting my helmet on an M16 barrel for a target. We take turns holding the helmet up for the sniper to shoot. He never comes close to hitting the helmet; and after about half an hour, he gives up, probably frustrated, or perhaps he caught on to our source of entertainment. I'm a little disappointed because a bullet hole through my helmet would be a great souvenir.

Around 0300 hours we decide to cook dinner. The enemy knows our position, so a barbecue is in order to have a little fun mocking the sniper who is trying to kill us. Tim gets out his C4 and starts a fire to warm our C rations. I'm having ham and beans with hot chocolate. I say, "I wonder if the sniper can smell the food we're cooking." Tim quips, "We should invite him over for some chow." I comment, "He probably would bitch about the taste of the food and that we have no rice." We laugh and keep making fun of the poor bastard getting his ass bombarded by our artillery. The remainder of the night we converse back and forth to Big Lou, Whitey, Ralph, Don, Larry, and a few other guys.

Early in the morning, we go out to retrieve the Claymore mines and discover the two mines in front of our foxhole have the detonation cords sliced in half from falling shrapnel. We check all the positions in our sector, and only two of the sixteen Claymores are functional. The rice paddy is littered with shell fragments, and it appears to be a miracle we didn't sustain casualties from all the flying debris last night. The previous day the woodline looked like a lush jungle bordering the rice paddies. Now the area is totally devastated. The vegetation on the standing trees is completely shredded, and the ground is still smoldering from fires caused by numerous explosions. I can't imagine anyone surviving the night in this jungle area.

The Third Platoon and the troops on our flanks are given orders to hold our positions, while other Ninth Division forces sweep the bombed area for dead enemy soldiers and weapons. During the sweep, the Third Platoon is alerted to saddle up. Pete Wood and Bo Senical inform the platoon that choppers are on the way to take us to another firefight, which is in progress as they speak. Apparently, a battalion commander spotted a group of NVA soldiers a few miles away in another woodline. These soldiers probably escaped from the circle jerk. The battalion commander said Cobra gunships have killed five to ten NVA and the fight is still going on. An infantry unit is needed to sweep the area to flush out the remaining enemy soldiers.

When we arrive, the battalion commander is circling the woodline in a Loach, a small bubble-shaped reconnaissance helicopter. Two Cobra gunships also circle the area and fire at suspected targets. After our insertion, the platoon moves through sparse vegetation to a more dense jungle area where the Cobra gunships encountered the NVA. A group of men including Billy West, Clyde Poland, Don Sarault, Joe Simmons, and Delbert Stancill is given orders to enter the jungle area where the remaining NVA soldiers are suspected of hiding out. When the squad enters the dense vegetation, they split up and firefights erupt everywhere. I remain with other platoon members waiting outside the dense growth. We listen to the small firefights begin and end continuously for quite a long time. The firing subsides, except for a few small bursts of probing fire. We wait anxiously for word on the outcome of the enemy contact.

Pete Wood directs the ground operations with the battalion commander, who keeps him abreast of the platoon's engagement and maneuvers. Bo Senical moves over to my position and asks me to retrieve the enemy weapons from the soldiers who were killed by the Cobra helicopters. I enter the woodline in a crouching stance, fearful that I may become an enemy target. As I move forward, I check a rocketed enemy position where four NVA bodies are located. I carefully secure the area and examine the soldiers, making sure they are dead before I strip them of their weapons. While I'm in the process of taking the weapons, a small firefight commences directly in front of me. Hustling out of the woodline, I carry a Chi-Com machine gun, an RPG launcher, and two AK-47 assault rifles. I take the weapons to Bo and say, "Bo, these guys are better equipped than we are. There are more weapons and loads of supplies and ammunition on the bodies." He tells me, "Go back in and bring it all out. Make a pile here with these weapons." I reply, "Okay, I am on my way."

I reenter the woodline and grab an armful of enemy field gear and another AK-47 rifle. When I turn to leave, the Second Platoon tiger scout passes by me with his M16 resting on his shoulder. I'm surprised to see him and yell at him, "Smirk, there are gooks in the nipa!" He smiles at me and says, "No sweat! No sweat!" Smirk smiles again with his goofy grin and walks into the dense jungle with his rifle on his shoulder. Seconds later, gunfire erupts where Smirk entered. I drop the enemy supplies, jump into an enemy foxhole, pull a dead gook over me, and peer around his head, awaiting the arrival of enemy soldiers. After waiting a few minutes until the firing stops, I look out of the foxhole. I see two soldiers running on my right flank, and I'm afraid to fire because I can't determine if they are friend or foe. Just as they are almost out of sight, I realize they are NVA regulars. I hasten back to Senical and announce, "Bo, two gooks are running through the woods toward our right flank." Senical gets on the horn and alerts the Cobras. Soon we hear the helicopters open up on a target. A pilot radios back to Senical, "We nailed them."

I tell Senical I think Smirk was shot by the two NVA soldiers whom the Cobra just killed. I ask him, "Do you want me to continue bringing out the equipment?" Senical says, "Let's wait for the situation to stabilize." That is music to my ears. I take a little time to reflect on what has happened. I feel some guilt and responsibility for the death of the two NVA soldiers. Until now I've been able to avoid being directly responsible for someone's death. This war, like all wars, is insane. I know the time will come when I'll have to kill someone to save my life or the life of one of my buddies. Sadly, I know in my heart I'll be ready when that day comes. A cartoon I read before I came to Vietnam describes the plight of the American soldier and his enemy. Both soldiers are given training and propaganda stating the other is terrible. Then they are sent to a war zone and issued weapons. When facing each other in combat, the decision to kill becomes a futile action because the warlords have predestined their fate by placing them in harm's way.

Another half an hour passes with no activity. From the undergrowth appears the squad of men who were involved in the fighting. All the guys are visibly shaken up. They describe the fighting as being at point-blank range. Joe and Clyde had NVA soldiers pop out of foxholes behind them to shoot them in their backs. In both situations, the enemy soldiers' weapons jammed, which allowed Joe and Clyde ample time to react to the click of the jammed weapons by turning around and killing their adversaries. Don had a firefight with a machine gunner, whom he killed at close range. The squad of men had six enemy kills.

The men confirm Smirk was killed. Luckily, due to jammed enemy weapons, our loss is minimized. Pete calls for an extra Huey to pick up the enemy loot we have captured. The pile contains four AK-47 assault rifles, two Chi-Com machine guns, two RPG rocket launchers, one Russian SKS rifle, mortars, grenades, field equipment, medical supplies, mines, and even a hefty supply of pot. These NVA troops were well supplied and possessed top-notch equipment. The AK-47s that jammed did so probably because the NVA didn't have time to clean them since they were on the run from the previous night. The total confirmed body count is twelve—four by Cobras before we arrived, six by the squad, and two later by the Cobras. There may have been more enemy casualties and weapons, but we limit our search because our loss is minimal and our leaders want to keep it that way.

The commanding officer tells Pete the platoon was exceptionally brilliant in wiping out the enemy force. He praises Pete and his men for a job well-done. He recommends the key soldiers be honored for their heroism and valiant efforts. The next day, Billy West and Joe Simmons are awarded Silver Stars. Clyde Poland and Don Sarault are awarded Bronze Stars for Valor.

8

Home Sweet Home

Last night I agreed to take Doug Taylor's guard duty because it's our last night in Thu Thua and Doug wants to celebrate with his friends. Around 0200 hours I develop a real need to take a much-needed piss. Instead of using a latrine, I decide to take a leak off the top of the sandbagged wall outside the guard bunker. The tops of the sandbags are slippery from the dew formed from the heavy moisture-laden air. I'm careful walking on the sandbags, trying to find a good spot to relieve myself. I select a clear area where I can take a leak through the barbed wire into the paddy below. After I finish my business, I insert "Mr. Nice" back into my fatigues and turn sideways to retrace my steps back to the bunker. As I turn, I slip on the wet surface of the sandbags and fall off the wall into the barbed wire that is strung in a rolled fashion next to the wall. I lie in the barbed wire with both arms and legs spread eagle. I try to get up, but the more I move to free myself, the more entangled I get in the wire. I'm really getting cut up, and I'll never be able to free myself.

Embarrassing as it is, I yell, "Help! Help! I am entangled in the barbed wire!" I hear Lee, who is also on guard duty, cry out, "Where are you?" I keep hollering, "Help! Help!" Finally, Lee locates me in the darkness. He grabs my arm and tries to pull me out of the wire, but his efforts fail because I'm getting more snagged in the wire. Lee says, "We need four men to get you out of this mess. I will get more guys to help." I lie in the barbed wire, being careful not to move. Soon Lee returns with the other men to rescue me. They need to remove sandbags in order to reach my arms and legs to pull me out of the wire. Each man grabs an arm and leg, pulling and twisting my limbs in different directions until they release my body from the barbed wire. My fatigues are ripped, and I'm a bloody mess from puncture wounds and tears in my skin. I'm really concerned about my wounds because I pissed on the barbed wire that is already rusty from probably one hundred other grunts pissing in the same place. I do my best to clean the very sore cuts. My left calf has many puncture wounds and is in especially bad shape.

In the morning Doc Struzik attends to my injuries and gives me hell for not seeing him sooner. Doc advises me to get a tetanus shot as soon as we arrive back at Camp Scott. He cleans my cuts with antiseptic and warns me about possible infection. I inform Senical about my accident and my intention of going to the medic's aid station for a tetanus shot when we get back to base camp. By the time we arrive at Camp Scott, I'm in a lot of pain and discomfort. My left calf has swelled to twice the size of my right calf. I look as though I'm suffering from elephantiasis. I hurry over to the medic's aid station to get my shot. The medic in charge tells me not to worry because I had a tetanus shot before I came to Vietnam and that shot should protect me. To ease my mind, he gives me another shot and medicine for the infection. I return to Delta Company area (Home Sweet Home) and inform Senical of my condition. Bo takes a look at my calf and says I should be on complete rest until the infection clears up.

The next day I learn that our sister platoons had four men killed recently. There is so much activity and socialization within one's platoon that the other two platoons in the company become a part of the outside world. The only time I catch up with other company news is when I have downtime from the field. I was told that PFC Wayne Knowlton, of Floren, Louisiana, was killed on January 18. On January 23, the following men were killed: PFC Keith Cantrell, of Amarillo, Texas; PFC Peter Alagna, of Santa Ana, California; and Sergeant Dennis Guthrie, of Quenton, Oklahoma. I don't recognize the men by their names, but I'm sure I knew their faces.

I take the time to write letters back home to my three best friends: Johnny Baumhauer, Jimmy Giancola, and John Dulin. In Johnny's and Jimmy's letters, I give them statistics on our company's casualties since my arrival. According to my records, our company has had eleven men killed and twenty-one wounded since the first week of December. The Third Platoon has suffered the loss of one man killed and three wounded.

The First and Second Platoons have been hit hard. The Third Platoon has had the same number of enemy contacts as the other two platoons but fortunately has fared better from the casualty standpoint. I attribute our success to excellent leadership, great guys working together, and the luck of the draw. On our last combat encounter, we could have had two or three men killed, but the men drew aces instead of deuces. In John's letter, I'm not graphic about what is going on. I tell John and his wife, Kathy, about the noncombative functions I perform. I ask John about their new home he is building. John is a talented fellow who has the courage and belief he can accomplish anything. I am truly blessed to have such good friends. Thank God they're not here with me.

In the last two days I've been leading the *Life of Riley*. The infection has cleared up, and I'm ready to return to the field with the platoon. I feel guilty when the men leave for the field or get assigned duties around base camp. All I've done for the last few days is rest on my ass, write letters, read, and drink beer. Bo walks into the billet area to check on my condition. I tell him I'm ready to return to the field. For some reason, I don't feel like a true infantryman unless I'm out in the field being a grunt. Bo says, "Rest another day, then you should be ready for field duty." Bo asks me, "Are you up for a movie tonight?" I reply, "Sure, the last movie I saw was *Wait Until Dark* before New Year's." I ask Bo, "What movie is scheduled for tonight?" Bo laughs, *The Green Berets* with John Wayne. I laugh, "No shit, we can't miss this flick!"

Bo and I put a couple of beers in our fatigue side pockets and proceed to the EM club to purchase a hoagie for the movie. This is the first time I've socialized with Bo on a one-to-one basis, and I feel good being in his company. I respect the man very much. We decide to carry our M16s with an ammo belt to the flick just because John Wayne would have approved of our look. We arrive early for the show and choose seats in the middle of the bleachers. Bo and I enjoy a beer waiting for darkness to set in. We open our second beer and begin to eat the hoagies when the movie starts with the introduction of the stars. I see John Wayne's face appear on the screen when all hell breaks loose in base camp. The base camp is under a ground attack with mortar and small arms fire. Bo says, "Let's get back to our perimeter." Off we go, leaving John Wayne in the sunset, with tracer rounds going by and probably through the movie screen. As we run back to Delta Company's perimeter, I think to myself, *You can't even see a John Wayne movie in peace!* I wonder if the Vietcong shot John on the movie screen. There is sure a lot of irony in war. Bo and I help man the perimeter, firing a few magazines for effect. When the attack is over, we decide to call it a night.

Today is January 29, and I return to the field with a clean bill of health. I'm amazed how quickly the infection and swelling in my calf responded to treatment. My leg looks normal, and I feel no pain when I walk or stand for a long period of time. I'll get a true sense of my recovery when I trek the rice paddies in full field gear. Our first LZ is a rice paddy near a blue. The intelligence report suspects enemy movement in this location within the last few days. The point team of Larry Boneck and Don Sarault get their orders from Pete Wood about the direction in which to move. Momentarily, Larry and Don split up, with Larry going toward a woodline while Don follows fresh footprints leading to the blue. Don walks through knee-high vegetation to the blue. Once he gets there, he sees no signs of the enemy and retraces his original path back to the rice paddy. The remainder of the platoon waits to see if the pointmen find something worth investigating. As Don retraces the trail he made to the waterway, the platoon witnesses Don getting blown up. One moment he's walking toward us when a loud boom occurs with a small ball of smoke. Don falls to the ground while members of the platoon scream that familiar and chilling word, "Medic!" Doc Struzik doesn't need anyone to yell for his assistance because he immediately runs in the direction of the blast. We instinctively cry out, "Medic or Doc!" The platoon secures the area around the blast as Doc works to stop the bleeding. Pete calls for a dust-off.

The MEDEVAC helicopter arrives, and Don is carried on a litter to the chopper. He raises his thumbs in the up position. The status of Don's condition is severe wounds to the legs and feet, but his balls are okay, as he indicates with his thumbs-up position. Everyone is relieved to hear that his family jewels are fine. When an infantryman sets off a booby trap, his lower extremities are very susceptible to critical injury. The surgeons can repair your limbs, but your balls are a different story. To the infantryman, an injury to the family jewels is more crucial than an amputation. Tim and I have become good friends with Don, and we'll miss him dearly. I'm especially grateful that he doesn't have life-threatening injuries.

Bo walks over to me and says, "Milliken, I need you to walk point with Boneck the rest of the day." I respond with surprise, "Okay," trying not to choke from the big lump in my throat. I don't know anything about being a lead man. The men who have experience are blown up or shot on a regular basis. I walk over to Boneck and say, "Larry, I guess you'll have to put up with me the remainder of the day." He grins, "Oh shit, you're my backup." Then Boneck laughs and says, "Don't worry. We will be fine." I'm comforted to a small degree that he doesn't seem too upset about my walking point with him. Larry appears calm about Don's misfortune; his body language exudes confidence and an undeniable resolve that he won't share the same fate.

At the next LZ, Boneck gives me instructions of how to walk point behind him, covering his flanks while he tends to the business directly in front of him. I do exactly as he says because he has an instinctive ability to search for the enemy in this tropical environment. When Boneck walks lead point, a swagger in his walk denotes an air of cockiness, suggesting he's the *baddest mother F in the valley*, a term frequently used by many GIs in Nam. The enemy is looking for an easy hit to kill the pointman, but Boneck appears to be a difficult score by using his uncanny ability to sense danger and make appropriate steps to ward off enemy contact.

Although Larry is only nineteen, he is a seasoned veteran of the wild. He has years of experience as a skilled hunting guide in the West around Reno, Nevada. In the strange terrain of Vietnam, Boneck looks at home tracking Vietcong, as though he's stalking a trophy animal for a client. When following behind him, I can't believe how relaxed he seems performing his duties as pointman. Just the way he carries his M16 suggests he is master of the weapon. I'm sure this comes from carrying, firing, and maintaining weapons at a very young age. I know if I have to walk point, this definitely would be the man I would choose to be my partner.

Larry calls for me to come closer to him. "Milkman, I want to show you a few things." He gestures toward some small branches bent on a bush. He says, "Gooks have recently been in this location. They probably went in that direction based on the bending of the plant branches." I'm surprised he notices such a minute detail. I would have never noticed his findings. Truly he's in rhythm with Mother Nature and her environment. Boneck says, "Let's go in this direction and see if we can find the VC." Larry approaches an area where the plant growth is approximately six feet tall and instructs the platoon to wait outside while we check for enemy signs. I follow closely behind him.

The foliage is dense. Larry motions for me to join him. He asks me, "What do you think that is?" I look at a conical-shaped object that appears to be made of reeds. I reply, "I don't know. I have never seen such a strange thing." I ask him, "Is it a booby trap?" Larry grins, "No, it's a rattrap. Gooks catch rats in these traps and cook them for dinner." I wonder how he knew this is a rattrap but do not question his explanation because it seems quite logical. It makes sense because the enemy has little meat in their diet, and the main staple of rats is rice. I knew of people back in the United States who ate muskrat legs as a delicacy. Neither Boneck nor I venture very close to his discovery. Finally, Larry announces, "It's time to quit for the day." As we retrace our trail back to the platoon, I sigh in relief that I made it through the day. Tomorrow Clyde will be walking point with Larry. Senical will have to select a third man for the point team. I hope it's not me.

The next five days were more of the same. I went to the field on Eagle flights during the day, and at night I pulled duty on three ambushes and two listening posts. It seems I carried a different specialty to the field every time we saddled up. This week, beside my regular gear, I carried Claymore mines, starlight scopes, blasting caps, detonation cord, ropes, and additional grenades. Depending on our mission, the requirements changed according to the gear we took to the field. The days were relatively free of enemy contact, but every day brings an interesting challenge or learning experience. Tim volunteered to be our demolition man. In addition to his regular gear, Tim carried a load of C4, blasting caps, and detonation cord.

Two days ago the platoon found a huge enemy bunker that was well constructed with large wooden beams. Tim called down the ranks for me to bring additional C4 and detonation cord because this bunker was going to be a challenge to destroy. I watched Tim go to work, packing C4 in critical beam joist support areas of the bunker. After half an hour, the inside of the bunker looked like a decorated Christmas tree with C4 packed everywhere. Blasting caps were inserted into the explosive, with detonation cord traveling from one load of C4 to another. I observed the demolition process, and the only part that bothered me was Tim using his lips as a holder for four blasting caps while he set up the charges. The final step was to run a wire hooked up from the explosives to an outside safe position where a striker can be connected to ignite the charge. Tim completed the demolition process by attaching the striker. He asked if I wanted to do the honors in squeezing the striker. I declined and said, "This is your baby to blow up." He squeezed the striker, and a huge explosion completely destroyed the bunker. Most of the guys congratulated him on a well-done job. Tim reciprocated with a huge smile.

Tim Firestone runs after blowing up enemy bunker.

We received a distress call yesterday, when we're on Eagle flights, that a Huey had lost power. Within minutes, our chopper pilots spotted the Huey gliding down with the rotors barely moving. Our pilot maintained a conversation with the pilot of the troubled Huey, giving instructions of our planned rescue effort upon impact. The Huey pilots positioned their choppers on both sides and to the rear of the crashing helicopter. We expected a bad crash and maybe a fire on impact. Our mission was to enter the craft seconds after impact and free the crew before it exploded or a fire broke out. The Huey hit the ground hard and toppled over on its right side. Our choppers landed simultaneously with the crash. Men exited from our helicopters and were on the crashed helicopter like a swarm of bees protecting their hive. All four crewmen were extracted in less than a minute from the crash site. As soon as they were safely rescued, we moved a short distance from the downed Huey and set up a defensive perimeter until a Mosquito chopper came to retrieve the chopper for salvage. The crew members suffered only minor cuts and bruises. They were appreciative of our rescue effort.

Tonight I'm in charge of the four-man listening post located at the rear of New Life Village. I've been getting this detail a lot lately. I developed a friendship with a Vietnamese soldier, who is the leader of the ARVN soldiers who man the bunker with us. The bunker is manned nightly by four US soldiers and eight ARVN soldiers or popular forces. I take gifts to the Vietnamese leader I call Sarge, who has mastered an adequate English vocabulary. I give him this nickname because I always forget his Vietnamese name. The gifts are cigarettes, soap, and a large bag of candy. I use these gifts as a bribe to get his cooperation in controlling his men on guard. As a further incentive, I always take Sarge and his men to breakfast the next morning.

I give the bribe to Sarge because he is my link in communicating with the other ARVN troops. The ARVNs love to recon by fire and send up illumination rounds just for the hell of it. The US soldiers must get permission to fire or have a good reason to request illumination from this LP position. Sarge is a definite asset in managing the ARVN troops.

Sarge invites me to leave the bunker and go into New Life Village for food and drink to celebrate the Tet New Year. He says the villagers are going to have pickled fish, duck, rice, and rice whiskey. I decline his invitation, stating I'll get in trouble leaving my men while on duty. I thank him for the invitation and send greetings to his family for a happy Tet New Year. Sarge and I check on his men before he leaves for the village. All his men are inside the bunker, while my squad from the Third Platoon maintains security on the outside. When I look inside, I see a mass of eight bodies sleeping together with arms and legs intertwined. The scene looks like an orgy from the Roman Empire. Sarge looks at me, smiling, and says, "No problem."

Sarge returns a couple of hours later with fish and rice for me. I graciously accept the small portions he offers me. Of course, I comment, "Number 1!" after every bite. I take out photographs my parents sent me from their Christmas holiday. I show Sarge pictures of my father, mother, and sister. I describe them as papa-san, mama-san, and baby-san. Sarge is impressed with the size of my parents' home

—

and all the Christmas decorations. I even show him a picture of my 1965 Chevrolet Super Sport convertible. I can tell Sarge is confused by what I shared with him about my life. Finally, Sarge questions me, "Why did you come to Vietnam to fight?" I'm startled he asks me that question. Sarge continues, "You come from a wealthy family." I ignore the first question because I don't have what I think is a suitable answer for him. I explain to him my family is middle class and not wealthy based on American standards. We talk for ten more minutes before Sarge retires for the night. During this time, I can feel a deeper relationship developing between us as human beings, not as merely friendly soldiers.

The next morning at 0600 hours, we leave the listening post with the ARVNs for our base camp breakfast. The ARVNs pig out on eggs, bacon, cereal, and baked goods. I encourage them to load their pockets with bananas and rolls. I tell Sarge I'll probably see him again in the next two weeks.

For tonight, our base camp is on high alert for a major ground attack. The army brings in eleven tanks to bolster the defense perimeter adjacent to the Vam Co West River. Intelligence expects a large force to cross the river and attack the base camp from this location. This side of Camp Scott would be great for a surprise attack, but if the attack fails, the enemy will be slaughtered retreating across the river.

Senical briefs the Third Herd on the expected ground attack tonight. Bo says we should load additional magazines, and if the guys choose to do so, it may be a good idea to sleep on the berm. Senical gives out details for tonight, and of course, I'm in charge of the LP adjacent to the river. He says battalion wants the four LP locations to report early to headquarters for more details pertaining to the ground attack.

I'm concerned about being placed between the river and eleven tanks. I decide to take a walk over to the tanks to determine if I can find a safe position to set up our nighttime LP. The tanks are aligned in a row with their guns aimed at ground level. I strike up a conversation with one of the men assigned to the tanks. He informs me the tanks will be firing beehive rounds tonight for maximum effect. I imagine this will be like firing a shotgun with hundreds of pellets expended into the air, only under a more grandiose scale. After viewing the tanks and learning the plan of defense, I know I better come up with some alternatives for my LP.

I walk down the river road and look for a good spot to establish a nighttime position where the squad will have protection from the enemy and the firing tanks. To my relief, I see the perfect location. The engineers have dug a huge hole in the ground to bury garbage. This will be the ideal place because it's not too close to the river and will provide us ample time to run back to base camp if we see approaching soldiers. Also the hole protects us from both enemy fire and the tank beehive rounds that concern me. I feel very satisfied with this protective site of observation and cover.

At dusk we walk to battalion headquarters for our briefing. A first lieutenant is in charge of the briefing. He begins by affirming the intelligence report stating command is 99 percent sure of tonight's ground attack. He reviews measures the battalion has taken to bring in tanks and have gunships on alert. He tells us that all the companies are on stand-down. The vulnerable areas for attack have been identified with preventive measures taken.

The lieutenant says that each LP will radio in immediately after he has set up in his nighttime position. Sit reps (situation reported) will be radioed every fifteen minutes instead of the usual hourly report, which is given during the night. He asks each LP to line up to receive his nighttime position that he's going to assign. I think, *Oh shit! I don't believe he's actually assigning a setup location.* When our turn comes, he asks who is in charge. I speak up and reply, "Sir, I am." He looks directly at me and says, "Your LP is a crucial alert site for the base camp. Intelligence reports reveal a large force of North Vietnamese soldiers will cross the river and attack from your LP area. We want you to go down the left side of river road and position your squad in the graveyard with a good view of the river. Radio immediately when you see the enemy. Remember sit reps every fifteen minutes. Do you have any questions?" I reply, "No sir." I turn around and march out of the briefing room in a really pissed-off mood.

As we walk toward river road, I think to myself there is no way that I'm going to obey those orders. The guys with me are new in the company. One of them gets the courage to ask me if we're going down by the river. I look at him and reply, "Do you think I'm crazy? They're not using us for cannon fodder." His concern reminded me of my first LP on river road with Eddie Foster in charge. Now I am in charge and will do what Eddie taught me.

I halt and motion all of the men to get closer to me. I announce to them there is going to be a change in our orders. I continue, "This afternoon I selected our nighttime position, which is located midway between the river and the tanks. The position is a large hole in the ground that will give us excellent protection in the event of a major ground attack. The change in orders will be our little secret." I can see in their eyes they have no problem with my changing the night setup position. Before we leave the camp's perimeter, I walk over to a bunker guard to alert him that our squad is on its way to our LP site on river road. I tell the guard exactly where we'll be in case we have to run back to the perimeter during an attack. Usually, this practice of alerting the perimeter isn't necessary, but everyone is on edge, and it's important to take additional safety precautions. The guard says he'll inform the other men on his bunker.

We arrive at our nighttime position, and I radio that the squad is in position as ordered. Every fifteen minutes we call in our status (sit rep—negative). After two hours of negative responses, the lieutenant calls and asks if we see any activity. I respond with another negative sit rep. A minute later after my report, the tanks open up firing their beehive rounds. Then the entire base camp goes crazy firing every type of weapon in their arsenal. I instruct the guys to get down low in the hole because the tanks are firing directly over our heads and we can hear the fleshettes from the beehive rounds whizzing by. I look through the starlight scope, expecting to see NVA soldiers, but don't see any enemy activity. I lower myself in the hole and radio the lieutenant and ask, "Sir, what the hell is going on?" His frantic-sounding voice replies, "We are under a ground attack." Due to the deafening noise, I scream on the radio, "There are no gooks out here. What the hell are you firing at?" I look again and see no enemy in sight. Just as I alert the guys to prepare for moving out, the firing ceases from the base camp. We relax in the hole while I call in another sit rep—negative.

I don't know what started the firing from the base camp, but tomorrow I'll address some issues with the lieutenant. I tell the men I'll stay up all night with them rotating on guard. Apparently, no one is interested in sleeping after surviving the firepower from our base camp. If the NVA are nearby, I'm sure their plans of a surprise attack have been postponed.

The next morning at the crack of dawn, we emerge from our hole and walk toward the river to see the damage the tanks inflicted on the terrain. The graveyard where we were ordered to establish an LP was pulverized from the beehive rounds. The tombstones were destroyed or severely chipped away from the shelling of the tanks. We knew if we would have used this position, the graveyard might have been our final resting place.

The squad and I walk to battalion headquarters and meet the first lieutenant who is still on duty. I ask him why the tanks opened up when our sit reps were negative. He says the base had incoming mortar fire, which made him believe the attack began, so orders were given to commence firing. My second question to him is, "Why were we not notified about the tanks and troops firing in our sector?" He had no response to that. I inform him that our squad could have been easily wiped out from friendly fire by his lack of concern for our welfare and his dereliction of duty. I look him squarely in the eyes and say in a threatening tone, "Sir, don't let this happen again!" I turn around and the squad follows me. The lieutenant doesn't respond to my statement.

The next day our platoon spends the morning and afternoon on Eagle flights. Late in the evening we set up our usual L-shaped ambush. I'm at a position with some of the Begoni clan. It's very late at night when we notice someone walking up the dike on which the ambush is located. I realize the time is past 0200 hours when most enemy activity ceases for the night. We wake the guys near us and prepare to shoot the intruder. At the last moment, I see the person is not carrying a weapon, so we decide to capture the person. I jump up from my lying-down position beside the dike and tackle the gook. The gook is light as a feather and offers no resistance as we hit the ground together. Just as I make a fist to punch the gook, I hear a scream and realize this is a woman. The guys surround us, holding their weapons in a combat stance. I get up and grab her arm, raising the mama-san to her feet. The Begonis and I are very upset because she was only seconds from becoming history. I can't imagine having this old woman's death on my conscience the rest of my life. We motion with our M16s that we were going to kill her. The poor bitch is scared to death and doesn't really understand what we're trying to tell her. Civilians know they are supposed to stay in their hootches until daylight; otherwise, they are fair game for any soldier. We make her remain with us for another half an hour until daybreak. At first light, she continues her trip, probably to a nearby market.

Today, February 11, is a day that will remain with me for the rest of my life. Last night Senical informed me that I was chosen to be the new member on the point team with Larry Boneck and Clyde Poland. I expected such a decision but buried the thought of walking point in the back of my mind. The casualty rate for pointmen is very high, which elevates my status of getting wounded or killed to a new level. I had a talk with myself to encourage me to do my best and not get psyched out about the increased probability of being a casualty.

I'm terrified about my new assignment as a pointman mainly because I lack the confidence in my ability to do the job. In this position, the result of a mistake or bad judgment can cost your life or the lives of your buddies. Larry and Clyde assure me not to worry. Larry says Clyde and he will continue walking lead pointman until I've experienced a few weeks of training.

Bo Senical briefs the platoon on our first mission of the day. The platoon is going to take a *Chieu Hoi* who has prearranged the surrender in the field to our forces. A *Chieu Hoi* is a former Vietcong who has agreed to defect from the enemy ranks to the American side. Most often the army tries to make tiger scouts out of the defectors because of their knowledge of the Vietcong's habits and methods of fighting. The main reason for Vietcong defections is that their own forces have killed someone in the defector's family. Senical tells the platoon that Sam, our former tiger scout, has arranged through battalion headquarters for this defection. Senical and Sam will orchestrate a fake capture, so no reprisals will be taken against the defector's family. Our job as a platoon is to make everything look realistic.

On our first landing, the platoon is inserted in a dry rice paddy near a woodline that conceals two hootches. Immediately Sam heads toward one of the hootches while others inspect the second home. Sam exits the hootch with the defector and puts on a big show as if he just captured a Vietcong. He yells at the defector and slaps him a few times for the benefit of the Vietnamese onlookers. The defector's hands are tied behind his back while the platoon remains in a defensive posture awaiting a pickup helicopter's arrival. Sam and the *Chieu Hoi* are flown back to base camp for interrogation.

This is a propaganda poem written by a Vietnamese soldier.

Chieu Hoi propaganda pamphlet.

On our second insertion, we enter an area loaded with *Tu Dia* signs. I tell myself this isn't my idea of an easy way to break in as a pointman. Pete gives orders for the point team to move in the direction of a nearby woodline. Boneck and Clyde take off in that direction with me following. We pass another *Tu Dia* sign in front of a small area of knee-high vegetation. Boneck avoids penetrating the high grasses and instead walks around a sharp bend of vegetation to a clearing of short scrublike weeds. The clearing juts into an opening containing a row of trees. Boneck spots another *Tu Dia* sign and passes the word back to Clyde and me. He stops to study the area for signs of booby traps and instructs us to do the same. I stand in a frozen position, gazing at the ground for anything that doesn't look like vegetation. After a few minutes, I notice something odd next to a small bush in the middle of the clearing. I scream, "Booby trap! Booby trap!" Boneck and Clyde look at me with Boneck responding, "Where is it?" Then I feel embarrassed and reply, "I'm not really sure if it's a booby trap." I have myself so psyched up that I blurted out, "Booby trap!" just from fright at seeing something strange lying on the ground.

Ba, the Third Platoon Vietnamese tiger scout, comes up to me and says, "Where? Where?" I point to the location by the bush, and he goes over to examine my find. Ba shouts, "Booby trap!" I walk point for only half an hour and I miraculously find a booby trap of two grenades rigged to a trip wire. We leave the booby trap for Firestone to blow up.

Pete comes over and announces that the platoon is pulling out of this area before we have a casualty. I like Pete's decision. *Tu Dia* signs are posted everywhere, indicating the location is heavily booby-trapped. When the choppers arrive for our pickup, I overhear chatter among the guys in disbelief that I found the booby trap.

The next two LZs were normal situations for Boneck and Clyde, but everything to me is a new adventure and learning experience. I notice when I walk up front, I become more aware of my surroundings. I try to focus on a particular sense to develop it. Using that sense then becomes more natural, and I don't have to make a concentrated effort. If I can achieve this with most of my senses, I'll be in harmony with my surroundings. Now, when I walk point, I concentrate on looking for objects that don't fit in the local picture and sounds that aren't natural to the setting. Hopefully, in time, my efforts will enable me to easily recognize danger. My goal is to become a good pointman like my partners.

We return to base camp for a few hours to grab a hot meal, relax with a beer, and prepare our gear for the night's mission. Tonight we board the LCMs (landing craft mechanized boats) we refer to as Tango boats. The boats are going downriver to an insertion point in the Testicles. What a terrible way to end my day on point. I hate the boats because of their roaring engine noise, slowness in the water, and lack of firepower. This craft is designed for off-loading GIs from troop carrying ships during World War II. The Vietcong in the delta can hear the boats coming a mile away, which gives them ample time to prepare ambushes near the insertion points. To compound my frustration, I hate the Testicles because this area is crawling with Vietcong, who frequently engage us in firefights.

The Vietnamese Navy drops us off in the Testicles around 2200 hours. Boneck and I walk point tonight. Clyde is getting a much-needed rest back in base camp. The pointmen are rewarded with rest breaks. Walking point for three nights is followed by a night of downtime.

Larry and I are the first ones to exit the boat, with Larry leading the way through the nipa palms to the rice paddies. We walk for about half an hour at night when we come under attack from quite a distance. Pete recognizes the firing as US forces, so he gets on the radio and tries to communicate with them. Within a short time, he contacts the force that just fired upon us. Apparently, they thought we were the Vietcong group that ambushed them earlier. They spotted us in a starlight scope, but due to poor visibility, they mistook our unit as an enemy force. They apologize for the mistake. Thank God we were not at close range when they fired on us because we might have taken a casualty.

An hour later, Larry and I walk about five meters apart in a dry rice paddy. The moon does not provide a source of light; therefore, we keep close quarters in our movement through the paddy. The air is very still, which creates an eerie feeling with the pitch-black darkness of the sky. I walk into a large object directly in front of me. I raise my rifle and inflict a few blows to what I believe to be an enemy soldier. On the third blow, I realize this weightless object is falling toward me, so I strike it a few more times. Boneck begins to laugh at my antics and asks, "Did you kill the rice shock?" I'm totally embarrassed but look at him, saying, "The gook is dead." Boneck roars in laughter and says in jest, "Good job, I'll report the kill to Pete." I reply, "Maybe Pete will put me in for a Bronze Star for Valor." Larry eases my embarrassment by making a joke out of the incident. I believe he can somewhat empathize with my fears as a pointman.

Larry tells me that when he walks in the dark, he always gets an orientation of the major land formations and buildings before he moves out. His advice is to walk the length of a paddy, stop, and check if there has been any change in what was previously observed. He does this as a practice when a starlight scope isn't available. He admits to me he observed the rice shocks through the starlight he has with him. He constantly checks the terrain with the starlight from paddy to paddy when there is little natural light from the heavens. This is an excellent practice in thwarting enemy ambushes at night.

The platoon walks the paddies until 0200 hours in the morning before Pete informs Larry to find a place to rest the remainder of the night. Larry chooses a place near three hootches. The platoon moves in to set up defensive positions. Feeling uneasy, I decide to check the perimeter of the hootch where I intend to bed down. I walk around the structure in a low crouch, stopping briefly to watch and listen. I almost encircle the hootch when I step on something, causing me to falter. "Jesus Christ, what the hell are you doing?" yelled Doc Struzik. Oh no! I just stepped on Doc's chest while performing my search. In a pissed-off tone Doc blurts out, "You're going to make a great pointman!" I look at him shamefully and utter, "Doc, this job is yours for the asking." After my response, Doc turns over in disgust and closes his eyes.

9

Walking Point (February 16 to 28)

Today is February 16. Many of us received orders for promotion to a higher rank. I was promoted to specialist fourth class effective January 31, 1969. I'll get a small increase in pay, which will make my life a little better. My net private's pay is $142 per month, which includes $65 per month combat pay. Oh, how generous the US Army is with monetary reward to the troops! I figure I make almost 20¢ per hour ($142 divided by 720 hours, 24 hours per day × 30 days). Presently I have a $75 monthly car payment that creates havoc with my finances. I left an $800 per month accounting job with Sun Oil Company to be a crusader in Vietnam.

A few days ago, all the men in the Third Platoon were put in for an Air Medal. The medal is awarded for a large number of infantry combat assaults out of a helicopter. In December all the members in Delta Company participated in a major ground attack. Those soldiers who didn't have the Combat Infantryman Badge were recommended to receive the award for defending the base camp perimeter. Within days after the ground attack, all the eligible men would have earned the award anyway for combat operations out in the field. Many of the men in the company have received Bronze and Silver Stars for Valor. I have managed to keep a low profile to date and have no interest in receiving medals. The awards are necessary for soldiers who plan to further their military careers. The mail just arrived. I received some hometown newspapers, which I go through in a hurry to see if there are any articles on people

I know. Then at a later time, I thoroughly read the paper. I notice that Phil Tinari, a high school friend, was recently married. Also there is an engagement announcement about Larry Etherton, who is in the army stationed in Germany. Larry was a year behind me at Grove City College and later took a job as a management trainee with Sun Oil Company, following in my footsteps. Larry and I would sometimes thumb rides together across the Pennsylvania Turnpike from Grove City to West Chester, Pennsylvania.

Leroy Sherfinski broadcasts that he's a recipient of a Dear John letter. Everyone pays their condolences to Lee in a mocking form of behavior. Dear John letters are common among the troops. When the letter comes from a wife, the men are more sympathetic, but we celebrate if it's a girlfriend. Lee takes a picture of his girlfriend out of his locker. He posts the bikini-clad girl's picture on the barracks wall. Then Lee produces two darts and requests the guys to join him in a contest to desecrate the photograph. The Begoni Clan helps themselves to beers, then forms a line for their two throws at the former girlfriend. When someone scores a hit in the face or boobs, the men go crazy hooting and hollering. The photograph is a complete waste after one round of darts. I ask Lee what he's planning to do with the picture. He informs us he plans to mail it to her, describing the fun we enjoyed at her expense. Wow! I thought that will be humiliating to her.

I have compassion for Lee and all the other GIs because of the difficulty of maintaining a relationship thousands of miles away in a war zone. On a daily basis, Lee is under great stress just to survive. His wants and needs are few. He appreciates the simple aspects of life having a hot meal, wearing clean clothes, getting rest, and taking a shower. His former girlfriend is probably more concerned with her social life and the material world back in the States. I'm sure both parties recognize changes in their loved ones that are difficult to understand. The separation from a loved one creates change in a relationship. Differences become magnified. This prevents couples from recapturing the same feelings for each other, which each of them previously cherished. Thank God I don't have a girlfriend because I'm sure it would be only a matter of time before I would receive my Dear John. Personally, I find it difficult to deal with the internal conflicts I'm experiencing. I couldn't imagine sharing my intense feelings with another person who would have no clue about my new views and appreciation of life.

—

The Vietnamese are celebrating the Tet Lunar Year tonight. Our company has taken extra precautions to guard against a major ground attack. We fortified our bunkers with more sandbags and filled the bunkers with ammunition and grenades. Barrels of napalm and additional Claymore mines have been placed outside the perimeter. The company added a .50 caliber machine gun to one of the large bunkers, with a 90 mm recoilless rifle available in an emergency.

Senical told us earlier that it would be a good idea to sleep on the berm tonight. Tim and I agree to share the same bunker. We depart for the berm early, and to our surprise, many of the guys are already in position for the night. Our bunker is a two-man hole dug in the side of the berm and is utilized as a firing position. I have brought forty magazines of ammunition plus a box of grenades. Tim has a similar number of magazines but will share the grenades with me. The battalion is on stand-down tonight because of the major enemy offensive last year during Tet.

At midnight, the local Vietnamese ARVNs shoot flares and tracer rounds in the sky to celebrate Tet. Tim and I tensely watch the display, anticipating a ground attack may follow. After ten minutes of celebration, the short, happy hour ends. The only activity experienced so far tonight is the usual few harassing mortar rounds fired inside the base camp. The night is relatively quiet. The Vietcong and NVA must realize we prepared for a battle this year.

Tim and I are on our way to an early breakfast this morning. I have a morning road-clearing detail with the engineers. This is my first time performing this detail, which encompasses an eight-mile stretch of road that needs to be cleared of mines and booby traps. At 0700 hours, I meet the engineers and three other infantrymen at the gate to our base camp. The sweep is expected to take two hours before we meet another road-clearing force coming in the opposite direction.

The infantry job is to walk in the rice paddies on both sides of the road, looking for trip wires and booby traps. The four of us will rotate, with two men walking in the paddies on either side of the road, while the other two men walk on the road. Rotating from the paddies to the road gives rest to those walking in the paddies. Many of the paddies are filled with mud and water. Walking for miles becomes difficult and tiring. The army engineers walk the road using their minesweepers.

After we travel about a mile from base camp, we come upon the first sign of enemy presence from last night. The Vietcong have lined both sides of the road for a long distance with little Vietcong flags. The flags are made from a woven paper with one side colored like the flag and the other side covered in brown paper. They're fifty feet apart and attached to sticks placed in the ground. The road looks like a parade route. The flags are checked for booby traps before being destroyed.

I suspect this is the Vietcong's best representation of psychological warfare. I laugh to myself because their best effort for ruining the celebration of Tet is occupying a road for a few minutes while posting crude homemade paper flags. At the side of the road in the middle of all the paper flags is a large cloth Vietcong flag attached to a pole. The engineers find a booby trap attached to this flag. The booby trap is blown up, and the cloth flag is taken for a souvenir. I take one of the paper flags for a war trophy.

Before we finish our sweep, the Vietnamese travel on the road with their mopeds and other small vehicles. That is an indication to us the road is probably clear of mines or they wouldn't be using it. Regardless, we must continue our mission and meet the other unit sweeping in the opposite direction. We complete the sweep in three hours because of the slow process of checking the flags for booby traps.

I return to base camp in time for Eagle flights. It is 1000 hours, which is a late starting time to go to the field for search-and-destroy missions. Our first drop-off zone is rather routine and boring for me, even though I'm walking point. In less than an hour, the choppers return to take us to our next landing zone.

On the second LZ, Boneck takes point and immediately sees a *Tu Dia* sign with a grenade drawn on the sign. Boneck tells me to pass the word down the line for the men to follow directly in our footpaths and don't go off our trail. Boneck walks in a wet rice paddy about ten feet from a paddy dike. Ahead of us is a small group of hootches positioned at the end of the paddy in front of a woodline. Normally when you see *Tu Dia* signs so close to habitable hootches, the people living there are responsible for setting up the warning signs. If they did not set them up, they know who did. The point team moves toward the hootches to search and ask questions about the signs.

Larry and I are in a hootch questioning a woman when we hear an explosion. We both look at each other in amazement. How is it possible for someone to hit a booby trap after we already had cleared the area? We hear the calls for Doc and exit the hootch to see what happened.

Pete and Bo Senical approach Larry and me. Pete goes into a tirade, screaming at us for not properly clearing the walking path. Larry and I listen to his wild assertions while Bo silently doesn't add a word. Pete flies off the handle while Bo is more composed and didn't direct blame. I understand how Pete feels; he expects a lot out of the point team to protect the main column of men. It's frustrating when a leader loses men. The leaders take it personally as though they failed their job.

After Pete's brief and unsavory lecture, the four of us rush back to the location of the explosion. When we get there, Doc is working on Sergeant David Roland, who has suffered leg wounds from a booby trap explosion, which is probably caused by a grenade. Sergeant Roland is in pain but doesn't have any life-threatening wounds. Larry and I notice Roland tripped the booby trap when he got up on a dike. He hit the booby trap in an area we avoided and didn't clear. Boneck tells Pete that Roland was walking a dike that the point team bypassed. Pete asks Roland and a few other guys why they walked near the dike. Their response is they did not get the word to follow our exact trail. I thought he should have had better sense than to get too far off the path plus never get on dikes in enemy territory. Oh well, we learn another lesson about communication the hard way.

Doc Struzik finishes working on Sergeant Roland. He goes over to Earl "Hillbilly" Henderson to treat him for injuries received from the explosion. Hillbilly sustained a concussion. Debris from the explosion, mostly mud and vegetation, were thrown in his face. Doc treats his face for superficial wounds and cleans debris out of his eye. Doc tells Hillbilly to go to the medic's aid station back in base camp to have his eye thoroughly cleaned.

The dust-off helicopter arrives, and we all say good-bye to Sergeant Roland. Hillbilly remains with the platoon. Larry and I go back to the hootches and try to intimidate the Vietnamese into divulging information about the local Vietcong. Their answer is *no biet* to every question. That is their typical response to our questions. In other words, they don't understand what we're saying, which is a damn lie. I quickly reply with "no bic my ass." We leave after a frustrating search and questioning period. Sometimes you want to beat the hell out of the Vietnamese until they tell you what you want to know, but as American soldiers, we must make a good impression, using proper conduct when dealing with the civilians.

Our third insertion is around 1400 hours and seems to be more of the same. Larry, Clyde, and I walk the paddies ahead of the platoon when I notice rice shocks lying on the ground in an adjoining rice paddy. I mention to the guys it's odd that the rice shocks are lying on the ground. I tell them to hold up the sweep while I check out what I think is a strange situation.

There are five piles of rice shocks dispersed throughout this paddy. I pick out the nearest pile to inspect. I reach down and begin to move the rice sheaths and notice this pile of harvested sheaths is camouflaging enemy supplies. I yell to Boneck and Clyde, "Get the hell over here!" They don't question me and proceed to hurry over in a quick and careful tempo. Clyde questions me, "What did you find?" I move the sheaths back, revealing an NVA poncho and gas mask. Clyde says, "Be careful, these supplies might be booby-trapped." Boneck responds, "Let Milliken clear this pile, then the team will individually check the others. If they are booby-trapped, only one of us will be caught in the explosion." We agree I'll proceed to uncover this cache, and if it's clear of booby traps, it will be highly unlikely to find a booby trap in the other piles. Boneck notifies Pete of our find and informs him the point team will inspect the other sheaths of rice. Boneck and Clyde wait until I finish investigating my find.

I take approximately ten minutes to carefully check the cache. I find six NVA ponchos, one gas mask, many AK-47 magazines, camouflage cloth, food, and two hundred rounds of .30 caliber machine gun ammunition. Boneck reports my findings to Pete, who immediately informs higher-ups of the cache so the platoon can get recognition for a job well-done. We expect the four other piles to produce more of the same and hopefully some weapons. Each of us examines another pile until the remaining four are checked. We're disappointed to not find enemy supplies under the remaining piles. Luckily, I chose the correct one to initially inspect. Otherwise, we would have missed the small cache. I believe anytime we find supplies, it makes the enemy's life a little more difficult and, in turn, gives us a psychological edge. We destroy the food, which includes a large supply of rice. I take a souvenir of NVA camouflage material, which I'm going to use as a neckerchief during the day and a face-protection mask for mosquitoes at night. The material is of high quality, very light, and tightly woven, which makes it durable and almost impossible to tear. The remainder of the cache is apportioned among the men to take back to base camp.

For the past five days, the platoon was out in the field both day and night, performing routine search-and-destroy missions. We experienced light enemy contact, blew up enemy bunkers, and found one enemy booby trap with four grenades attached to a trip wire. During one of the daily Eagle flights, the choppers inserted us in an area that appeared to be more like a jungle growth area than the normal woodline. The point team noticed dried nipa leaves and other mixed wilted vegetation lying on or near a trail in the jungle area. On close inspection, we determined the wilted vegetation concealed Vietcong punji pits. We uncovered a few pits that contained many sharp bamboo stakes that looked like they're covered with human excrement. Luckily for the point team, these booby traps were easy to spot because of the dead vegetation. If a GI fell in one of these camouflaged dug-out pits, his injury would disable him and he'd run a high risk of developing infection.

On two different nights when Larry, Clyde, and I searched hootches, we experienced an unusual situation. We've developed our own method of entering and searching the surroundings when our point team enters a hootch at night. Generally, we approach the thatched buildings and listen for sounds of activity inside, and if possible, we peer through openings in the thatched walls, looking for movement. Usually, we hear and see nothing because the residents of the hootch are bedded down inside their dried mud bunker area. The bunker is shaped like an igloo, having a small tunnel that must be crawled through to get to the bedding area.

This night we heard and saw nothing; therefore, we prepared to enter the home. Larry and Clyde positioned themselves on both sides of the entrance, and it was my turn to knock the door down. If I fail to find a latch to release the door, I take a small run and break down the door with my body. When I fall forward into the hootch, my counterparts will enter and secure my flanks. I can't find a latch to open this door, so I ran and hit the door head-on and flipped over in great pain. To my astonishment, this hootch had a heavy metal bar midway across the door that hit me in the abdomen when I tried to break in. I lay at the entrance with the wind knocked out of me, while Larry and Clyde continued the search. I wondered if this papa-san knew of our tactics and prepared an obstacle for us.

The next night we used the same entrance procedure and entered a hootch, which, to our surprise, housed a water buffalo in a small pen. The water buffalo went crazy when we entered and had to be calmed down by the owners. If the pen had been larger, the water buffalo would have had room to knock the pen apart and attack us. If that occurred, we would have been forced to kill it.

Today is February 23. The platoon is going to the field with two army dog handlers, accompanied by their German shepherds. The dog handlers and the shepherds walk point with the point team following. I'm nervous because the handlers move too slowly with the dogs. The shepherds might be good for detecting booby traps, but they're entirely too slow in case the enemy sees us and decides to set up an ambush. Finally, the handlers turn over the point job to our team. Around dusk, we take sniper fire and the dogs get excited. We refrain from returning fire because we can't identify the location of the sniper.

Later in the evening, while resting in our nighttime location, we spot a Vietcong position that is mortaring a nearby ARVN base. Pete gives our base camp coordinates of the suspected Vietcong mortar emplacement and artillery opens up on the site. Immediately the mortaring stops from the nearby woodline.

I rest by one of the dog handlers and his shepherd. I notice the handler and the dog are best buddies. They both have mutual trust and respect for each other, but neither the handler nor the dog interacts with the troops. I lie on the ground and fix my eyes on every movement the dog makes. The German shepherd sits on his hind legs with his head in an erect position, surveying the field in front of him, using his eyes and ears like a radar beacon. I stare at the animal and believe every infantry unit should have a dog as a sentry for pulling guard duty in the field at night. This dog will never go to sleep and possesses keen senses that will alert its handler to danger in ample time to react to a particular situation. Dogs are helpful to intimidate prisoners or detainees in order to learn information. I remember seeing a dog compound in Dong Tam, but this is the first time I ever saw them with an infantry unit. They are most commonly used for base security.

Today is February 25, and the platoon is walking into base camp after spending another two days in the field. Unexpectedly, we got caught out in the field on an extended stay with little food. The last few days we supplemented our C rations with coconut milk and meat. We shot groups of coconuts out of high trees and first make a hole to drink the milk before breaking open the coconut to carve out the white coconut meat. I hate coconuts, but because of a lack of food, I became a connoisseur of the fruit. Pete informs base camp about our hungry platoon, and the mess hall will open for an early breakfast.

It is around 0600 hours when the platoon marches into base camp. We proceed directly to the mess hall and form a line outside, waiting to be served. Battalion Sergeant Major Whitby positions himself in front of the chow line, checking dog tags. The mess hall opens, and the men walk by Whitby, displaying their tags. When I come up to him, I take my tags out of my fatigue pants pocket and show them to him. I had my dog tags wrapped in tape so they would not jingle and make noise while I walked point. I explain this to him, and he tells me to get out of the line and that I can't eat breakfast until the tags are properly displayed around my neck. When I begin to argue with the sergeant major, my buddies intervene and tell me to go back to Delta Company and they will bring breakfast to me. It takes me a good hour to cool off.

Apparently, the battalion is having an IG inspection today. I guess that is why I had to put up with the base camp bullshit in the chow line. First Sergeant Hullette enters our billet area, giving stupid, harassing details for the IG inspection. Again I lose my temper and voice my opinion about an inspection that creates work for those with a rank of E-4 and below. I tell Top that we do most of the fighting in the field, so why doesn't command recognize our efforts? We should get proper rest in base camp so we can do a better job in the field. I'm concerned about the men in the Third Platoon getting worn-out and making careless mistakes. Top listens to me but still proceeds with the details. He assigns me to clean inside our billet area, which is a real mess. I should consider myself fortunate because I didn't get a shit-burning detail, which is usually reserved for shammers in base camp. I don't know Top very well, but I am sure he has made his mind up about me as being a troublemaker and maybe a shammer.

Senical informs the platoon that we have the Tango boats tonight. The boats are expected to arrive around 2000 hours at the base camp river's edge. The platoon waits for two hours before the boats show up. Then we travel the blue for four hours before the platoon is inserted in the bush. At 0200 hours, we begin to hump the paddies until 0440 hours. Finally, we set up an ambush site, which is ridiculous because the natives will be awake in another hour to work their fields. This entire mission is a waste of time. I feel bad for Pete and Bo, who have to obey and execute command's asinine orders.

We hear good news when we arrive back at base camp early in the afternoon. Tonight the company is going to have another one of those famous "all you can eat" barbecues. I have off tonight and expect to spend a little time in the EM club with Ralph, Whitey, Boneck, and whoever shows up. Sometimes ten to fifteen guys from the platoon frequent the place when we have downtime.

I just received my mail, which includes letters from my mother and best friend Johnny Baumhauer. Mom and Dad purchased their first color television. Mom describes the wild-looking colorful suits Johnny Carson wears on *The Tonight Show*. She really enjoys her new television, which makes me feel good. She is a wonderful woman who always sacrifices to make life better for others. I'm fortunate to have such a loving mother and family.

Johnny describes an ordeal he experienced when his car broke down in a snowstorm on a return trip to college in New York. He said his car generator went bad so he abandoned the car. He found a police station where he bummed food and lodging for two days before he received money his parents wired him. I laughed when I read his letter because for a bright guy, he always manages to get into innocent trouble. I enjoy reading letters from family and friends. I assume they think their letter writing is trivial when I'm in a war zone, but that is far from the truth.

It's amazing that I survived my training period walking point. Larry and Clyde are more confident in my abilities. I'll be rotating as first pointman because I have gained experience in the last few weeks. I adopted the following rules about walking point that Boneck and Clyde have ingrained in my mind:

1. Never walk dikes.
2. Never walk paths in woodlines.
3. Avoid intersections of paths and dikes.
4. Never enter a woodline in an open-entrance area. Enter in dense foliage that appears undisturbed.
5. Check the situation from paddy to paddy when walking at night. Utilize a starlight scope or get close to the ground to observe silhouettes.
6. Always exit the woodline in a dense area.

7. Always take immediate command of the situation when raiding hootches.
8. Never feel sorry for civilians, women, or children. Keep your guard up.
9. Expect the unexpected.
10. Check weapons frequently to ascertain if the safety is on or off.
11. Concentrate, utilizing all senses.
12. Use tricks to get civilians to talk. Hide enemy material in their homes.
13. Never be intimidated by command. *You* are the boss.
14. Avoid contact with enemy if possible.
15. Get firepower over enemy when in contact. Don't be afraid to shoot.
16. Walk in an unorthodox fashion when approaching a woodline. Move slowly, fast, and sideways, which makes it difficult for the enemy to shoot you.
17. Use stall tactics to give troops rest and keep them fresh.
18. Walk with an authoritative, alert stance.
19. Try to draw early fire at a safe distance when approaching a suspected enemy target.
20. Never align yourself to a marker, such as a tree, which makes an easy target.
21. Respect *Tu Dia* signs!

The list is much longer and seems to build on a daily basis. If a pointman follows these rules to perfection and has a lot of luck, he might survive his tour on point.

Boneck, Clyde, and I board the lead helicopter called Smokey for our daily Eagle flights. I expect we will have the opportunity to use many of the pointman guidelines that I now refer to as my unwritten Bible. I carry a small Salvation Army Bible that has a metal plate enclosed as a good luck charm. The Bible fits in my upper-left fatigue shirt pocket over my heart. For some goofy reason, this symbolism of the Bible and metal plate protecting my heart gives me hope that I will survive.

We receive word that a Cobra helicopter spotted Vietcong running into a woodline. We try to locate the VC for the Cobra gunship. Smokey lands in a paddy near the place where the VC entered the woodline. As we approach the suspected area, the VC open up on our position. It appears there are two Vietcong firing from a camouflaged large bunker in dense undergrowth. Pete radios the Cobra pilot and informs him we will mark the bunker position with red smoke for his rocket attack. Pete asks me to go to the platoon's right flank to prevent the VC from escaping in that direction. The platoon is already positioned on the left flank and directly in front of the enemy bunker. I low crawl behind a paddy dike for about twenty meters to the right flank. I rise up to view an open area of high grass. Then I see movement in the grass, coming from the direction of the enemy bunker. I raise my M16, waiting for my target to get closer. Also, I want to be sure there is only one Vietcong in the grass. The target gets closer, and I notice it's an unarmed woman moving through the high vegetation. I decide to try and take her prisoner. I rise up and yell at her, "*Lai dai* mama-san! *Lai dai* mama-san!" She sees me aiming my M16 at her and raises her arms to surrender. I motion to her to come toward me as I lower my body for cover.

As soon as she makes it to my position, I throw her on the ground. Then the Cobra begins its rocket attack on the bunker. While the Cobra fires on the bunker, I try to search the woman for weapons, but find it difficult because of the shrapnel flying overhead. I grab her white blouse and rip it off, motioning for her to do the same with her black pajama bottoms. She is lying next to me naked, probably thinking I want to rape her. Now I feel a sense of relief since she is not concealing a weapon. She is probably the girlfriend or wife of one of the VC the Cobra is going to kill. Finally, the gunship has a direct hit on the bunker, and the two men are killed.

Pete calls for me to return to his position and is surprised to see me walking toward him with a naked woman. I explain to him who she is, and he calls for a chopper to pick up the prisoner. Meanwhile, while I talk with Pete, men in the platoon start to gather in the area to get a look at the naked Vietcong. When Pete notices what is going on, he motions her to dress. The guys boo Pete, and everyone starts laughing. I wonder what she is thinking.

Our next landing zone is a routine preplanned drop-off in a suspected Vietcong target area. Boneck walks first man while Clyde and I cover his flanks. Boneck informs Pete we found some enemy bunkers that we are going to blow up, so the platoon should take a rest break while we do our job. The point team moves out of sight of the platoon and proceeds to throw a few grenades as though we're destroying bunkers. We throw grenades but aren't blowing up bunkers. This is a delay tactic we use to take a rest break. I know Pete is aware and realizes some of the shit we pull, but he goes along with our antics, especially when a rest break is in order. If we did not look after ourselves in the field, command would have us moving constantly until exhaustion would become another enemy and a liability to our own safety.

After a short rest, Clyde and I decide to walk over by the woodline while Boneck checks with Pete about orders. Clyde and I approach the woodline and hear a metal click. Simultaneously both of us hit the ground in a prone position. Clyde looks directly at me and says, "Someone just flipped his weapon on automatic." I concur, "You are right, let's low crawl to the dike." Clyde asks me, "What do you think we should do?" I vent my concern, "They missed their chance to kill us, let's low crawl to the next paddy and get the hell out of here. I sense that woodline is crawling with Vietcong." Clyde says, "Follow me." I laugh while he stares at me in confusion. Clyde asks, "What is so damn funny?" I reply, "'Follow me' is the motto used by future officers in Officer Candidate School." He laughs and reiterates, "Follow me, dumb ass." We proceed to low crawl out of the area. We meet Boneck and tell him what happened. Obeying the commandments of walking point, we walk in the opposite direction of the woodline. Our pointman policy is "Don't fuck with us and we won't fuck with you."

The platoon sets up near a small village for our dinner of C rations. I have my dinner with Tim, Lee, Ralph, Whitey, and other members of the Begoni Clan. A young Vietnamese girl comes over to talk. She speaks very little English. I become mystified by her gold smile. Almost all her teeth have gold crowns. I never saw such a sight in my life. She is definitely proud of her teeth, which I think are gross looking. Her mouth must be worth a fortune! I'm surprised she hasn't been killed for her gold teeth. I have witnessed tiger scouts extract gold teeth from dead enemy soldiers. I think if I were her, I would keep my mouth shut.

I put on my sunglasses to get my eyes used to darkness before we walk point at night. I never wear sunglasses while walking point during the day because they interfere with my vision to spot objects glistening in the sunlight. Many times these objects are booby traps. If I bring sunglasses with me, I put them on and go into a hootch and wait until

---

dark. When we move out, I have an edge because my eyes have already adjusted to darkness.

Larry is ready to walk first man and does so in a manner that doesn't telegraph our direction of travel. It's important not to give the enemy an indication of the direction you might pursue after a rest break. This minimizes the enemy's opportunity to set up an ambush site. We walk for about an hour and come near some hootches that look suspicious. We have a short meeting with Pete and decide that only Larry and I will check a specific hootch while the men guard our entrance and exit.

Boneck leads the way, and we enter the hootch in unison. Inside are two women, several children, and an old papa-san. We find it odd that all of them are out of their bunker as though they're having family time. Larry and I know something isn't right. At this hour of the night they should all be sleeping in the bunker. Larry puts his M16 to the papa-san's head, asking the whereabouts of the VC. The women start to cry, and I point my M16 at them to silence their crying. We search the hootch and decide we should leave since the people are difficult to handle.

As we exit the hootch, we see three armed Vietcong soldiers walking on a dike to our left flank. Larry agrees to follow them while I cut between two hootches in order to ambush them. I tell Larry to let me spring the ambush since I've a greater distance to move. Larry leaves to follow them down the dike while I start my run between the hootches. I run in a low crouch between the hootches when I fall into a deep pit. I try to get up but sink deeper in the pit. Oh my god! I have fallen into a Vietnamese shit hole.

The more I move, the quicker I sink in the shit. Now I realize I must cease all movement or there will be no tomorrow. I still sink, but at a much-slower rate. I place my M16 out in front of my body, parallel to the top of the hole. Finally, I stop sinking, but my body is submerged in this mess up to my armpits. I hold my rifle directly in front of my body, stabilizing myself from further sinking. I can't seek help because the Vietcong may hear me calling for assistance. Hopefully, Larry will realize there is a problem when I don't spring the ambush. All I can think of is the probable headlines in my local newspaper "Local Vet Drowns in Shit in Nam."

I can see a figure approaching me, coming between the hootches. The figure is moving slowly. Then I hear someone in a soft, quiet tone say, "Milkman, Milkman, where are you?" I'm relieved to hear Boneck's voice calling for me. I reply in a whispering voice," I'm over here." Boneck replies, "I can't see you." I say, "Be careful. I'm at ground level in a shit hole." He carefully maneuvers my way and positions himself at ground level near the hole. Boneck sees my plight and says, "Hang tight while I get help from the platoon." He disappears and reappears with help. Apparently, Pete became concerned about Boneck and me and moved forward with the platoon. With great difficulty, the men extricate me out of the hole. The shit has formed a tight vacuum around my body, like a fence post curing in cement.

My body is covered from shoulder to toe in shit. The stench is so bad that everyone backs up far away from me. Immediately we move out to locate a bomb crater full of water so that I can take a bath. Soon we find a pool of water in which I can partially clean my clothes and equipment. We move out again, and I follow behind the platoon at a distance. I sense my body can be smelled a mile away. Every free moment of the night, I spend cleaning myself. Eventually, we pick a nighttime position, and I am stationed by myself. I distance myself from the rest of the platoon, but I suspect there is a lot of bitching going on about the foul odor. The next morning we walk into base camp, and I trail at an even greater distance during daylight. I guess this is one way to get off walking point! As soon as we reach the company area, the guys encourage me to take a private shower. I thoroughly clean myself, then get my clothes ready for the laundry by washing them by hand. It takes all morning to clean my web gear and equipment. I clean everything with a toothbrush. Dried shit is caked in the holes of my web gear, canteen holder, helmet, bandoleer, and each item attached to my web gear. I fieldstrip my M16 and clean all my magazines and ammunition. After I finish cleaning, I put my field equipment together to let it dry in the sun. Then I proceed to take another long shower and change my fatigues. It's now lunchtime, and I have spent the entire morning cleaning shit from my body and equipment. I take my clothes to Ms. Ahn's laundry before proceeding to lunch by myself.

10

March 1969 (Body Count)

Today is March 1. During the last two weeks, enemy activity has noticeably increased in the Mekong Delta region. The rumor circulating Delta Company is that our motto for the month is "Body count." In sports, teams and players are measured by wins, batting averages, or points scored. In combat, as sick as it may be, battalions, companies, and platoons are measured by body count and weapons captured or destroyed. Our platoon measures success by bringing all the men back safely to the Delta Company area after a mission. The Third Platoon definitely has a conflict of interest according to Army Command's standards.

The platoon arrives back in base camp from Eagle flights. On our first insertion, two prisoners of war were taken. The remainder of the day is uneventful. We come back to base camp early because Delta Company is planning a surprise attack on a suspected Vietcong R&R center. Battalion obtained information from a highly reliable source about a rest-and-relaxation area the enemy is utilizing not too far from base camp. I find it amusing that they have an R&R center that close to Camp Scott.

Usually we never travel by chopper after 1700 hours, but tonight two platoons of Delta Company leave by chopper at 1800 hours. Prior to our boarding the choppers, Bo Senical begins to brief the platoon on our special mission tonight. Bo says the intel report expects twenty to thirty VC to be at this R&R site. These soldiers are taking a rest break from the past months of fighting. Bo says the choppers are going to pass over the target area at a high altitude to get an idea of the terrain. By passing over at a high altitude, the enemy will think the choppers are on another mission and won't be alerted to our forthcoming attack. The helicopters will circle back at treetop level and the attack will commence. To me, this is a great plan, but I'm skeptical because our intelligence reports are often incorrect or outdated. Hopefully, the reports are accurate this time.

At 1800 hours, the platoons board the choppers; and within a short time, our pilot informs us that we're flying over the target area. The choppers fly at a high altitude, preventing the troops from recognizing any activity on the ground. The Hueys turn around and begin a rapid descent to treetop level. We move at a fast rate over the tree canopy of woodlines from paddy to paddy. The choppers travel so low that it is possible to kick the tops of trees if one were standing on the rungs of the helicopter. The word spreads throughout our chopper that the clearing after the approaching woodline is our target site. Everyone takes a firing position on the side of the choppers, even though for safety reasons we aren't permitted to fire out of the helicopters.

Eight choppers pass at treetop level over the last woodline and circle the target area. The VC soldiers are caught off guard and run in every direction. The Huey machine gunners start to rock and roll, ripping up the ground with their firepower. Our chopper passes over two fleeing soldiers, and the guys open up on them. The one running to the left is shot, and the one running to the right, whom I fire at, is missed. Everything is happening so fast that you only have seconds to fire. It's impossible to aim due to the speed and the maneuvers the choppers make in flight. The choppers land a few minutes after the initial attack. I jump off the chopper and immediately begin to fire at fleeing VC. The Vietcong run to the woodline nearest their location when they're attacked. They retrieve their weapons, which are concealed in the woodline. I move down a paddy dike toward what appears to be a dead enemy soldier. Before I reach him, I fire a few rounds in the body to make sure he's dead. I check him for weapons and papers. He has nothing on him.

The platoon leaders make a hasty assessment of the attack by counting the dead and the number of prisoners taken. We have only two confirmed kills and took two prisoners of war. Possibly there are more wounded and killed who aren't accounted for.

Pete Wood comes over to my position and says, "Milkman, I need you to enter this woodline to check for additional dead and wounded

VC." Frightfully I knew this would be my next order of the day. Pete emphasizes, "Milkman! Be careful, and goddamnit, do not risk your life!" When Pete is overly concerned about one's safety, he dictates orders in a loud, authoritative voice, cussing profusely. I look at him and understand what he really wanted to say but can't because of his position. He really wants to say go in the woodline and lay low until he gets orders to move out. The clue to what he actually meant is "Do not risk your life!" Hell, every man in the platoon risks his life on a daily basis.

I enter the woodline in a dense area where I saw a few VC run for cover. As soon as I enter, I kneel down and observe the area for signs of blood, footprints, and damaged vegetation. I listen for sounds of movement and possible moans from a wounded soldier. I see and hear nothing, except for a gunship that is still hovering over our location in case we need assistance. Slithering through the vegetation like a huge boa constrictor, I look for prey. I low crawl and wind my way through the maze of vegetation, then rest and listen for movement.

Believe it or not, I use tactics I learned as a little boy playing the game Kick the Can. The goal is to remain quiet for a long period of time and let your adversary get uneasy and make the first move. I remain quiet and listen for movement or unusual sounds. Then I move ten feet and repeat the process. Visibility is so poor that it's difficult to see anything more than five feet in front of me. The dense jungle can also provide cover for an enemy soldier who is twenty or thirty feet away and using the same tactics. Unbeknownst to me, my foe could be using similar concealment techniques, preparing for the appropriate time of action.

Darkness begins to settle in for the night. I hear someone yelling for me to exit the woodline. I feel relieved to get that order but remain cautious about not making a hasty retreat. Instead, I turn around slowly and slither out the same way I entered. I move quietly, resting and listening for activity. Within a short time, I exit the woodline. My fatigues and equipment are soaked and covered with mud, but I'm not complaining because I was successful in following orders.

The platoons form to move out. Pete selects me to guard one of the prisoners of war. The POW I guard doesn't look like the typical VC we encounter in the field. He is dressed in a white shirt with matching pants and wears thongs for footwear. He gives the appearance of being dressed like he is going to a movie rather than a foot soldier. Darkness pervades, and we move out at a slow pace. I follow at the rear of our platoon with the prisoner. The column moves only a short distance when a sniper fires a few rounds at the platoon.

I notice the prisoner's white clothes stand out in the darkness of the night. I don't want to attract sniper fire, so I have him strip down to his dark undershorts. I coat his back and chest with mud to camouflage his skin. I motion for him to do the same on his legs. This poor bastard is a pathetic sight, swatting at mosquitoes that are making a meal of him. The platoon starts to move again, and my prisoner begins to make sounds to signal snipers of our whereabouts. I warn him to keep quiet by pointing to his mouth. He continues making noises, so I let him have a rifle butt to the chest, knocking him to the ground. That got his attention, and he honors my demand for silence. After about an hour, the formation stops. We experience more sniper fire. This is the first time snipers have followed us for quite a distance. Now the platoon moves in short intervals: stopping, then moving only a short distance, and then stopping again. I approach an area of nipa palms and heavy vegetation. Then I see what appears to be a large blue directly in front of me. That explains why the column is moving so slowly and stopping frequently. Our platoons are crossing this damn river at night.

I get the chills thinking about the river crossing since I'll have to cross the blue with this prisoner. I move closer with my prisoner to check out the procedure being used for the crossing. Within a short distance, I run into one of the biggest cluster fucks imaginable, which undeniably is a good sniper's dream. There are about ten to fifteen men waiting in a bunched group for their turn to cross the blue. John Harrington, our company commander, is with the group. Keeping in character with my big mouth, I say the sniper could be a poor shot and still kill a few of us in this massive cluster fuck. John heard what I said and ordered the men to spread out.

The crossing is assisted by a recon team, which brought an inflatable raft to transport us across the blue. The procedure is for one recon member to get in the water, swim, and guide the raft. The men in the raft paddle with their M16s to help the swimmer. The procedure is working well, but no one has had to cross with a prisoner. Now my turn comes to cross with the prisoner, and John Harrington decides to ride over with us. John gets in the front of the raft, the prisoner in the middle, and I sit at the rear. For security I tie the prisoner's hands behind his back in case he has any wild ideas about jumping in the blue.

The raft is loaded, and we begin to paddle with the recon man guiding the raft. We leave the edge of the bank, and a sniper fires directly over the raft. I grab the prisoner by the ropes, hold on to him, and jump in the water. John yells at me, "What are you doing?" I yell back, "What in the hell do you think I'm doing? I'm returning to the shoreline until the firing stops." Without hesitation or further comment, John jumps in the water behind me. Fortunately for me, the water is still shallow at the edge where I can easily maneuver and drag the prisoner back to the banks of the blue. John follows me, and the recon guy returns with the raft. We wait for about ten minutes before we make a successful trip across the blue.

On the other side is a recon unit that is taking turns ferrying the raft across the blue. The men are spread out on the other side, waiting for the last man to cross. The crossing takes about an hour. Now we'll hoof a short distance to base camp.

After sleeping several hours and eating a hot breakfast, our platoon is on our way via Eagle flights to the field. Our second insertion is changed at the last moment because an observation Loach helicopter spots approximately twenty-five to thirty enemy soldiers going into a woodline. We land in a hot zone amid enemy and aircraft firing. The platoon takes immediate cover behind a paddy dike about fifty to sixty meters from the enemy's location in the woodline. Artillery and jets pound the woodline to our far right. Pete Wood motions for me to come close to his position. When I get there, Pete gives me that worried look and says, "I need a blocking force by the blue in the woodline to the left of our position. Take a few men and secure the blue against VC who may try to use the water to evade the artillery and jet barrage." I reply to Pete, "Okay, but make sure the damn jets and artillery know our position." Pete shakes his head in agreement. I know he doesn't need to be told that, but I always communicate my feelings.

Quickly I return to my position and select two new guys to be my backup in the woodline. I'm not sure of the new guys' names, but I believe they go by the nicknames Chico and Vance. I inform them of our mission to act as a blocking force. We leave our position behind the paddy dike and run to the left directly toward the woodline. The platoon gives us plenty of covering fire while we make our way to the wooded area. Shortly after entering the heavy vegetated woodline, we encounter a small boa constrictor. The men and I cautiously make a detour around the snake and go only another fifty feet before we come upon a huge beehive. All three of us get stung before we see the hive positioned waist high in jungle vegetation. Another detour is necessary to reach our objective. We bring extra grenades to detonate in the waterway and hopefully discourage the VC from using this avenue of escape.

Ahead of us is the blue, which actually looks like a narrow canal. Then I hear a distressing sound. It seems as though jets are preparing for a diving run on our position. I yell to my men, "Let's get the hell out of here! Move! Run as fast as you can!" My instincts tell me a jet is about to bomb our location. The men follow me, running back through the wooded area to the paddies. I run as fast as I can, and they follow without questioning me or saying a word. I near the paddy dike where the platoon is located when a huge piece of shrapnel hits the wet paddy in front of me and throws mud all over my glasses. I dive over the paddy dike and see Larry Sandage, our combat photographer, take a picture of me diving over the dike. I turn around and see a jet dropping napalm in the position we just vacated. The woodline lights up in a huge ball of flame. I look to my right and stare at Pete, who shrugs his shoulders in disbelief. Fortunately, I had enough sense to recognize the danger.

Larry tells me he took a terrific shot of me diving over the paddy dike with napalm exploding in the background. Then Larry asks me, "I'm not sure the shot will develop. Would you do that again and dive over the dike?" I look at Larry, shaking my head in disbelief. "Are you crazy, I almost died on that last shot." Larry looks at me as though he is disappointed because I refuse to do a retake on the picture. Larry is a great guy, but he takes his profession too seriously. Many times he stands up in direct fire to get what he thinks is an outstanding combat photograph.

The bombing and artillery firing continue for almost another hour before the platoon gets the order to search for bodies and weapons. I check out the area of the woodline that the three of us traveled through to the canal. The area is completely scorched and has no sign of life. The beehive was vaporized, and there is a small skeleton, which appears to be what is left of the snake. I realize it was only a matter of seconds and we would have been a part of this devastation.

The platoon sweeps the bombed section of the woods. While sweeping, we find many enemy bunkers that are still usable. Men destroy most of these bunkers with grenades. I destroy two bunkers and come upon a third bunker. I look inside the bunker and everything appears

---

normal. I inform the guys I'm going to release a grenade and blow the bunker. I yell, "Fire in the hole!" throwing the grenade inside the bunker, and run to what I think is proper cover. The grenade explodes, creating a multitude of secondary explosions. I hug the ground and listen to one explosion after another for a few minutes. When we think the area is safe, a few men converge on the blown bunker. This bunker had a false bottom containing enemy mines, explosives, and ammunition. Tom Gabig and Earl Henderson retrieve the unexploded ordinance out of the bunker.

LToR Tom Gabig and Earl Henderson retrieve unexploded
enemy ordinance from a destroyed enemy bunker.

I move on to continue the sweep. The area is saturated with enormous bomb craters, making it virtually impossible to locate bodies due to the devastation created by the large bombs, napalm, and artillery shells. I take a break with some of the Begoni Clan when one of the guys notices a huge pile of mud in front of us is moving slightly. The mud is a hole formed from a direct hit of a bomb. One of the guys enters the pool of mud where we saw movement and pulls out an enemy body. The Vietcong soldier's body is unrecognizable until we spend a few minutes scrubbing him in clean paddy water. Apparently, this soldier survived a direct hit from a bomb on his bunker. This man is very confused about where he is and may have doubts as to whether or not he's actually alive.

As we celebrate this man's good fortune, one of the guys informs us the mud is still moving. On further inspection, we pull out another soldier who survived the direct hit. If we had not rescued them, both would have died from suffocation. The second Vietcong soldier is cleaned up while our celebration continues for our heroes who have miraculously survived a direct hit. We offer the prisoners food, water, cigarettes, and candy. The prisoners smile, but I believe they have no clue as to what happened and what is going on.

The sweep nets three Vietcong bodies, two prisoners of war, five weapons, mines, and ammunition. I'm sure there are many more killed, but the army would need a forensic team to locate portions of enemy bodies. More VC could have been buried alive by bomb blasts like the two VC whom we rescued.

Our unit returns to base camp for a hot meal and further assignments. My detail is security guard on Listening Post 3. Late at night our position is approached by five VC, whom we fired at but probably missed. Our search this morning revealed no blood trails. We return to base camp for breakfast before our daily search-and-destroy missions.

The choppers land to transport us around our area of operations in Long An Province. Every day Pete gives me approximately fifteen possible target areas to plot on his erasable field map. I like the job because I become more involved in the daily assignments, plus I gradually learn the areas in which to expect trouble. On an average day, the platoon searches four or five target areas. One day, recently, we were inserted nine different times. These airmobile operations keep the enemy on the run and make it difficult for them to mobilize for a major attack. The enemy must vacate a particular location after being there for a few days or else they risk a high chance of being spotted.

Our first LZ is uneventful and does not show any promise of engagement with the VC. If we fail to engage the enemy in the first half an hour, most likely we're wasting our time remaining in that

LZ. The second LZ makes me very uneasy. I get bad vibes because I know the woodline we're in is booby-trapped, even though I see no markings with *Tu Dia* signs. There is a main path in the woodline that has been traveled extensively. I walk parallel to this path in the dense vegetation. I come to an intersection of two trails and try to decide on my next course of action. To my rear I hear the enemy open up with the platoon returning automatic fire. I crouch down looking for enemy positions in my area but see none. I begin to wonder how I avoided the enemy earlier. Maybe they waited for me to pass by to spring their ambush.

I hear some of the men calling for me to return to the engagement. I start to retrace my footsteps, being careful not to hit a booby trap. I come to an open area in the woods and meet Big Lou, Ralph, and a few other guys. Gunfire is directly in front and to the right of our position. Big Lou is upset, looks directly into my eyes, and says, "Whitey and Jimmy Pearson are pinned down by enemy fire." Apparently, the men are taking so much heat from the Vietcong that Jimmy's machine gun sight has been shot off. Guys are shouting back and forth to Whitey and Jimmy telling them to hold tight and we will rescue them.

Big Lou asks me, "Can you go in there and rescue them?" I look at Big Lou with a tremendous amount of fear in my eyes and say, "I can't, I will die if I do." My body is frozen in fear and overcome with emotion, telling me death is certain if I try to rescue Whitey and Jimmy. Big Lou hears my emotional response and doesn't ask me twice. He drops his M60 machine gun, grabs an M16, and immediately enters the woodline with Ralph and others to rescue our buddies. They put down a lot of firepower, which enables Whitey and Jimmy to retreat to a safe position. When the gunfire stops, the men return to my position. I remain seated on a rock, still very upset about the thought of dying. Even though the others were successful in the rescue, there is no doubt in my mind I would have met my death if I attempted the rescue. Now I have to deal with an additional emotional trauma. I'm completely ashamed of myself for freezing up in a situation when I was needed.

Whitey says he got pinned down by three Vietcong located in a bunker. The VC had firepower over him, and he just positioned himself on the ground near a nest of red ants. He said the VC bullets shredded the nipa branches around him. He lay there terrified as red ants bit him unmercifully. He was continually hit by fragments of nipa palm that were severed by bullets. Jimmy Pearson came to his position and commenced firing his machine gun at the bunker. Within a short time, the sights of the machine gun were destroyed from an AK-47 round. Whitey threw two grenades at the enemy bunker and observed one of the soldiers fly in the air. At this time, Dave "Big Lou" Johnson passed smoke grenades to them, which they threw at the enemy bunker. Dave and others laid down a field of fire to provide protection for Whitey and Jimmy as they retreated under the cover of red smoke.

LToR Bruce "Whitey" Falkum, David "Big Lou" Johnson.

A gunship fires on the VC bunker that is identified by the red smoke. The gunship fires a rocket at the bunker, making a direct hit. Whitey returns to the bunker site with orders to find the dead VC. The bunker is completely destroyed, which makes it necessary for Whitey and others to dig in the mud to look for bodies. Two bodies and two AK-47s are found. That satisfies command, so we exit this booby-trapped area. I hope the fear I experienced today is not an indication of how I'll respond in future engagements.

Today I have downtime while the platoon is on Eagle flights. Larry and Clyde rotate walking first man on point. The point team talks to Pete about starting a rotation system on point, so we always have trained men with experience guiding the platoon. We agree the best scenario is for the lead man to have a month's experience, with the second man having at least two weeks' experience. The third man would be new and would remain in a training phase for two weeks. Walking point would be limited to a total of six weeks. Pete would select the candidates for walking point, leaving the training job to the point team. This is a fair system that gives men the option of leaving the team after six weeks of dangerous duty. This system also protects new pointmen by not selecting them to walk first man until they're fully trained. This rotation system will work, providing the point team doesn't get wiped out in a battle. Training and experience are the key elements that hopefully will prevent this from happening. If the point team is killed, men who previously walked point could train new men. Putting inexperienced men on point is a disaster. Other platoons have done it, and the result is the pointman gets killed or wounded, plus the platoon incurs high casualties.

I decide to walk down to the commo shack to check on the platoon's status in the field. I walk by the Second Platoon's billets when I notice a tiger scout called Jake going through somebody's footlocker. I stand next to the open door to observe what Jake is doing. Jake is rifling through the person's belongings as though he is looking for something specific. Then he finds the pistol that he knew was there. I keep quiet and say nothing to him but leave without his noticing me. I proceed to company headquarters to report my observation. The clerk promises to inform the first sergeant and the company commander, who are unavailable at the time.

I walk back to the Third Platoon quarters to maintain security in the vacant billet area. An hour passes when I receive word that Jake is gone. Apparently, he was caught with the pistol and was relieved of his duty as a tiger scout. Company headquarters keeps his sudden disappearance quiet. I wonder what his punishment is other than loss of his job. I feel sure he will be thoroughly questioned about the theft of the weapon. He could be taken as a prisoner of war since he was a former Vietcong or maybe sent to Long Binh Jail. Command probably merely discharged him from his duties and told him to leave base camp. I thought it would be ironic if our company ever got in a firefight and took Jake as a prisoner or killed him in battle.

Tonight the Third Platoon is going out on the LCMs. We travel by truck up to Ben Luc Bridge to board the craft. Near the bridge is a very small market area with an outdoor café where we socialize while waiting for the boat to dock. The boat arrives to take us to the field. I find it scary enough to be transported on the river via Tango boat, but my fear escalates when the Vietnamese Navy mans the craft. They remind me of a bunch of clowns in the Barnum & Bailey Circus. How fortunate we are to have the Vietnamese Navy tonight!

After about an hour-and-a-half ride, the boat approaches the shoreline for us to disembark. I wait in the front for the gate to be lowered so I can lead the men off the Tango boat. When the gate is lowered, I notice the shoreline is about twenty-five meters away. I yell at the Vietnamese to get closer to land. An argument ensues. They say the water is shallow, which prevents them from getting closer. I jump in the water and sink about fifteen feet under the front of the boat. I relax under the water and grab metal protrusions on the front of the boat to propel me to the surface. I'm laden down with my field gear and an M16 but have no difficulty getting to the surface. When I hit the surface, I start cursing at the Vietnamese Navy while the guys from the Third Platoon grab me and pull me aboard the vessel. I was so pissed off at the Vietnamese that my inability to swim never bothered me.

Pete orders the Vietnamese to move the boat next to the shoreline. The Tango boat maneuvers close to shore, and when the metal gate is dropped, everyone can walk ashore without getting wet. Now I'm really mad because I'm the only one soaking wet in the cool night air. I begin to get the chills even though the temperature is probably seventy-five degrees. I move out and walk for about an hour before I spot four Vietcong in the starlight scope. I watch them move quickly into a nearby woodline. If the VC had been closer, I would have called our sniper Bob Jaeggie to do his work. We regularly take snipers with us at night, and they do a tremendous job killing the Vietcong. The snipers use balanced M14 rifles with zeroed night-vision scopes. The M14s are equipped with silencers and flash suppressors, which make it almost impossible for the enemy to detect the whereabouts of the sniper. The remainder of the night is uneventful, thus affording me time to deal with my bad attitude toward the Vietnamese Navy.

I still have a "case of the ass" about last night. Today is a new day full of adventure. Sometimes I feel like an explorer instead of a pointman in the field. Every day brings a mixed bag of adventure and unwanted trying circumstances. We finish our third insertion with only one more remaining before we return to base camp for a few hours' rest, a hot meal, and several cold ones. The platoon is flying to our fourth target area when the choppers receive word of a hot LZ. Our destination is changed in midair to the new location. A gunship fired on a group of Vietcong near a small cluster of hootches. The VC ran into the nipa while the gunship waits for our assistance in routing them out. The lead chopper lands as Larry and I disembark in a hurry to run toward the hootches. Because dusk is approaching, we must act quickly in this LZ to get out before nightfall. We enter the first hootch and encounter a mama-san with five children of various ages. We question the mama-san about the location of the Vietcong. She gives us a confused, dumb look as though she doesn't understand what we want. I talk to Larry, "We need to get information quickly." Then I look at the kids and realize the answer to our problem. I grab the youngest child and threaten to kill him if she doesn't give us the information Boneck and I seek. The mama-san starts to scream and points in the direction the Vietcong departed. I have observed the Vietnamese family reveres the youngest child. If I had chosen an older child, she would have not told us anything. I use this seemingly cruel tactic to obtain pertinent information that may save my life or the lives of my platoon members. If she had called my bluff, I would have done nothing to any of them.

Larry notifies Pete of our intentions to enter the nipa. Pete tells us to head toward a bunker location that a gunship has just rocketed. Larry and I enter the nipa in the direction the mama-san pointed. Our destination is the rocketed bunker. Larry walks lead man, and I follow at a close distance because the nipa is dense. Larry wades in a small waterway completely surrounded by high vegetation. When we come to an area where the water is over our heads, we stop at the edge. The vegetation hanging over the waterway shields us. I tell Larry, "This is the end of the trail for me because the water is over my head." Larry knows this and says, "Cover me while I cross to the other side to check out the bunker area to our immediate front." I reply, "Go ahead, I have you covered." Just as Larry takes a few steps out in the open into deeper water, I hear a noise in the tree canopy. I open up with my M16 on automatic, directing my fire where I hear movement. I rip apart the tall vine-covered trees with automatic fire, and I see a body fall from the trees. I'm quite startled that I just shot a Vietcong sniper. I insert another magazine and continue blasting the tree canopy until I finish that magazine. Then I insert an additional magazine but stop firing. I listen for movement and possible sounds of a wounded soldier in the canopy.

When I began firing, Larry dove in the water and held his breath underwater. He emerges abruptly from his submerged position when he realizes I stopped firing. He yells at me, "What the fuck are you shooting at?" I yell back, "That dead gook lying in the water next to you." Larry looks over at the dead VC in disbelief. Larry says, "Where was he?" I reply, "I heard a noise in the canopy overhead and opened up. He dropped out of the canopy on my first burst."

It's almost dark, so we decide not to press our luck but instead retrace our steps to Pete, who is probably anxiously waiting to learn the reason for our firing. Larry informs Pete that we had one kill. Pete radios the battalion commander, who is overhead in a Loach helicopter. Pete says the battalion commander wants to see the dead gook. Larry and I are at wits' end because we now have to reenter the nipa and drag the body out to a position where the Loach can hover overhead to view the body. I guess he thinks we're lying about the dead VC.

Larry reenters the nipa with me following. He swims out and retrieves the body, which is now submerged in the water. Larry brings the body near me so I can help him drag the body back through the nipa. Larry notices the dead soldier is wearing a nice watch. He takes the watch off the wrist of the dead soldier to check if it still works. I look at Larry and ask, "Why do you want that watch?" He looks at me, replying, "It's a nice Seiko watch, and he has no use for it." I think about his reply. "You're right." This is the first time either one of us took anything personal from a dead soldier.

—

We drag the body to a clearing for observation and receive a compliment from the battalion commander for a job well-done. Pete, Larry, and I just shake our heads, anything to make command happy. It's a shame that a high monthly body count is the criteria used to measure the success of the battalion commander.

Larry and I head back to the paddies to await our late pickup by the choppers. We want to get out by nightfall because the VC will open up on us. The VC count on dusk for their cover and means of escape. Larry and I walk by the hootch where the mama-san gave us the lifesaving information. The woman is outside waiting for our return. She recognizes the watch Larry has on his wrist. Immediately she breaks down and begins to cry uncontrollably. I look at Larry and say, "Oh my god, I just killed her husband!" We continue walking, not acknowledging her distress. I wonder what she'll think for the rest of her life when she realizes she saved a child but instead lost a husband. My emotions have hardened because I really don't feel her pain and agony. I only feel good about getting the correct information to protect myself and the men of the Third Platoon. If I had to do it over again, I would do the same thing under the circumstances because I have no regrets. War is an unpleasant, horrific experience that forces one to expect the worst at all times. Our daily contact with the enemy is having an ever-changing effect on my personality.

Tonight many veterans of the platoon have off. The only duties needing coverage are bunker guard and listening posts, and the new guys are assigned to them. I have been in the country for less than three months and I'm considered a veteran. It's amazing how quickly a soldier must learn the skills to survive in a war zone.

Most of the guys are writing letters or reading army propaganda. Regularly we read the *Stars and Stripes, Octofoil* (a Ninth Infantry Division publication), and *The Old Reliable* (a Ninth Infantry Division newspaper). Larry Sandage, the combat photographer who spends a lot of time in the field with the Third Platoon, had many of his photographs published in *The Old Reliable*. The guys always look for his pictures of the platoon. Many of the Third Platoon members, including me, have had their picture on the front page of *The Old Reliable*. Larry is making a legend out of the platoon with his excellent photographic skills.

Front page photo
Jim Milliken, Third Platoon, Delta Company

Front page photo
Tim Firestone, Third Platoon, Delta Company

140

Whitey is writing a letter to his parents describing his recent combat experiences. I tell Whitey he's going to give his parents heart attacks telling them the truth about what is going on. He laughs at me, saying they want to know the real story about his encounters and life in Vietnam. I tell Whitey I write home regularly but discuss only what is happening in base camp and inform them of only listening post and guard duty detail. If my parents mention they saw fighting in the Mekong Delta and base camps being attacked on television, I explain to them that was another unit. I know they must question my little white lies, but I believe it gives them hope that I'm in a more secure area.

Big Lou gets out his guitar and strums a few of our favorite ballads before we retire for the night. His soothing, mellow voice prepares us for a good night's sleep. Everyone hits the rack early tonight. The constant action in the field is catching up with our endurance and ability to cope with the stressful conditions.

It was a blessing to have off last evening in order to relax and get reenergized for the coming day. Our daily Eagle flights begin at 0900 hours. The first LZ has many bunkers, which I blow up. I use my four grenades and have the platoon send replacement grenades until I destroy fortifications by throwing over thirty grenades into one bunker complex. I keep all the grenade rings and loop them together with the grenade pins as a souvenir of my crazy antics. The grenade rings make great key chain holders.

On our third LZ, we land in an area where the enemy has been spotted, and a Cobra is working over the location with rocket and machine gunfire. Larry leads the way to a suspected enemy position. Larry is first man, and I follow with Dinky Dau, our new tiger scout. Dinky Dau is a very small Vietnamese kid who lacks the qualifications to be a tiger scout. Even though he is sixteen, he has a fragile tiny frame, with the face of an old man. Dinky is terrified of everything, and the pointmen are concerned about his carrying an M16. Larry and I allow him to carry the M16 but discourage him from putting a loaded magazine in the chamber. He carries loaded magazines in his bandoleer and will load one of those magazines only when we give him permission. We believe he might accidentally shoot us if he carries a loaded weapon. He reminds me of Don Knotts, who played Barney Fife on *The Andy Griffith Show*. I've been told *Dinky Dau* translates to "crazy person" in Vietnamese. He has been in Delta Company for a month, but no one wants him for a tiger scout.

Larry finds a bunker that is manned by the Vietcong. We alert Pete about our find and request orders instructing us how to take out this position. Pete advises us to mark the enemy position with red smoke and mark our position with yellow smoke. Pete will alert the circling gunship of the red smoke target. He emphasizes the importance of letting the gunship do the dirty work. Larry and I pop red smoke around the enemy position before we fire a few magazines to keep the soldiers in the bunker. We move back to what we believe is a safe distance to mark our position with yellow smoke. The gunship immediately opens up on the target area. Larry, Dinky Dau, and I are lying prone on the ground but are taking close hits from the flying shrapnel. Larry and I notice every time shrapnel hits close by or flies over our heads, Dinky Dau's body flops off the ground like a frog hopping. Larry and I laugh uncontrollably at the sight. Larry throws a small rock near Dinky Dau and his body jumps again. We laugh even harder and continue our fun, even when the gunship stops firing on the position. We throw any stones we can find around us at Dinky Dau. He lies prone with his face buried in the earth. Every time he hears something hit near him, his body quivers and hops like a Slinky toy. This is truly a hysterical moment in combat, which is providing Larry and me with our fill of enjoyment.

After five to ten minutes, the gunship finishes its work. Because we remained too close to the rocketed position, both Larry and I take a few small hits from dead shrapnel, and we sustain superficial burns on our arms. Dinky Dau's area is littered with sticks, rocks, and dead shrapnel. He is still shaking when he gets up. We point to all the debris around him, and he smiles because he is happy he survived the flying shrapnel from the rocket attack. He doesn't realize the fun we had at his expense. I guess this will be the last time he walks point with us. He is great for a laugh, but we need a dependable extra gun.

Pete tells other members of the platoon to sweep the target area. The result is two confirmed kills with two weapons. Our amusement has ended and the platoon is on its way to another preplanned LZ.

I lie in a hammock next to the ammunition bunker to read my mail and enjoy a cold Budweiser. I receive a letter from my good friends John and Kathy Dulin, who are starting construction on their new home. John is going to have Amish builders frame the house. He plans to do all the finishing work. John is a talented individual who will do a great job on the new home. He mentions one of his good friends, Mike Cotter, got drafted. That was unexpected since Mike has a wife and child. I finish my Bud and open another cold one before dinner. Later I will resume my beer drinking with a planned trip to the EM club tonight.

Today is another beautiful day in Vietnam. It's a shame this country is destroyed by war. I love the tropical climate, sunny days, Asian culture, and artwork. I hear Saigon was the vacation spot of the Far East in the late 1930s and early '40s. Maybe the past will become the present again when this war ends. It seems everything on earth revolves around a life cycle. While we fly in the choppers, we pass over the gorgeous countryside at an elevation, which hides the scars of the many years of war. At a distance you see the vast waterways and lush vegetation intertwined with the many rice paddies. The view creates the best picture of nature's artwork. Upon closer examination, one notices destroyed rice paddy dikes, bomb-cratered land, exterminated animal life, and damaged man-made structures. Such devastation is wrought by years of conflict. When I fly from one LZ to another, I like to reflect on life and dream of what is possible if people were considerate and respectful of each other as human beings. Since life is so short, many of the people in Vietnam will never experience the restoration of their country.

Now I must deal with reality because the choppers are preparing to land in an unattended rice paddy. I alter my demeanor in seconds from a dreamer and lover of life to the reality of war, death, and destruction. Sadly, my life at this time is more of the latter than the former. We quickly exit the choppers, even in a nonfiring situation. The pilots like to spend no more than ten seconds landing, disembarking the troops, before leaving the LZ.

Pete directs Boneck and me to advance toward the target area. Boneck takes the lead and moves into an area that has seen significant bomb damage in the past. The surroundings look suspicious, but we see no signs of recent activity. I move to my left flank and inform Larry I'll check for signs of enemy presence. Larry acknowledges my intention and moves off in another direction. I walk through a muddy area that is a section of rough terrain. Then I realize I'm traveling on what was an old paddy dike. This is evident when I come to an undamaged section of dike. I take another step to get off the dike when my right ankle catches a trip wire. My momentum propels me forward, and I decide to pull the wire while I jump off the dike to a lower position. I dive to the ground and see a small crater in front of me where I direct my leap. I feel the trip wire release and yell, "Booby trap! Booby trap!"

Lying in the small hole in the ground, I protect my head with my hands, waiting for an explosion to occur. Only a few seconds passes and there is no explosion. Screaming for others to stay away, I yell, "Booby trap! I hit a trip wire." Still there is no explosion, which really puzzles me. Even though I've never hit a booby trap trip wire before, I feel positive the trip wire is snapped. I caution the men to remain in their positions and wait for almost five minutes before getting the courage to check out the situation. I'm right! I did hit a booby trap. Directly in front of me are two grenades attached to a small bush. It appears the VC who set the booby trap did a poor job because the grenade pins failed to pull. I see the trip wire and yell out, "I found the booby trap. Do not move! Stay back!"

I carefully exit by the same route. Pete calls Tim to blow up the booby trap in place. I show Tim where the booby trap is and caution him that others might be close by. Tim sets up a charge and proceeds back to our location when the booby trap explodes on its own. Damn! Our luck is undeniably good! Pete looks at Larry and me and says, "Milkman, it's time to leave this LZ!"

While the platoon waits for the choppers, I describe to Larry the feeling of hitting the trip wire. Thoughts rushed through my mind that I would be a casualty. I dove for a low point on the ground and hoped the booby trap would be positioned higher than my prone body. I remember thinking that if the blast occurs higher than my prone position, I probably will be only slightly injured. Most guys who hit trip wires don't act instinctively to protect themselves because they fail to realize immediately what has occurred. Diving toward lower ground, I imagined taking the blast in my face and losing my vision. If I had failed to hit the ground before the explosion occurred, I would have been higher in the air and most likely fatally wounded. The location of the grenades was much higher than the hole I dove into. If the grenades had exploded sooner, it would have been only a matter of timing how extensively I would have been injured. It is amazing that everything worked to my advantage as I made a split-second decision.

On our last LZ, Larry and I search some hootches. We check two hootches with no finds, just a group of women and children. I say to Larry, "How can all those women be pregnant, have four or five kids, and no men are ever in sight?" Possibly one man shows up yearly to promulgate

—

the population, like a bull does with a herd of cattle. The next hootch is more of the same, housing a mama-san and her young children. Now my turn comes to check the bunker inside the hootch. I kneel down to crawl in the small winding opening to the bunker. Larry and I find it difficult to maneuver in these narrow enclosures that are designed for people half our size. I flick a lighter for a source of light. I slowly low crawl, trying to juggle an M16 in one hand and hold a lighter in the other.

Just as I enter the main section of the bunker, something lunges at me, causing me to rear back with my M16 ready to fire. I realize an animal is in the bunker, but I can't identify what type. Then the dog begins barking incessantly, and it lunges at me again. The dog is huge. Thus I retreat hastily out of the bunker. In order for me to search the inside of the bunker, I will probably have to kill the dog. I decide the dog's life is more important than searching the bunker since we rarely find supplies in the bunker. I observe there is no one inside the bunker other than the dog.

I find the situation very strange because this is the first dog I ever encountered in the countryside. Dogs are found in the major cities and towns but not in large numbers. Most of the dogs are short-haired mongrels. I have never seen a purebred or long-haired dog in Vietnam. Many of the men in our base camp had dogs for pets. Delta Company had a dog named VC who had pups. VC, her pups, and all the other dogs were killed after a dog that bit a soldier was found to have rabies. When a soldier enters a hootch, he may be surprised about the animal life that shares the living quarters with the Vietnamese people. Our platoon has seen the people living with ducks, monkeys, water buffaloes, and pigs. These animals are a source of wealth to the peasants; therefore, many times they live with them to protect their investment.

Today is March 9, and the Third Platoon has had four insertions in the morning and afternoon. We found enemy bunkers, which we destroyed, but so far, we have had a relatively quiet day. During our fifth insertion, Clyde and I are on point when we find a sign marking a mined destination ahead. Clyde asks me, "What should we do?" I answer, "Beats me. Give me a minute to think about this." I am puzzled because I have never traveled through a marked mined area. Clyde defers to me to make decisions probably because I'm older and more experienced in problem solving. Being five years older and having a college education make a difference in one's level of confidence.

Clyde sees a small group of hootches nearby and notices a young boy staring at us. I tell Clyde to hold our position while I get a guide for the minefield. I walk toward the hootches and yell, "Lai dai!" to the boy. He remains still as I approach. I question him about the nearby minefield, but he remains quiet, which indicates he probably set the minefield or knows the locations of the mines. I take the boy with me at gunpoint to search three hootches. My search finds another boy about the same age as the one I plan to use as a guide. I escort both boys back to Clyde. Clyde remarks, "Do you think they will get us through the field?" I say, "We will soon find out." I point to the mine sign and indicate the direction to follow. Clyde and I give the boys a shove with our M16s, which encourages them to cooperate. The boys successfully take us through the minefield while we follow at a safe distance. When we feel safe, I lower my rifle and offer the boys a few cigarettes and candy, even though I suspect them to be Vietcong. At least they didn't do anything stupid that would require our shooting them.

Clyde and I approach another group of hootches. We notify 3-6 of our plan to run up to the homes with a surprise visit. I run into a hootch and immediately notice it has a back door, which is unusual. I hurry out the back door and see a figure running in high grass toward a woodline. I raise my rifle and instinctively prepare to fire at the running figure when I realize it is a child. I lower my M16 and talk to myself, saying, "Warn your daddy the enemy is here." I knew the child probably did this many times before because there was no hesitation on his part to alert his father. If I were in the child's situation, I would do the same to save my dad. When we left the area, I purposely avoided where the child entered the woodline.

Our last insertion of the evening is supposed to be our monthly suicide mission. All three platoons of Delta Company are going to participate in this mission. At dusk, Delta Company will fly into a Vietcong-controlled area where army units always take casualties. Command has dreamed up the goofy scheme that platoons should intentionally draw fire at night so artillery and gunships can decimate identified targets.

We approach the target area with an armada of choppers filled with Delta Company troops, who are escorted by two Cobra helicopters. This is truly an awesome display of firepower in the air! The VC run in every direction as we position ourselves over the target location. We fire from the choppers, and the Cobras go to town firing rockets into the woodline, prepping for our landing. The choppers are in formation as they come into the landing zone, but they don't land because of the intense firing. They descend quickly hovering three feet off the ground for the platoon's quick departure from the chopper. This affords the chopper a fast exit from the battlefield.

The fighting lasts only half an hour before the outmanned enemy seeks refuge in the woodlines. The word is passed around that, thus far, the company has three enemy kills and one prisoner of war for its efforts. The platoons remain in this location for the duration of the night to perform the suicide mission.

The platoons separate but will be in the general area to support each other. The Third Platoon takes a break for an evening meal of C rations. At dusk Pete gives the order to move out for a temporary nighttime position and await further orders about our mission. I sit next to Pete, listening to his conversations with command about tonight's operations. Pete informs the guys near him that the First Platoon is now on the move trying to draw contact. Within a short time, automatic fire begins in the location of the First Platoon. Artillery fire commences and stops after several volleys. The Second Platoon is ordered to move out with the same mission of drawing enemy fire. The same scenario occurs with the Second Platoon. The enemy opens up until the artillery silences their weapons.

In less than an hour, the Third Platoon is ordered to follow the example of the previous two platoons. Pete gives me orders to move out. I already informed Pete that there is no way I'm going to walk into an ambush or risk anyone in the platoon members getting shot for this asinine suicide mission. Pete listens and doesn't tell me otherwise; therefore, I surmise he is going along with my decision.

I move out and walk at a slow pace, checking my progress with a starlight scope more frequently than usual. I head toward some hootches to look for soldiers who might be wounded from the artillery fire. From the first two hootches the platoon searches, we take three men as detainees who could possibly be VC, due to the circumstances of tonight's mission. Rarely is military-age men found in a hootch at night. Hiding in the next hootch is a man dressed in black clothing. I become somewhat violent with him and try to find out if others are in the bunker. He refuses to respond to my questioning methods, so I tear off his shirt and give him a couple of love taps with my M16. I push him outside for others to

147

deal with while I continue to check the bunker. In the bunker were two women and two children. The family is probably Vietcong although we find no proof. The man is taken as a fourth detainee, but in my mind he is an enemy soldier. Probably all four are VC; however, we must list them as detainees because we find no weapons or Vietcong propaganda to change their status to prisoners of war. The detainees will undoubtedly be questioned and released tomorrow. We move out of this area and set up an ambush position with our four detainees. I wonder if higher command is pissed off that we failed to incur enemy contact by drawing fire like our sister platoons.

11

Contact Every Day

Now, it seems that every day I unfortunately get the opportunity to fire my M16. My rifle looks like a beat-up piece of junk, but it has failed me only once when Twiggy was killed. I keep the inside well lubricated. One time during a base camp ground attack, I fired so many magazines on automatic that the barrel glowed like molten steel and curved in a downward position from the intense heat. I stopped firing until the barrel cooled off, enabling it to return to its original shape. Incredibly the weapon was not damaged from the abuse.

As Third Platoon is flying between insertion points, I reflect on the weird feeling I experienced last night. When the platoon set up a late-night ambush after our suicide mission, I lay down looking into the heavens to reflect on my recent combat experiences. I was concerned about the probability of my number getting close to "checkout time" in Vietnam. The more I concentrated on my fate, the more images of many family soldiers from the far past appeared in my subconscious. These soldiers were wearing uniforms as far back as the Civil War. I was confused because I'm not aware of my family's military background, other than my uncle Jim, who served in World War II. I was named after my uncle Jim, but he didn't appear in my vision. These mute soldiers provided a support mechanism because they understood my personal conflict. Maybe someday I will research my family history to determine if there were many Millikens who served in combat. I feel as though I possess a myriad of guardian family soldiers who silently guide me to make the right decisions.

The platoon is alerted that our plans have been changed due to a sighting of thirty or more NVA soldiers. Cobra gunships report a few kills. Our battalion commander, Lt. Colonel Fred Mahaffey, is on location requesting our immediate insertion to sweep the area. It seems like we attract enemy contact on every day of our last insertion.

We land in the paddies, but the landing formation is broken up because of the close proximity of a Cobra, which is firing on a woodline. I jump out of the Huey and run to the nearest paddy dike to provide cover for others who are exiting the choppers. Pete and his RTO are located farther down the paddy. There is a lot of gunfire and confusion about what to do, so I take over and start to give orders to position men in various sectors of fire. I approach Big Lou and order him to position his machine gun on a particular sector of the woodline. Lou gets very upset that I'm giving orders and says, "Who the hell are you to give me orders?" I yell back to him, "Just do as I say, you can bitch later!" I think he gave me the F-word while he very reluctantly set up his gun. I yell to him again, "Pete and Senical aren't here to give orders. So unless you want to take charge, shut up!" I'm dumbfounded that Big Lou made that remark because he is easy to get along with and takes life in stride. Combat has taken a toll on all of us.

Soon Pete makes his way up the paddy with orders from the battalion commander. Pete wants me to go around the right flank of the woodline to check for enemy dead. The platoon remains behind the paddy dike to provide support in case the enemy fires at me.

I begin my walk around the woodline and notice bunkers on my left flank. I look straight ahead, but I use my peripheral vision to keep an eye on these bunkers. Directly in front of me I see enemy soldiers through a clump of trees. I raise my M16 and begin to fire at four NVA soldiers who are in the process of hiding their dead. The soldiers hit the ground while I reload another magazine to keep firepower over them. My body is completely exposed when I'm standing in a dry paddy and firing at the NVA. Behind me the Third Platoon opens up all around me in the direction I'm firing. I can hear the Third Platoon's bullets whizzing by my body. I use their cover firepower to run back to the paddy dike for protection. The Cobra moves into position to fire on the location where I spotted the NVA.

Pointman Jim Milliken fires at four NVA soldiers beyond the
tree line.

I tell Pete about the four soldiers whom I saw picking up their dead
and wounded. I thought I saw the soldiers trying to bury one of the
bodies under mud. Maybe this is a technique they use to hide bodies, thus
preventing us from getting an estimate of the damage we inflicted upon
them. Pete tells me at least thirty NVA soldiers are somewhere inside this
small woodline. I respond that the woodline is filled with enemy bunkers.
Pete waits for further orders.

After much chatter on the radio, Pete gives me orders to enter the
front of the woodline with a squad of men. I tell the guys to load up with
extra grenades because the bunker complex is larger than usual. The squad
follows me into the woodline. Once we enter, I take almost ten minutes to
observe the maze of bunkers surrounding me. Each bunker is positioned
at an angle to support fire from another bunker. I must be very careful
getting the men through this mess while I look for booby traps. I begin
the arduous task of blowing up one bunker after another. Half an hour
passes and I make little progress through the bunker complex.

Our battalion commander begins to scream at my RTO. The RTO,
who is a new platoon member, is getting quite upset with the abuse

Lt. Colonel Mahaffey is giving him. Finally, I ask the kid for the horn. The battalion commander shouts at me, telling me I'm taking too long to find the VC. I tell him we have to maneuver through a huge bunker complex. The lt. colonel is uninterested in my problems and screams again, "Hurry up!" Then I open my big mouth to the LTC and say, "Sir, if you can do any better, get your ass on the ground and lead us through this complex!" Now there is dead silence on the radio. I bet Pete is going to get his ass chewed out for my remark. I think it was the right thing to do because his tirade about our moving slowly was distracting us from our mission.

I run out of grenades and must bypass the bunkers as I maneuver through the complex. I hate doing this, but I have no choice. At the end of the bunker complex is a very dense section of vines and jungle undergrowth. To get through the vegetation, I must crawl on my hands and knees to clear a path for the squad to follow. Luckily, this dense section extends for only forty feet. On the other side of the vegetation, I peer through the vines at a huge cache of military supplies.

I crawl out of the vegetation with the squad following my trail. The men cover my entry into the supply area. There are boxes of equipment stacked six feet high under a canopy of vines. Between the stacked boxes is a path leading to the entrance of a cave. There are additional supplies and military equipment stacked in scattered piles outside the cave. I stay away from the cave entrance because I believe many of the soldiers are hiding in the cave. Quickly I move back to where the squad is providing cover for me.

I have the RTO contact the battalion commander. I beam with pride because I think Mahaffey will be very pleased to hear about this huge discovery. I report my findings of the military supplies and the cave entrance, telling the lt. colonel I believe the majority of the soldiers are holed up in the cave. I ask the LTC, "Do you want me to take some of the mines and other explosives outside the cave and blow up the cave?" The LTC responds by saying, "You got there too late." I think to myself, *What does he mean by that comment?* His answer disturbs me, but I reiterate my request to blow the cave and possibly kill those inside. The LTC responds in a louder, sterner tone, "Leave the area and the artillery will hit the coordinates tonight!"

I look at the RTO and the other men in disbelief. I want to destroy the supplies and cave so badly that I contemplate disobeying direct orders from Mahaffey. I can make up a story that the enemy came out of the cave, which necessitated a firefight that caused explosions. Then I realize if one of the men in the squad gets wounded or killed from my disobeying his orders, I will be court-martialed. I take a last look at the huge stacks and piles of equipment and order the men to move out and follow me.

As I walk out of the woodline to a clearing, I pass a dead NVA soldier whom the enemy missed when they concealed bodies. I come out near the area where I initially spotted the NVA picking up their dead and wounded. It's sad the LTC felt he had to show me whose boss by making such a stupid decision. I guess that is my lesson for telling him to get on the ground and lead us through the bunker complex. I will keep the incident to myself because Pete will raise hell with me for questioning and intimidating command. I hope the LTC does not create a problem with Pete because of my insubordination. Pete is accustomed to my telling him off and disobeying minor orders. He gives me leeway as a pointman and just refers to me as a "real pain in the ass" when I bitch so much. I agree with him the majority of the time although I'll never let him know. I like Pete because he is an officer who truly cares about his men.

It's Budweiser time. The platoon is back in base camp enjoying a few hours off before our night assignments. I just opened my mail. I received three letters: one from my parents, sister, and best friend John Baumhauer. My parents ask me if my base camp was attacked recently. They say the news media reports many base camps in the Mekong Delta have been under recent attacks. My sister, Connie, provides news about Clarion University and her college friends. Connie says she brags about her brother to all her girlfriends. Johnny writes he has a new girlfriend named Maria Lanzillo, with whom he went skiing in Massachusetts. Johnny said Maria wasn't impressed with his skiing ability.

Good news! I am free the remainder of the night. I intend to write a few letters before spending some time in the EM club. The entertainment is either an outdated movie or slot machines and music at the club. I prefer the club because I can socialize with other guys and get updates on what is going on in base camp. I usually average four beers a day, but I have a feeling this will be an eight-beer day. I probably would drink less beer if potable water were available.

Last night at the club, the jukebox played mostly current music. I heard a lot of Supremes and Temptations songs. I temporarily forgot the woes of Vietnam. Music is great for calming the mind and soul.

Our first two insertions by choppers are routine for March. On the second insertion, we chase some Vietcong into the nipa. The Cobra gunship accounts for two kills. The infantry and gunships make a great team to keep the enemy on the run. Our third and fourth insertions are uneventful. On the fifth landing, Larry and I walk point in a dense undergrowth of briars, which tears my fatigues when we maneuver forward. I yell to Larry, "My crotch just ripped completely out of my fatigues." Larry begins to laugh and says, "I never saw a guy have as many problems as you." I reply, "I have to get out of this vegetation because it's ripping my balls apart." I cautiously move out of the briars to an open paddy. Larry follows me to the paddy. He looks at me, laughing hysterically, "I wish I had a camera to get a picture of this." I look like a sorry sight with my private parts hanging outside the tear in my fatigues. I never wear underwear because the weather is very hot and wet. When we conduct our daily missions, sometimes we get soaked five to ten times a day, depending upon how many wet paddies we walk in or the number of blues we cross. Continuous exposure to water makes it necessary to wear boots and fatigues, which dry quickly. Thus underwear is never worn in the field.

Larry and I see a small village nearby. We notify Pete about our intention to visit the village for a rest break, and maybe I can find a mama-san to sew my fatigue pants. Reluctantly, Pete goes along with our change of plans.

I feel embarrassed as Larry and I stop at the first hootch in the village. I walk in the hootch and meet two mama-sans and their kids. The women look at me in amusement. I point to my crotch, motioning that I need my fatigues sewn. The younger woman laughs at my plight, but to my delight, she instantly produces a needle and thread. I take off my boots and give her my fatigue pants to repair. I stand bare ass nude, except for my fatigue shirt. Ten minutes later, the mama-san hands me my pants. I inspect her work. The seam where the pants were torn is repaired like new. The thread even matches the green of my fatigues. I tell the mama-san she did a "number 1" job mending my pants.

I ask Larry what is proper payment for her work. He says, "Do you have *piasters*?" I reply, "No, I don't have any Vietnamese money or MPC, but I have two US one-dollar bills." Larry says, "Don't give her that because one dollar of American money is worth eighteen to twenty Vietnamese dollars. That means if you give her two US dollars, it is equivalent to almost forty Vietnamese dollars." I laugh and say to Larry, "This is going to be the happiest woman in Vietnam when I pay her two dollars." Since the average Vietnamese family earns only ninety dollars a year, I'll give her almost a half year in wages for sewing my pants.

I immediately feel like a new man when I put on my pants. I appreciate having these jungle fatigues mended because they provide a much-needed protection from the elements, such as the sharp vegetation and the many insects. I take the two dollars out of my Salvation Army Bible and give the money to the mama-san. She begins to smile incessantly and acknowledges my gift by bowing to me as though I'm a god. The mama-san gestures to Larry and me, asking if we want her to sew more items. Larry and I do our best to explain to her that the two dollars will convert too many *piasters*. I have a feeling she understands what we're trying to communicate to her. People who live in a large village have an understanding of American money and the military payment currency. GIs often buy Coca-Cola, Seiko watches, and Vietnamese goods with currency other than the South Vietnamese *piaster*.

The platoon moves into the paddies to await the choppers for our return flight to base camp. Before dinner, Pete approaches me and asks if I will walk point for a company-size operation tonight. Without hesitation I say, "Yes, no problem." Pete tells me Delta Company will walk out from base camp at dusk to link up with a group of ARVN soldiers in the early-morning hours. The mission is for our company to support the ARVNs in a large sweep of suspected enemy territory.

At dusk the company mobilizes at the edge of base camp. The Third Platoon leads the company operation with Clyde and me as pointmen. Larry has the night off as pointman in the rotation. Darkness settles in as we leave base camp. I walk lead man with a starlight scope. Periodically I look back at the troops with my starlight. There are so many men walking in single file at night that we appear to be marching in a parade. I find it unusual to have such a long line of men behind me, which makes it impossible to see the end of the formation.

I walk for about an hour, frequently checking the starlight for enemy movement. I notice what appears to be a Vietcong runner who is following our column from a distance on our right flank. He has been going into hootches to alert people of our presence. I wish we had snipers with us so I could put an end to this potential danger. The runner seems overly confident because he is following us at a closer distance than before.

He moves in front of our column with another Vietcong. They head to a hootch that is directly in our path of movement. Clyde and I decide to ambush the two with the help of a few other men.

We start running through the paddy in the direction of the hootch. As the two Vietcong enter the hootch, we open up and try to kill them before they warn the occupants. We shoot a short burst of fire at the VC, directing our aim at the hootch. Clyde and I rush up to the hootch but see no one. The VC had already left the area. I knew it would be difficult to kill them at night without the aid of snipers. The four of us return to the column, which has stood in place for the last fifteen minutes.

Pete approaches me saying we are getting behind schedule for our linkup with the ARVNs in the early-morning hours. He says Captain Harrington is giving him orders to cut through a woodline to save time. I look at Pete, saying, "There is no way I'm going through a woodline at night." Pete and I get into an argument. Pete says, "You have to cut through the woodline because the orders are from Harrington." I reply to Pete in an empathetic way, "I don't have to do anything. Fuck the orders! That woodline is booby-trapped, and I will not lead men in there." Then Pete says Harrington will punish me for disobeying orders. I back off a little and retort, "Tell Harrington the woodline is booby-trapped and too dangerous to enter at night. Assure him I'll meet the deadline in linking up with the ARVNs."

Pete talks with Harrington and gets the authorization to avoid entering the woodline. I move out quickly, taking the paddies as my route around this large wooded area. I move fast because I believe all hell will break loose if we don't meet the ARVNs as planned. After considerable humping through the paddies, we reach our destination for the early-morning hookup for the ARVN sweep. We wait until dawn for the ARVNs. No one is surprised when they fail to show up. Pete gets orders to cancel the sweep.

I begin the return to base camp by taking the shortcut through the woodline. We maneuver through the woodline with no problem; however, when we come out on the other side, I locate a booby trap of a 155 mm round. If I would have hit it at night, many men would have been killed. The booby trap is easy to spot in the daytime since the shell is large. Thank God I was a persistent "pain in the ass." I show Pete the 155 mm round, and he communicates the find to Harrington. I guess Pete and I are still in the good graces of command. Tomorrow will be a different story, based on our perception of the orders to follow.

Delta Company returns to base camp just before lunch. The Third Platoon remains in the mess hall line instead of going back to the company area. We want to get a hot meal in case we get called out to the field later in the day. After lunch I return to the company area. Specialist Hicks delivers the mail. What a bummer; I don't receive any letters or newspapers. I will have to drown my sorrows in Budweiser while the guys read their mail.

Approximately one hour after dusk, all hell breaks loose with another ground attack on our base camp. We man the bunkers and fire our weapons for a prolonged period of time. This attack lasts for about half an hour, which is longer than usual. The Vietcong who attack this base camp at night must live in close proximity to the base camp because they always attack in the early hours. They would be spotted by air if they were coming from a long distance. I remain outside in the bunker area for the remainder of the night.

During my sleep I have a disturbing nightmare. I dream that I lie in a coffin with my parents standing over me. My family is extremely upset about the war in Vietnam taking my life. I feel their resentment and sadness in not understanding how and why my life was taken at such a young age. I wish I could console them and let them know I'm blessed to be on my way to eternity. My life was shortened because of the important values my parents instilled in me during my youth and teenage years. I died because I had the moral conviction of right and wrong and the courage to follow through on the toughest tasks. Yes, I died to save another man's life. Truly I wish they could comprehend the unselfish and heroic way I died to further the life of another human being. I feel bad about their harboring resentment for my death in Vietnam. I awaken with chills and the realization I had a bad dream.

First Sergeant Hullette stops by the Third Platoon billets to announce a Japanese company is coming to Delta Company around 1000 hours to take our photograph for a Vietnam yearbook. Hullette says the yearbook will include pictures of all the personnel in our battalion. Most of the men express little interest until he informs us the yearbook will include names and home addresses of all the men. I would love to have the book just for the addresses.

The Japanese photographer shows up according to schedule. He begins by taking photographs of the three platoons outside as buddies get together for special photographs. When those photographs are completed, he sets up a makeshift studio in company headquarters to photograph each member of Delta Company on an individual basis. After each picture is taken, the photographer requests the individual to fill out a form with one's home address. Later the photographer explains that his company will go on a field operation to enhance the yearbook with those pictures. Finally, he moves to a table to take orders at $12 per yearbook. As much as I hate the idea of a Vietnam War yearbook, I do want a complete list of addresses. Most of the guys in the Third Platoon, including me, order the yearbook.

The company is on stand-down for today. Maybe that is why today was selected for the men to have their pictures taken. In the early afternoon, the word spreads rapidly to saddle up. The Third Platoon is ready within five minutes, hurrying to the main road to board choppers. Usually a unit is in serious trouble when we're called to report when on downtime. Pete, Senical, and the squad leaders brief the men on the choppers what to expect on this emergency flight.

Senical tells the men on our chopper that another Ninth Division unit has encountered a small NVA advance-party force that precedes an NVA battalion. Currently, the fighting rages in the Plain of Reeds. The Ninth Division needs additional troops to prevent the advance party from fleeing back to Cambodia for refuge. Apparently, the NVA are using local Vietcong as guides and aides in setting up the logistics for the incoming NVA troops.

The LZ is very hot with fighting going on in all directions. Pete gets orders to move out and secure a specific area of the battlefield. The point team becomes a part of the infantry unit when all the men walk in a line formation. The men fan out over a large area to sweep through the tall grass to find the fleeing NVA soldiers. Helicopters hover overhead, trying to locate enemy soldiers hiding in the high reeds. Our goal is to take some officers as prisoners. If that isn't possible, command wants the troops to kill them so the advancing NVA battalion is unaware of our presence in the Reeds. A helicopter pinpoints a hiding soldier to our left flank. I walk toward the position with approximately ten platoon members. An NVA officer rises up with a weapon and ducks for cover when he sees us approaching. The ten of us fire at him on automatic while we continue to walk toward him. Eventually, overwhelming firepower kills the officer.

He is dressed in an impressive uniform, which denotes an officer of importance. The search of his uniform produces many documents that will be given to intelligence.

Quickly we move out in a different direction where a Loach helicopter has spotted another enemy soldier. This time, Larry, Clyde, Senical, and I walk point close together because of the high concealing grass. The platoon follows us from a distance. The platoon remains in a fanned-out formation, enabling all of them to fire at a suspected target.

Point Team
LToR. Jim Milliken, Clyde Poland, Lt. Peter Wood, Larry Boneck.

The four of us approach the location where the helicopter pilot pointed to the whereabouts of the enemy soldier. We move slowly and are very close together but do not see the NVA soldier. We pass the pinpointed area. The enemy must be low crawling in the grass. Again the Loach hovers over the original targeted area and points to the ground. Oh my god! The soldier just shot at the Loach. The helicopter is disabled and is forced to land in the high grass to our right flank. The chopper has been downed by the NVA soldier!

All four of us on point are shocked that we walked within a few feet of this guy who downed the Loach. We walked directly past the area where he shot down the Loach. The four of us retrace our steps to the suspected area. Meanwhile, the platoon stops their forward movement. In an instant, Senical opens up on the soldier to whom the Loach pilot was pointing. The three of us fire in the same direction. Bo moves forward and grabs the body of the dead soldier to search him for documents. The officer is carrying a Chi-Com 9 mm pistol and an AK-47 rifle plus documents. Bo Senical takes the nine millimeter pistol as a war souvenir. The documents reveal the officer is a battalion commander in charge of 650 soldiers. If the opportunity presents itself, I would like to have a pistol and a Vietcong flag as remembrances of combat in Vietnam. Immediately we take off for another location, leaving the fate of the chopper and pilot to others.

When the fighting ends, we have one casualty, killed nineteen enemy soldiers, and took two prisoners of war. The enemy dead are NVA soldiers and Vietcong. The entire advancing party is wiped out, including a North Vietnamese battalion commander and a chief of staff. After spending a short two hours in the field in a supporting role, we board the Huey choppers for "home sweet home."

Today is March 16, and the battalion is halfway through the "body count" month. If the second half of the month follows suit as the first half, the battalion commander, LTC Fred Mahaffey, will have impressive numbers to report. Larry is walking first-man point, with me and Dave Pickering following. Recently, we have been training new guys as replacements for us. Dave Pickering, Carl Williams, and Bruce "Whitey" Falkum are filling in when we need a third man. On our second LZ, we take some sniper fire. Dave Pickering uses his M79 grenade launcher to fire in the direction of the harassing sniper. Dave is fairly accurate with the M79, but the point team discourages him from carrying it as his main weapon on point. Today he also packs an M16, which gives the team more firepower. Even though he is carrying an M16 he still carries his M79 until another member of the platoon is assigned to carry that weapon. The point team begins to search hootches to give Pickering some experience about our tactics. Dave is a clean-cut tall, slim young man about nineteen years old. He is nervous, which is only natural with his lack of experience on point. He has a lot to learn and seems willing to take on the task.

The first hootch houses a young mama-san and two children. We keep our weapons aimed at the occupants of the hootch while I perform a body search for weapons on the mama-san. I proceed with a very fast but thorough search. After I finish, Dave asks me, "Can I do that?" I look at him and say, "Do what?" He replies, "Search the mama-san." I laugh and say "why not?" to myself. I wonder his motive but decide the search should be a part of his learning process. I watch Dave intently while he conducts the search. He maintains a proper stance and distance from her while performing the one-hand search, keeps his weapon secure, and is authoritative in his demeanor. Pickering is following my example well with the only difference being that the woman begins to smile. Dave finishes the quick search. I yell to Dave, "Enough practicing. Let's get the hell out of here!" We exit the hootch and move back to the paddies.

On our next LZ, I find an old sewing machine that is probably used to make Vietcong flags. I surmise that because there is quite a lot of propaganda material next to the machine. The propaganda includes pictures of American soldiers who are rallying behind the cause of the North Vietnamese. The captions and declarations under the pictures of the American defectors or POWs are ridiculous. It is obvious the enemy has no clue about the American culture and values. One of the purported defectors alludes to Walt Disney characters in his confessed statements. If any of this propaganda is true, it is clear the men are sending a message they are not cooperating with the enemy. We destroy the materials because they appear to be false. I have never heard of the Vietcong or NVA keeping prisoners in the Delta.

The final insertion of the day is near a local road that we follow into a small village. One of the guys tries to use Confederate States of America money to purchase a Seiko watch from a Vietnamese panhandler. The men are surprised when he believes it is valid US currency and accepts the Confederate money. The money is passed out to many of the men to go on a shopping spree. Within an hour, the Third Platoon has purchased two pigs, two ducks, Seiko watches, hammocks, and sodas with fake money. The Vietnamese grin with delight while the men are ecstatic about our coup of purchases. We hope Top will have a pig barbecue for us. The choppers arrive, but because of safety procedures, the pilots prohibit us from boarding with the animals. The sight of pigs squealing, ducks flapping their wings, and pilots screaming at the troops is something no one can imagine. We reluctantly turn loose the pigs and ducks as the Vietnamese watch from a distance.

Tonight Boneck and I raid hootches as the platoon lies back to cover our entrance and exits to the structures. Larry and I leave the second hootch, taking about ten steps before someone ambushes us. We both hit the ground simultaneously when the first rounds are fired. We keep ourselves very low to the ground, due to the barrage of automatic weapons fire on our position. Larry and I are fortunate that they missed their target on the initial burst of fire. At night it's very difficult to shoot a soldier unless one is firing at a close range of five meters or less. We change our fixed position by low crawling to an intersection of two dikes. The firing originates from a location approximately fifty to hundred feet away.

After a few minutes, Boneck says to me, "That is friendly fire. It sounds like M16s." I concentrate on the noise generated from the weapons and reply, "You're right." Larry yells over in the direction of Pete and the platoon, "Friendly fire, friendly fire, let them know we are GIs!" Just as Boneck starts to yell, the firing ceases. Pete recognized the friendly fire before we did and already radioed to our sister platoon to cease fire. He tells them they were ambushing the pointmen from the Third Platoon.

Larry and I remain on the ground until Pete and the platoon arrive to check on our status. Pete tells us the First Platoon wandered into our locale and ambushed Boneck and me. He recognized the friendly fire and radioed the platoon leader, who was the guilty party. Pete knew the First Platoon was operating in the same general area. Boneck and I are lucky the ambush ended quickly before grenades or M79 fire were used to flush us from our cover. Pete radios the first platoon's first lieutenant citing no casualties. Both platoons move out in separate directions.

The next day I pay a morning visit to the latrine. When I open the screen door to the six-hole shit house, I see Barry Osborne looking at a *Playboy* while doing his business. I sit down two holes from him and grab one of the many available *Playboys*. I say out loud, "Thank God for Hugh Hefner!" Barry looks up and says to me, "We almost killed you last night. The First Platoon spotted you in the starlight scope and thought you were Vietcong." I laugh at Barry, saying, "When was the last time you saw a VC wearing a metal helmet?" Barry laughs and says, "Last night." I reply with my ridiculing humor, "Thank God the First Platoon guys are lousy shots!" Barry chuckles before quipping, "Thank God we were lousy shots last night."

A new tiger scout enters the latrine and heads for the hole between Barry and me. He stands on the wood toilet, pulls down his shorts, and commences to bomb away. Barry and I are astonished but remain silent. After the tiger scout leaves, Barry and I roar with laughter. I think what a picture we would make for a *Playboy* advertisement. Two GIs sit on the john looking at *Playboys* while a third party stands between them taking a crap. Barry says, "This would only happen in Nam." I agree with him.

Barry tells me he has already been wounded three times. He says the wounds were minor except for one. I tell him I heard if a soldier is wounded three times, he can request to be relieved from the field for a better job in base camp. Barry said he's aware of the practice but enjoys the comradeship with the guys in the field. I tell him he should jump at the opportunity to get out of the field. Barry and I leave the latrine; he promises to practice his shooting.

Later in the morning, we catch a late flight on the birds to the field. We get off to a good start on our first insertion. I walk first man with Clyde as my backup. When we hump through wet paddies, the water is often a dirty brown color, but this paddy water looks black. Halfway through the paddy, I feel something on my leg. I raise my boot out of the water to check my leg. When I pull up my loose pant leg, I notice three leaches getting ready to have lunch. I yell back to Clyde to get out of the paddy. The black coloring is the result of millions of leaches breeding in this paddy. I never saw such an incredible sight! If one stands in the paddy for ten minutes, hundreds of leaches will hook onto you and suck your body dry of blood. It almost seems as though a rice farmer is raising leaches in this particular paddy. All the other paddies look normal.

I move into an area by a small stream that has evidence of current activity. I tell Clyde to remain in his position until I check the undergrowth on both sides of the stream. When I enter near some cactuslike growth, I notice a small campfire for heating water. The VC soldiers are close by; maybe they are watching me. The camp is loaded with food, sleeping gear, and cooking supplies. I move down a small bank toward the stream to look for weapons and pick up a shovel by the stream. There are dirty pots and pans nearby.

I scale the bank of the stream with the blade of the shovel cupped in my hand. Just as I reach the top of the bank, a sniper fires at me. I hit the ground in a prone position, suffering a severe gash in my left index finger from the shovel. The deep gash cuts to the bone. I try to attract additional firing, but this appears to be a "one shot and run" situation. My hand bleeds profusely, and my left arm is completely covered in blood.

I leave the camp area and run past Clyde, looking for Doc Struzik. I run up to Pete and Bo Senical shouting for Doc. Sitting down next to Pete and Bo, I tell them of my find. Doc Struzik runs up to me and throws his medical gear on the ground. Doc says, "Are you shot in the arm?" I look at him in embarrassment and say, "No, I cut my finger on a shovel when I was fired upon by a sniper." He heard the shot and assumed I was shot in the arm when he saw my blood-soaked arm and fatigue shirt. Doc Struzik cleans the wound and wraps my finger in gauze. Then he stabilizes my finger with a small splint and bandages my hand. Doc says he will call in a dust-off to get me out of the field for the remainder of the day. I decline his offer saying I'll be fine. Doc says he will put me in for a Purple Heart because I was injured while under enemy fire. I tell him, "I appreciate your concern and help, but I don't want my parents to be informed about an injury that is only a minor wound." Doc continues by saying, "The Purple Heart might help you to receive benefits when you leave the military." I tell him, "Please don't put me in for the medal for such an insignificant wound." Doc agrees to forget the matter.

I advise Bo and Clyde, "Let's check out this camp and destroy the contents." A further search reveals marijuana drying in the sun. I find an AK-47 rifle in the cactus bushes. The rifle is lying on limbs of a bush about two feet off the ground. It is well concealed, but I was determined to find a weapon because of the large bounty of supplies and equipment nearby. I enjoy destroying the enemy's small cooking pots and eating utensils. We throw rice over the area, especially in the muddy areas where it will be difficult to salvage any of the food. We set the marijuana on fire and basically destroy everything in sight to make their harsh life a bit more difficult.

I continue to walk point the remainder of the day. The white bandage on my hand bothers me because it can be seen from a distance in the wooded areas. I could use some camouflage material to make me less of a target in the woods. The afternoon is hot and causes me to feel woozy from the blood loss. Reluctantly I ask Clyde to walk first man at a slow pace. The day ends with no additional encounters.

Today our battalion is in heavy contact in the Plain of Reeds. They are fighting a company of NVA soldiers. These enemy troops are probably associated with the advanced party of officers we wiped out a few days ago. According to our communications room, the fighting has progressed through the day with additional units of the Ninth Division called in for assistance. Many enemy soldiers have been killed, plus the troops have found huge caches of B-40 rockets, Chi-Com grenades, mortar rounds, AK-47 rifles, and various stockpiles of ammunition. I have today off but keep myself busy with periodic checks at the communications room. It seems every time I get an update, the troops discover new hoards of weapons and supplies.

Tim Firestone, our demolition expert, has been sent to the field to blow up many of the rockets, mortars, and ammunition uncovered in the Plain of Reeds yesterday. A Ninth Division general requested his services. Tim is developing a reputation in the Ninth Division for his many skills. He will do anything that is asked of him. He has carried almost every conceivable weapon to the field, including the 90 mm recoilless rifle. He has served as an RTO for our platoon and higher command. He is an excellent self-taught demolition expert. Recently, he has been asked by higher command to blow up the large caches that are found. A Ninth Division general asked Tim what schools he attended to learn his skills as a demolition expert after he blew up a huge stockpile of ordinance. Tim told the general, "I taught myself in Vietnam." The general almost choked in disbelief. Next week Tim is going to Dong Tam to serve as a general's orderly for a short period of time.

The choppers are late in taking us to the field today. On our second insertion, we have an eerie experience. We walk in a shallow wet rice paddy when the ground under us begins to move as if an earthquake is occurring. Many miles away B-52 Stratofortress bombers hammer a target location. I find it difficult to conceive what it would be like directly under a B-52 strike. We have been told by captured NVA soldiers that their greatest fear coming down the Ho Chi Minh trail is the B-52 bombers. The prisoners say the strikes usually kill half their men before they reach their southern destination. The NVA troops who reach southern Vietnam will incur high casualties when they engage in combat with the GIs. The American troops find it amazing how loyal these soldiers are to General Ho. Many of the NVA soldiers carry a photograph of Ho Chi Minh, which is given to them before their trek to southern Vietnam. The North Vietnamese remain loyal to their leader even when they know death is probably their ultimate fate when they make the march to South Vietnam to wage war.

I am glad to get back on the choppers because the B-52 bombing really gave me the creeps. The bombing lasted for quite a while. The large bombloads carried by these planes will destroy a vast area of beautiful countryside in minutes. We land in our next LZ and begin our humping through the endless rice paddies. I pause in the middle of a paddy to view the approaching woodline. One of our M79 grenadiers shoots a few probing grenade rounds into the woodline. A huge water buffalo runs out of the woodline in the area the grenades landed. The water buffalo sees me in the center of the paddy. The buffalo snorts and shakes its head and charges toward me. I aim my M16 at the buffalo, ripping off an entire magazine at the animal. I see the bullets hit his body and glance off his tough hide. The buffalo's blood spurts in the air from the many indirect hits. I insert another magazine and continue firing until the water buffalo comes to a complete stop about fifty feet away. I stop firing but keep my M16 in the ready position. The water buffalo stands in front of me, dripping in blood from the ten to fifteen bullets I fired in him. I shot thirty rounds and estimate half of them hit him. The water buffalo calls a truce with me. He is definitely dazed by my poor shooting, but I believe he will survive.

I gingerly move backward, keeping eye contact with the buffalo until I reach a safe distance away from him. Larry watched the ordeal, saying he was about to fire when the animal ended his charge. I tell him, "Sure you were! You probably wanted to see me as a trophy impaled on his horns!" We laugh as both of us exit the water buffalo battlefield.

I say to Larry, "It would be ironic if we have mystery meat for dinner tonight." Water buffalo steak, which we call mystery meat, is so tough that one must chew a small slice for five minutes before swallowing it. Your jaws tire from the effort of chewing. Most guys never finish their portion because their mouths are fatigued.

Pete instructs us to prepare for the choppers to land and return us to base camp. One man per helicopter positions himself in a paddy, holding his M16 parallel over his head to denote where the chopper is to land in front of him. The other men wait on the side to board the helicopter when it lands. The men on the side board the helicopter first and the guide man enters last. Larry directs the landing of the chopper at our position. Surprisingly, we had chicken for dinner tonight. It would be ironic if the mess hall had fed us water buffalo meat.

Today is another beautiful day for Eagle flights. Larry is off today, so Clyde and I take turns walking point. The first two landing zones are normal situations when Clyde walks point. The third LZ is next, and I walk first man for the next two landings.

After our insertion, Pete directs me to a distant woodline. So far we have walked in only dry rice paddies, which is a treat. I think the platoon will break a record if we stay dry today. I enter the woodline and notice a clearing of trees one hundred feet in front of me. I point to the area to show Clyde my route of travel. As I get closer to the open area, I see three structures located on lower terrain under a clump of trees on the other side of the opening. These structures are larger than typical hootches and seem to be more temporary in construction.

I approach the opening but avoid going directly toward the structures. Instead, I move to my right flank to get an overall view of the situation before I enter the suspicious surrounding. As I move to my right flank, two Vietcong run directly in front of me toward my left flank. I fire at them on automatic, expending one magazine of ammunition. The second VC is hit by one of my rounds. His body jerks and twists from the impact of the bullet, but he remains on his feet running. I yell to Clyde, "Gooks are running toward you!" Then I hear Clyde open up on them. Both of them change direction and run down a ravine path in the wooded area. I yell back to Clyde, "Get up here with me!" Clyde arrives saying, "The gooks got away. I missed them." I state to Clyde, "I think one of them is slightly wounded because the second one faltered when I shot at them." Clyde stays where he can see all three structures while I investigate. I approach the structure from which the VC ran and look inside the structure. I see two wooden beds situated two feet off the ground. Two Chi-Com grenades are visible lying under one bed. This hootch contains only two beds and two grenades. The other two structures have little contents in them. None of them have bunkers, which the local Vietnamese use for protection and sleeping quarters.

I go back to Clyde, showing him the grenades. Clyde says to me, "You did hit one of the gooks." He shows me a blood trail he found. We agree to get more men to follow the blood trail. The enemy soldier should be close by because of the amount of blood we see on the ground. He is seriously wounded and must be running on pure adrenaline. Clyde gets three men to help us trail the wounded soldier.

We start where they ran down the ravine path. The path looks like an old dirt road that is covered with grass and vegetation. The road is surrounded by high jungle plants and vines. I immediately find blood, move slowly down the trail, and listen for any sign of a wounded soldier. The blood trail is easy to follow because this man is bleeding profusely.

At the end of the trail is an intersecting path at the bottom of the ravine. I approach the bottom of the ravine and hear a low moaning sound directly in front of me near the intersecting paths. I motion with my hands for the guys to get on line with me.

The guys move up to my position, and we advance, listening to the dying soldier's moaning. He is concealed in two-foot-high vegetation on a bank where the paths intersect. All of us open up on the position with a short burst of fire. We stop firing and listen to the dead silence our rifle fire creates in the jungle area. The vegetation where the soldier hides is in shredded pieces. We see his motionless body. There is no more moaning, and the five of us turn to retrace our path to the platoon. All of us feel that man could have easily been one of us. I have a personal policy of not taking wounded soldiers prisoner. The danger of capturing someone who thinks he may die is too great. The feeling to fight until death is all too familiar to me. I also have a policy of not inspecting dead bodies because a grenade could be booby-trapped on the body.

We return to Pete and Bo Senical to report the VC kill. Pete and Bo commend the men on a job well-done. The men are always happy to survive contact with no casualties. I decide to get rid of the enemy grenades by pulling the pins and throwing them in the heavy underbrush. The practice is to destroy enemy grenades and explosives in the field. The platoon often brings captured weapons, such as Chinese AK-47s and Russian SKS rifles, back to base camp, and we train with them. The reason we train with a captured weapon is to learn how to use it effectively in case that is our only option in the field.

The platoon returns to the barracks. The men are informed that we have a short turnaround before the platoon is trucked to the Ben Luc Bridge to catch the Tango boats tonight. I clean my M16 and grab some C rations for a nighttime snack. We arrive at Ben Luc in the early evening and wait for the Tango boats to dock.

Vietnamese music is heard in the distance. The music sounds like a band coming in our direction on a backstreet. The Begoni Clan, who are music lovers, rise up to investigate the festivities. We walk down to a side street to see a Vietnamese wedding march in procession. Everyone sings and dances down the street behind the bride, groom, and musicians. The wedding march passes by, and we jump in line to join in the fun. Surprisingly, the men are welcomed with smiles and laughter. The march continues until the next intersection of the street, where the wedding reception is located. We stand back and view the proceedings.

One of the guys gets our attention in another direction. The sight we see is unbelievable, hilarious, and disgusting to witness. An old man and a mama-san are trying to breed a boar with a sow. The hog is so huge that the two people are unable to get the boar in a mating position on the sow. We begin to laugh unmercifully at the pathetic situation of these two small people trying to breed the hogs. The American GI comes to the rescue. Four guys go over and help to raise the hog on the sow and quickly depart when that is accomplished. The boar completes his assignment as the mama-san pays the breeding fee to the old man. Only in Vietnam would anyone see two hogs mating next to a wedding reception. In this country one must always expect the unexpected.

The Tango boats arrive, and we board for our slow trip to wherever. When we get off the boats, we make our way through dense nipa palm to the paddies. We walk for a long period of time before setting up our nighttime L-shaped ambush. Everyone in the platoon is exhausted from our many days of constant contact with the enemy. The hot temperatures, little rest, and stress take a toll on the Third Platoon. I have guard duty and find it very difficult to stay awake. I keep poking my eyes and pinching my face to stay awake. Even when I do that, I have doubts whether I'm awake or just dreaming about my efforts to stay alert. I look through the starlight scope and notice everyone in the platoon is asleep except for me. Usually I would wake other men, but I say to myself I will remain on guard and let them sleep. I can see all the platoon's positions through the starlight, so there should be no issue unless I fall asleep.

I take another look through the starlight and see a column of enemy soldiers moving perpendicular to our ambush position. The soldiers walk in the paddy at the edge of the woodline. It looks like a company-size force of men who are heavily armed. I wake up Clyde and another guy, apprising them of the situation. I tell them everyone is asleep and not to wake them unless the enemy turns in our direction. Fortunately, the enemy moves quickly out of sight. We keep the sighting to ourselves. It would have been futile to call artillery or gunships on the fast-moving, fresh troops.

Yesterday I remained in base camp while the platoon engaged in field operations. The platoon had contact with several VC. Our new tiger scout, Mung, was shot superficially in the foot trying to get the VC to surrender. After that incident, the gunships came in to record another two kills. Lately I have been trying to make friends with Mung. I give him candy and supplies to express my appreciation for having him as an experienced soldier for our new tiger scout. Mung has been a soldier for the last twenty years. He has been fighting longer than the age of most of the men in the Third Platoon. Hopefully, Mung will return to the Third Platoon after being treated for his wound so he can help me learn the ways of the Vietcong soldier.

12

Bad Day in Nam

I thoroughly enjoy the excitement, adventure, and responsibility of walking point. Every day is a challenge to survive, while each chopper insertion brings new turf to conquer, if only for the few moments that we occupy the land. I am overly confident in making the right decisions in the field. Sometimes I feel no one can do a better job—and it is absolutely insane for me to believe to that extent in my ability. Deep down in my innermost conscience, I know the longer I walk point, the greater the odds of something happening to me. Hopefully, God or Lady Luck will intervene on my behalf when that time comes.

Today the platoon is inserted by Huey choppers in an area of Long An Province. Our company has often frequented this location. The paddy-laden province is not very large, which makes it an easy area to cover by helicopter insertions. Over the last three months, I feel as though the platoon has walked every square inch of Long An Province. Before moving out, Larry and I converse for a few minutes about our maneuvering plan. Both of us feel uncomfortable about the terrain. The paddies border a dense woodline that indicates there could be danger ahead. Larry leads the way into the woodline as Clyde and I guard his flanks. Once inside the woodline, we can tell by the beaten-down undergrowth that the Vietcong have recently been in this location. Larry moves to a clearing in the woods, then stops and takes a long look at a situation that reminds him of many past scenarios where the enemy was present.

He motions for Clyde and me to join him. Boneck says, "Guys, I don't like the vibes I sense about this place." Boneck continues, "Clyde, go back and bring the platoon up to this position. Hold tight here until Milkman and I clear the area beyond us." Larry and I move forward while Clyde leaves in the opposite direction for the platoon.

I observe cacti-type undergrowth directly in front of me about twenty-five meters away. The VC hide weapons in this vegetation because the prickly spines provide a natural barrier that searching troops prefer to avoid. I say to Boneck, "Cover me while I check this vegetation for a cache." I carefully approach the cactus, expecting to find booby traps. Larry remains in the rear to my right flank. The vegetation is so thick that it could tear through skin if one tried to penetrate the spiny foliage. I get down on my knees to view the cactus at different angles while I look for enemy weapons and equipment. On previous missions I found weapons using this method of searching.

As I concentrate on looking up from a kneeling position, something lunges toward my face. I jump backward and almost fall down because of my sudden movement. I back up at a slow pace in a low-crouching stance, trying to see what startled me. A second later, a huge python exits the thorny underbrush and comes after me. I begin to backpedal, running, keeping direct eye contact with the python. The damn snake is actually gaining ground on me! I have no choice but to fire at the python. The bullets hit the snake, but it continues attacking. Larry rushes toward me, firing at the snake. Finally, one of us shoots the snake near the head, which slows him down and enables us to take better aim. We both fire at the python until we think it is dead.

The python measures eight to ten feet in length. Its length is difficult to determine because the body is twisted in many places from the many rounds we fired into it. The snake has a wide girth that is the size of my thigh. Even when we think the python is dead, neither one of us gets near the snake. The damn thing must have been really hungry to want me for a meal. I believe the snake could have strangled me, but I think my body is too large to be ingested by him.

Larry says, "I want to report our kill to 3-6." I reply, "With all the gunfire we shot, Pete probably thinks we ran into a company of NVA." We return to the spot where we asked Clyde to position the troops. Larry and I nonchalantly walk up to a small depression in the ground where the platoon is taking cover. Pete is on the radio talking to command. He sees us and yells out, "What the hell is going on?" We begin to laugh because we anticipated that response. Boneck says, "We have one body count for you to call in—a python!" Pete looks at us in disbelief. He never knows what to expect from us.

I forgot to bring my Instamatic camera to the field today. I ask around but no one is carrying a camera. I really have a "case of the ass" because I desperately want a photo of the python. I think this is the first time nobody in the platoon has a camera. Of course, Larry Sandage is unavailable to take a picture. Knowing Larry, he would want someone to drape the python around his body for a spectacular shot. He is always looking for that attention-getting photograph. I feel like I should become a wild game hunter in Vietnam. In the last week, my encounters in the field include a water buffalo and python. That is strange because most of the wildlife has disappeared because of the destruction of its natural environment. The python must have lived on rats or, hopefully, a few Vietcong.

The next day the Third Herd is in the air for about fifteen minutes before we get the signal to prepare for landing. The choppers land in a rice paddy near a small village. Larry and I agree that we will secure the village while the troops disembark the choppers. Clyde is rewarded with a day off from field duty.

As soon as the first chopper hits the ground, Larry and I jump out and run at a fast clip toward the village. Pete hates it when we take off on our own before he gives us orders for a specific LZ. We only do this when a hootch or village is near the landing zone, which is normally once a day. God bless Pete because he puts up with a lot of our crap, to say it nicely.

Larry takes the first hootch on the right while I run to the next one on the left. I check out a mama-san in the second hootch when I hear Boneck scream, "Milkman, get over here. Now!" I know there is a problem when he is that curt and emphatic in addressing me. I run to the hootch he is searching. I stop outside before I enter in a ready position to fire. Boneck has his M16 pointing directly at a young woman. Larry says to me, "Do you notice anything strange about her?" I look her over and reply, "The dirt on her hands." Boneck says, "You're right. We probably caught her in the act of hiding something." Larry keeps his M16 trained on her while I try to question her about her dirty hands. I grab her dirty hand and yell "number 10," which indicates that is a bad sign for her to have dirt on her hands. She repeats, "No biet," meaning she doesn't understand me. She is doing her best to act dumb about my questioning.

I say to Larry, "She has hidden weapons or documents in this hootch." Larry responds, "The bunker needs to be checked." I announce a plan, "We should bluff her, with me pretending to throw a grenade in the bunker. I fear kids might be in the bunker because there are none in the hootch, which is definitely out of character." Time is critical. It is necessary for us to gain control of the situation.

I show her the grenade, then point to the bunker entrance saying, "Baby-san! Baby-san!" She fails to respond to my concern about children being in the bunker. I position myself near the entrance of the bunker and pull the grenade pin as though I am about to throw the grenade inside the bunker. The woman screams loudly in Vietnamese. She continues to scream and then begins to sob uncontrollably. I stand beside the entrance with my hand around the spool of the grenade. Now we definitely know there are people in the bunker.

Larry screams to me, "There is a hand rising out of the dirt at the bunker entrance!" I put the pin back in the grenade and grab my M16. We're startled to see the ground moving with an arm then a head emerging from a shallow burial. I back up, putting my M16 on automatic. Then another head appears from the burial place. I holler to Larry, "This bunker is filled with gooks." Larry calls out for 3-6 and Bo Senical.

I motion to the mama-san to have the VC exit the bunker. I find it amazing how a grenade will get the cooperation one seeks. The two VC wrestle their way from underneath the dirt, crawling out of the bunker. We position the three together with Larry guarding them. I leave for Pete, Bo, and additional support to continue our search.

I return with reinforcements to provide security while we continue our search of this village. Ba, our tiger scout, crawls in the bunker and finds some buried documents. One of the scouts reads the documents while another interrogates the prisoners. The interrogation gets out of control when a tiger scout smashes his M16 over the head of a prisoner. The interrogation deteriorates from a question-and-answer situation to a merciless beating of the two men prisoners. The tiger scout shows no mercy to the Vietcong, which I find interesting since they are former VC themselves.

Larry and I leave the area while the prisoners are hit. We have no interest in witnessing this cruelty. We discuss how shocked we were at the sight of the Vietcong's hand rising out of the ground. The VC people are incredible to be able to hide bodies so quickly. Both of us wasted no time departing the choppers to enter the village. Those men were buried in less than five minutes with the ground looking undisturbed. The men must have formed small air pockets around their noses and mouths to survive the burial.

The tiger scout accomplishes his mission of getting pertinent information about the village and the people. According to one of the VC, who identifies himself as a local district chief of the village, the village serves as a hospital convalescent center for wounded soldiers. The district chief reveals there are eight nurses in the village and the center has medical supplies.

Larry and I take several men to search the remaining hootches. We spend another hour and come back to Pete with eight candidates for nurses. All the women are in the same age bracket, probably their early twenties. We find medical bandages and bottles of medicine in the possession of two of the women. The medical supplies are destroyed. The women are questioned by the tiger scouts for a short period of time. The women are released, but the three POWs are held for additional interrogation by a Ninth Division intelligence unit. A chopper arrives to pick up the POWs for further questioning by professionals.

The next day the point team is informed that Sergeant Billy West will be walking point with us. According to Pete and Bo, this is Billy's last day in the field. Billy requests to walk point on his last day for a final hurrah before his retirement to base camp duties. Normally, a veteran would not walk point on his last day, but Pete and Bo honor his request because of his many contributions as a fine fighting soldier. Boneck and I express our displeasure about the idea of Billy being up-front with the point team. At one time Billy walked point, but his methods and reckless ways are contrary to our cautious style of walking point. We express our displeasure with their decision but are still overruled. Clyde moves back in the ranks of the platoon with Boneck walking first man, followed by Billy and me.

The first LZ is marked with *Tu Dia* signs at the edge of the woodline. The point team is in the woodline walking through waist-high vegetation. We spot several *Tu Dia* signs, causing us to divert in other directions. The signs seem to encircle us in every direction. Boneck, West, and I are in disagreement as to what course of action to initiate. Boneck and

I want to fake the situation and just leave the location before someone hits a booby trap. However, Billy wants to push forward, believing the point team will find something. The only discovery I ever made with the sight of *Tu Dia* signs is a booby trap. I firmly believe the enemy feels the American soldier's curiosity will be an overriding factor in investigating booby-trapped areas. To me, the sign is an ego buster, indicating that if you bypass the posted area, you could be labeled somewhat of a coward.

This is the scenario Boneck and I were afraid would happen. The point team is in a dangerous situation with us arguing about the course of action to be initiated. Larry, Clyde, and I never argue about what we plan to do. We think alike, especially when backing down in dangerous situations. One of the most critical factors in walking point is to remain cool and not get emotional or mad. When this happens, you lose your ability to focus and make the proper decision. All three of us are mad and very emotional about the decisions being made. A good point team has now become a walking time bomb.

Boneck moves out with his body language expressing his anger in every step he takes. I hope he cools down because we need a composed man walking point. Larry walks up a narrow waterway that appears to be an old canal. The waterway is enclosed in a canopy of vines and dense tropical vegetation. Our movement is slow in the waist-deep water, and our progress is compounded by a foot of mud. This is the safest way to traverse a booby-trapped area by walking a waterway or wet paddy. We have moved approximately thirty meters in this canal and are able to see the land around us. Our heads are just a few feet above ground level, which affords us an excellent view of silhouettes and movement in the woods. Our low position in the canal also provides a great place for protection in case of a firefight. Larry makes the correct moves investigating this booby-trapped site.

The platoon is stationed at the entrance of the waterway, awaiting our reconnaissance findings. I notice Billy getting out of the water in a small clearing. Boneck must have spotted something to get out of the canal. I follow Billy and climb up the side of the embankment. When I get on the bank in the clearing, I realize we are on a path. The path in front of us borders the edge of the canal. I question myself, "What in the hell is Boneck doing? Is he going to walk on the path?" Just as I complain about getting on the path, Boneck takes a few steps forward toward a small tree. A huge, deafening explosion occurs. There is dead silence. Debris flies in the air surrounded by a cloud of smoke. I expect to fall to the ground in pain; however, I feel absolutely nothing except for a ringing in my ears. Billy whirls around with his face directly in front of my face. We are only three feet apart. I stare at his blood-covered head and can see a nail sticking in his right eye. The blood is spurting from his eye. Billy starts to scream, "I'm blind! I lost my eye!" I grab Billy and gently lay him down on the ground. Billy keeps repeating, "I'm blind! I'm blind! I'm blind!" I try to comfort him by lying to him about his eye. I tell him a nail punctured his face above his eye, causing massive blood loss that blocks his vision. My lie seems to calm him down for the present time.

My immediate concern is that Billy will go into deep shock, which could be life threatening and more traumatic than his loss of an eye. I get my canteen out and trickle water over his forehead as I talk to him in a soothing voice, reassuring him that help is on the way. I tell him to remain calm and still because of the nail penetration near his eye. The sight of the nail sticking directly out of his eye upsets me so much that I must refrain from the urge to remove the nail. I know that directly pulling on the nail will completely dislodge the eye. The surgeons will have a delicate operation to perform without causing additional damage to his face.

Boneck is screaming in pain. I tell Billy that I should check Larry's injuries. I go over to Larry to examine his wounds. His fatigue pants are torn into shreds from his being on top of the explosion. Larry's legs are full of nails, pieces of metal, glass, and whatever else was used in the booby trap. I pick some nails out of his leg that hit his leg sideways. These nails hit his body with such force that they remain lodged in his skin without penetrating the flesh. Other nails are deeply impaled in his legs and will require surgical removal. These nails are so deep in his leg that it looks as though a hammer was used to pound nails in him.

Boneck keeps whimpering and wincing in pain. I look directly at him, saying, "Don't be such a pussy, quit whining." I tell him I should go back to West, who needs help more. Boneck says to me, "I'm not a pussy." I repeat, "Okay, but quit moaning about your pain." I leave to attend to Billy, knowing Boneck probably thinks I am an asshole with my comments about his behavior. Billy is going into shock, which is a natural body reaction to such a traumatic injury. He is cold and shivering in the hundred-degree temperature. Even though West is in shock, he remains relatively calm emotionally. I know Billy is coming to terms mentally with the realization he will be permanently blind in his right eye. I wish a dry blanket were available to put over him. Wearing soaked fatigues from wading in the canal and going into shock cause him to shake unmercifully.

Pete and Bo emerge from the canal to help us. Both of them are visibly upset, screaming for Doc to get up to our location. Doc Struzik arrives and begins to work on Billy. I get out of the way to check my body for wounds. I'm so high on adrenaline I could be lightly wounded and not even know it. I inspect my body to find myself free of wounds. Billy was a perfect barrier to protect my body from the close blast. Larry's and Billy's bodies shielded my frame from the spray of shrapnel, glass, and nails. I escaped from being seriously injured because they were directly in front of me.

Pete asks me to move forward to find a dust-off LZ location. I tell Pete it would be crazy to move forward in this booby-trapped maze. Pete is extremely upset and begins to yell at me, "Damn it, Milkman, move out!" I yell back at him, "If we move forward, we risk the chance of hitting another booby trap. Let's not fuck up again!" Pete has allowed his emotions to overrule his good judgment. I tell him the only sure and safe way to exit is to retrace our path back through the canal. Pete takes a moment then calms down in a rational voice, blurting, "Milkman, you're a pain in the ass!" With that response, I know 3-6 and I are in sync about our plan of exit.

Bo gets men to carry Boneck and Billy out via the canal. When Boneck is picked up, he screams in pain. He continues to scream as the men carry him to the LZ. He must be more seriously hurt than I thought. It seems every time someone touches or moves him, he cries in pain. He is probably suffering from nerve damage in his legs. I guess I should not have called him a pussy, but that is the infantryman's way of being a hard-ass. I follow the contingent of guys transporting the men to the dust-off location Pete has elected to use.

When I exit the woodline, I go over to sit down with my buddy Tim Firestone to await our extraction from this unforgettable LZ. Tim remarks, "I thought all three of you were killed by the force of the explosion." He continues, "The blast was so loud it sounded like a 105 or 155 mm howitzer round detonating." I tell Tim the booby trap was a large container of nails, glass, and metal objects packed with explosives. I explain that Boneck and West shielded me from the blast. I continue, "My number is still in contention. I survived the explosion without even getting a scratch." Tim replies, "Thank God! I thought I would be accompanying your body back to the States." When we arrived in Delta Company, Tim and I made a pact that if either one of us was killed, we would request a temporary leave to accompany the body for stateside services to comfort the family.

Bo Senical comes over to Tim and me. Bo asks, "Milkman, how are you doing?" I reply, "I'm okay, just a little shook-up." Bo realizes the impact losing Larry and Billy must have on me. The entire platoon is in a state of disarray and shock. Bo makes me this offer, "Milkman, I'll walk point the rest of the day and will arrange for your return to base camp." Almost in tears, I utter, "Bo, thanks for your concern, but I need to keep busy to rid my mind of the what-ifs." Bo understands how I feel but again volunteers his services if I decide differently. I think it takes a lot of courage and unselfishness on his part to offer relief in walking point, especially after this tragedy. Bo's suggestion exemplifies his strong leadership and manly character.

Bo leaves while Tim and I continue talking. I tell Tim many of us feel guilty about what happened, but I really feel deep down inside no matter what course of action was taken today, the event was destined. Pete and Bo probably blame themselves for allowing Billy to walk point. Undoubtedly Billy feels it was a foolish mistake to walk point on his last day in the field. Larry is probably questioning his decision of walking on the path. I deal with my reluctance to not speak up in a more authoritative manner to influence the decisions that were made. We all struggle with our consciences and wish there were an opportunity to change the outcome of the day. Guilt is felt by all, but no one is to blame for what happened. I keep reminding myself this is a war zone. As much as we gain experience and train for the unexpected, we maintain little control over our fate.

Tim and I receive word the choppers are on their way to pick up the platoon. Our next LZ is a hot one. Our platoon is to provide support for another Ninth Division unit that is in heavy contact with the Vietcong. I recover from the shock of the last hour, knowing I must be prepared for combat within minutes. Immediately I switch from a fearful, doubtful attitude to a pissed-off mood, ready for a good fight. My heart begins to pump with excitement in anticipation of my opportunity to even the score with the enemy.

The birds arrive to usher us to the next hot LZ, which is only ten minutes away. The radio transmissions reveal a few enemy soldiers have been killed and the Vietcong are on the run. A force of thirty or more VC were spotted and fired upon. As our choppers approach our landing in a dry rice paddy, we see small groups of enemy soldiers running for the woodlines. I jump off the lead chopper and spot six Vietcong running at the edge of a woodline directly in front of me. I take off running in their direction, firing my M16 at them while I run. I empty a magazine with no visible hits on the soldiers. I stop in the paddy and insert another magazine. I continue to fire at them, trying to keep my aim low to the ground, hoping to score some hits with low-grazing fire as the bullets ricochets off the ground. The soldiers pass a hootch and run to a specific point in the woodline.

Pete screams at me, "Milkman, get your ass back here! Hurry up! Hurry!" I know 3-6 is ticked off from my charging at the VC. I react on emotion, trying to seek revenge for our earlier casualties. While running back to his position, I think about the stupid move I just made. Only idiots and heroes charge the enemy. Since "the Milkman" is definitely not a hero, I expect to get my ass chewed out when I approach him. Instead, Pete is immersed in his responsibilities to perform the task ordered by command.

Pete gives me orders to head for a blue south of our landing to search for two VC who are hiding. I move out quickly, keeping my eyes trained on two approaching woodlines. To my left is a small woodline consisting of what looks like an island of trees in the paddies. There is a major woodline to my right where I focus my attention. I cautiously approach the woodline to the right but occasionally glance to my left. I stop to get a last-minute observation of my surroundings before I make a fast dash to the woodline on my right.

Again I look to my left flank and see two Vietcong hiding behind a paddy dike. The VC lie on the ground behind the dike shielded by trees. The enemy looks the other way to conceal themselves from the choppers hovering above. I plan to take them as prisoners since they aren't aware of my presence. The noise from the chopper rotors will drown out my movement toward them. I raise my M16, ready to kill them if they notice me or try to defend their selves. I get within a short distance and aim my rifle directly at them lying on the ground. I yell to them to surrender. They look in my direction and see me with my M16 aimed directly at them. The two soldiers raise their arms to surrender. I motion for them to get up as I keep my aim on them. They get up, revealing they are not armed.

I move closer to them to check for weapons around the dike. There are no weapons in sight, so I motion them to move north in the direction I came from. I remain extremely cautious with the prisoners because I haven't frisked them for weapons. These guys are definitely VC because of the attire they wear, plus the uncooperative attitude they display while I escort them back to the platoon. The only way I can get them to move faster is by shoving my M16 in their backs.

I take a different path back to Pete's location. Once I go around a bend in the woodline to my right, I should meet up with the platoon. As we approach the bend, I see a *Tu Dia* sign to my right marked with a drawing of a grenade. These guys probably set the booby traps. I want to see their reaction when I show them the *Tu Dia* sign. I lead them over to the dike and point to the sign. The prisoners start to panic, thinking my intention is to have them walk down the dike. Both of them drop to their knees and plead to me in Vietnamese. The one grabs at my legs, which takes me by surprise. I give him a rifle butt directly to the head and proceed to do the same to the other prisoner. I move back from them, motioning for them to get up. They both bleed from the blows to the head. I guess their action further confirms their status as Vietcong. I scream at them to move in the direction I point with my rifle. Now they walk at a brisk pace as I prod them along with the barrel of my M16.

We come to the bend where I see Pete and the platoon moving in my direction. I direct the prisoners toward Pete. I expect to get hell for the bloody condition of the prisoners. When we meet, I'm surprised to see our company commander, John Harrington, with Pete. Both Pete and Harrington congratulate me on a job well-done. Both are happy to get prisoners for interrogation. Nothing is asked about their bloody heads. I offer no explanation about their head wounds but give them the circumstances of their capture. I ask Pete if I can follow up on my initial contact with the six VC. Pete approves my request and assigns a squad of men to follow me.

I proceed across the paddy to the hootch the VC ran past. I ask the old papa-san and mama-san about the whereabouts of the VC. The people are close-mouthed about my questioning. I leave the hootch to walk slowly in the direction that the VC had run. I walk in a clearing leading to a waterway surrounded by nipa palm. Now I know why the VC ran in this direction. I find three enemy sampans that Ralph, Tim, and I sink with M16 fire. For good measure we throw a grenade in the sampans to make them irreparable.

The squad checks the location for weapons or anything that may have been dropped in their haste to escape. I notice a suspicious place in the ground where the soil has been tampered with. Palm leaves have been placed over the disturbed ground in a hasty manner. Closer inspection reveals that something is buried in a hole. I don't see signs of a booby trap, so I slowly move back the leaves to discover a Vietcong handmade cloth flag. There are also two eggs in the hole with some documents. One of the eggs had cracked and leaked on the flag. I gloat over finding a VC flag, which is the only war souvenir I want besides a pistol. The eggs are tossed against a tree. The squad and I return to the platoon. Pete has already had the prisoners evacuated for interrogation. I give Pete the additional documents I discovered but keep the flag.

According to command, twenty-one VC were killed with a few prisoners taken. The gunships accounted for most of the kills. I fired almost three magazines at the six fleeing VC, but there was no evidence of any blood trails when the squad checked the escape route.

The Third Platoon returns to the company area. Tim and I plan to spend the evening together. Lately we haven't seen too much of each other due to his special assignments and my pointman responsibilities. I read in the *Daily Local News* that Lang Gerhard got engaged. Lang is a good high school friend who moved to New York City. His mother is a gracious woman who always made one feel very welcome in her home.

Tim and I leave for the mess hall. After dinner, we go to the EM club with other Third Platoon members. Our platoon is scheduled to have downtime until tomorrow night, so tonight will be a drinking night because we'll have rest and recuperation time tomorrow. Battalion has a new policy to grant more downtime to the troops based on the increased enemy contact. Just like in sports when an individual needs rest between athletic events, soldiers need downtime when they return from the field to prepare for the next enemy encounter.

Tim, the Begoni Clan, and I drown our sorrows at the EM club. I win a few dollars at the nickel slots. I buy a round for nine Third Platoon members, who sit together getting wasted. At dusk Tim and I go to see a movie. Tim buys us six beers for the movie. After the flick, we return to the company area to listen to Big Lou serenade us, which is almost a nightly ritual before bed. Tonight will be special since Larry Sandage made a bartering trip earlier today to Saigon to buy some Chivas Regal and film for the guys. I gave Larry an AK-47 to sell to the US Navy sailors.

The day's end approaches as we pass around a bottle of Chivas. I need a couple of shots for a good night's sleep. Today has been my worst day in Vietnam to date. I will greatly miss my buddy Larry Boneck. Spending time with Tim tonight has helped me to temporarily forget the unforgettable.

Today I got caught up in my letter writing, reading, and menial chores. Tonight the Third Platoon is taking a river cruise on the Tango boats. I hate the damn boats because I have a premonition that, eventually, the platoon will have something tragic happen while we're transported in the boats. I will be walking first man tonight with Dave Pickering backing me up. I hear the engine throttles cutting back for our insertion.

When we ride inside the boat at night, there is no light. Guys talk to each other in such a low tone that only the person next to you can understand what is said. The boat is filled with whispering, garbled conversations. The part I hate is the lowering of the landing craft front gate to unload the troops. Every dropping of the gate is an adventure for the pointman.

The gate is lowered in front of a grove of nipa palms. I must maneuver through this jungle vegetation to the clear expanse of rice paddies. About two months ago, we followed another platoon's pointman through a similar site. The pointman found a booby trap in the jungle area right after we departed the boats. Everyone was amazed he found a trip wire in the pitch-black jungle. Two platoons crossed under the wire at night. Each soldier had to show the man behind him the trip wire. The only way to see the wire was to get on your knees and look to the sky. That is how the pointman found the wire, by looking for profiles in the horizon. His face touched the trip wire. The next day two 155 mm howitzer rounds were found attached to the trip wire. A terrible tragedy was avoided by the pointman finding the wire.

Without too much effort, I reach the paddies. I wait for Pete's instructions as to which direction to follow. He wants me to go forward straight into the paddies, staying clear of the woodlines. Tonight is a clear night to use the starlight to move from paddy to paddy. We always check our progress moving through the paddies, especially when we disembark the boats. The enemy can hear the boats from a long distance, which makes it easy for them to prepare ambushes. I move forward about three hundred to four hundred meters when I hear some gooks to my right flank. I see what appears to be a Vietcong roughing up a villager. He is probably robbing the villager of money and food. I move back to Pickering and notice he is quite upset. I look at him and realize this is his first night walking point. I have taken too much for granted with him because I'm so used to having experienced men around me. I give him some words of reassurance, then a few words of harsh encouragement, "Dave, get your shit together! I need your help!" I tell Pickering, "Inform Pete that gooks are to our right flank. Tell Pete to send up the snipers. I will wait here for the snipers."

Pickering leaves to carry out my request. Soon he returns in a calm manner with the two snipers, Jaeggie and Langhurst from the number 3 sniper team. Bob Jaeggie is a former member of the Third Platoon, and fortunately for our platoon, his sniper team frequently accompanies us on night operations. The Third Platoon has had John Price and John Dinsmore trained at division headquarters sniper school. John Price and his partner Middlestead comprise the number 5 sniper team. Price likes his job as a sniper and has been very successful in demoralizing the enemy with many kills. Price says he has been getting the majority of his kills firing from helicopters and boats at night. I have lost contact with John Dinsmore since he became a sniper.

I tell Pickering to remain in this location in case I need his assistance to communicate with Pete. The snipers and I move forward for a short distance. Jaeggie and Langhurst take their M14 rifles out of their cases. The rifles are equipped with night-vision scopes, silencers, and flash suppressors. Both of them get out sandbags to use to rest their rifle barrels. I point to our right flank where we still hear commotion. All three of us peer through our starlight scopes at the enemy target. Langhurst agrees to take this hit. The target is quite a distance from us at night, probably seventy-five meters away. Langhurst fires with a direct hit to the enemy soldier. The Vietcong is blown in the air right out of his sandals.

We continue to look through our scopes for more targets. I notice a group of Vietcong hiding behind the next dike in an ambush position. Damn! Our men are lucky that I stopped and took time to view the surroundings. These guys are keeping their heads down because I looked ahead to that dike a number of times and observed no activity. Both Jaeggie and Langhurst fire at them from their end positions, hoping to kill a few of them before they figure out their plight. The VC heads keep bobbing up like they expect our arrival. The snipers target what they believe to be the end positions of the ambush. We watch through our scopes. Jaeggie's man pops up, and Jaeggie scores a direct hit in the head. Another guy pops up next to Jaeggie's hit. Langhurst scores another hit. The enemy soldiers have finally realized we know their location. We wait for a long time but see no more activity. Apparently, they have low crawled out of the area.

Pete and Pickering join the snipers and me. We wait for a while before the snipers return their weapons to the cases. Pete has me move out to my left flank to find a nighttime ambush position. Later in the night, we spot more VC, but they remain far away. Earlier the VC must have been terrified to see their buddies get shot without any trace of sound and gun flash from the weapon. The only way they could tell the direction of the fire would be to look at the dead bodies for the entrance wound.

The remainder of the night is quiet. The next day Pete receives a report from the company commander that our sister platoons also had two kills for the night. Lately Delta Company has frequently used snipers in night ambushes. The snipers are extremely effective. Jaeggie has eighteen kills to date and Langhurst has thirty-three. Many people think they perform a dirty job, but I can attest to the fact the snipers are valuable assets in guerilla warfare and have saved many American lives. The Ninth Division should recruit more snipers to remain in the bush for up to five days to cause havoc with the VC. If the woodlines were saturated with snipers, the enemy would find it difficult to continue effective operations. It would take dedicated, patient, skilled, and hard-core men to undertake such a task.

Pete alerts the point team that the platoon is near the village where we found the VC buried a few days ago. Higher command orders our platoon to reenter the village to look for the confirmed VC whom we captured. Pete tells us that the VC were interrogated and let go because of the way we previously treated the prisoners. Pete looks at me in disgust, saying, "Milkman, if we find the VC, we have orders to kill them." I reply, "You mean murder them." Pete says, "Let's hope we don't find them." I know where Pete is coming from because he really has no intention of carrying out those orders. He knows I'll do anything to avoid such a situation. Command is playing with our minds again. Due to the tiger scout's interrogation methods, they reprimand our platoon for our terrible treatment of prisoners. Now to show who is boss, they give us orders to execute the former POWs. We enter the village from the opposite side of our last encounter. I walk through the village directly to the hootch where we found the buried VC. To my displeasure, I find the VC woman who buried the men, breast-feeding a baby. She surprises me as a new mother. Previously, the baby must have been moved to another hootch. The woman recognizes me but continues her breast-feeding. I tell Pickering to get Pete.

Pete enters the hootch and sees the woman. In jest I look at Pete and say, "I found her. You can kill her." Pete frowns and replies in a loud, pissed-off tone, "Damn it! Milkman, tell that woman to get lost! Furthermore, tell her that if GIs approach this village in the future, she should leave immediately." Pete leaves while I do my best to convey his message by yelling, "Didi mau! Didi mau mama-san!" *Didi mau* means "get lost" in Vietnamese. The woman seems to understand the fact she is a marked VC in this village. With the aid of my M16 and pantomime gestures, I communicate to her that she may be killed. I expect, in the future, she will be less reluctant to remain in the village when US soldiers approach.

Pete tells us to saddle up for a paddy close by that he designates as our extraction location. Charlie Company is in the middle of a battle with the VC. Our platoon has been called to support their operations because of our close proximity to the conflict. The Third Platoon of Delta Company is inserted south of Charlie Company. Our mission is to sweep north from our location. We hear sporadic gunfire in the distance but see no enemy to engage in a firefight. Our sweep results in the capture of two VC mortar tubes. After we complete our mission, the platoon is airlifted back to base camp. Later on, we receive word that Charlie Company had one man killed and another wounded while recording three enemy kills.

Today work details build a system of ramps to walk on in the company area during the rainy season. The ramps are constructed out of corrugated metal that has many holes for drainage. The walkways are approximately eighteen inches off the ground. I get the impression the monsoon season will be difficult to cope with. Many of us receive footlockers to store our limited wardrobe and valuables. It's amazing how a footlocker makes your life a little easier. Senical comes by to tell the platoon the battalion is having a down day tomorrow. The battalion will have another floor show for the troops. I feel suspicious of how nice command is being to the troops.

I enjoy a huge breakfast of bacon, scrambled eggs, pancakes, and orange Kool-Aid. I walk back to the company area with Gary Reitan and Ivan Wilber. Both of these guys are extremely competent RTOs. Gary has served as Pete's RTO, and Ivan is currently Bo Senical's radio operator. Gary has been assigned to various positions, including rifleman, pointman, squad leader, and radio operator. Before he leaves Vietnam, Gary will probably expand his repertoire of skills. Ivan has been Bo's right-arm man and sidekick since joining the platoon. Both of them are always near the action because Bo has a sense of allegiance to the platoon and chooses to stay in the forefront.

I decide to empty my duffel bag and arrange my belongings in my new footlocker. We even have locks for security. This is great to have a place to store one's belongings in an orderly manner. I hate rummaging through a duffel bag for something that is always on the bottom of the bag. The locker is a convenient place to store my writing materials and the few war souvenirs I kept. I now possess a Vietcong flag, a pair of black VC pajamas, and some VC camouflage cloth that I use for a neckerchief.

After lunch, a group of the guys from the Third Herd go to the EM stage show. The floor show consists of four young women musicians from Flint, Michigan. The girls call themselves the Socialites. The girls perform rock songs that last five to ten minutes per song. All of them sing while playing instruments. The girls are dripping wet from constantly moving in their soul-searching songs. As they sing, I look around at the audience. All the GIs are spellbound from their performance. What this group needs is a successful agent to get them the right exposure other than performing at USO shows. After the show, I sit for about ten minutes, delighting in the experience. I liked them as much as the Supremes.

The next day while walking first man in a woodline, Pete requests that I cross a large paddy to a parallel woodline. Ivan Wilber approaches me and takes me aside, saying that he heard on the radio that there could be an estimated force of two hundred enemy soldiers in the next woodline. I look at Ivan and say, "Only two hundred!" Wilber doesn't appreciate my sense of humor. Instead, he reprimands me for being too cocky and taking unnecessary chances. I listen to him because I know he is truly concerned about my welfare by telling me the truth. I thank Ivan for the tip and assure him I'll take every precaution entering the woodline.

As I exit this woodline, I stand out in the open, giving anyone plenty of time to see me. Pete is instructed to keep the platoon at a distance from me. The closer the platoon is to me, the more danger they create for an ambush. I move slowly toward the woodline, trying to draw fire from a distance. As I approach, my pattern of movement becomes more erratic stopping, turning left or right, walking at angles, before I begin running. My goal remains to draw fire at a distance, but due to my unconventional behavior, my body becomes less of a target. I reach what I consider the non-comfort zone of the woodline. Now it's time to charge the woodline at an angle as fast as the terrain permits. I run, expecting to hear a shot that would cause me to dive to the ground. I hear nothing and enter the woodline. An immediate search reveals bunkers but no recent activity.

Pete and the platoon meet me at the edge of the woodline. We proceed to blow up some bunkers. We thoroughly search a portion of the woodline, but our efforts produce no signs of enemy soldiers. Happiness is when intelligence is wrong again. Another LZ is a bust like the remainder of the day.

At the last LZ, the men take a Coke break. Frequently, when the platoon is near a populated area, the young children bring Cokes to sell to the troops. I buy a Coke from a young girl and hold the bottle to the direct sunlight, examining it for impurities other than the cola. Many times one sees the contents contaminated by dirt and food particles that settle to the bottom of the bottle. Shaking the bottle and holding the contents directly to light will reveal whether or not the Coca-Cola is fit to drink. I tease the Vietnamese child by indicating I plan to drink the soda later. She wants me to drink the cola now because she waits for the bottle. The old Coke bottle is worth as much as the cola. This bottle appears to have been refilled over one hundred times due to the worn condition of the bottle. Ralph, Whitey, and Lee summon many of the guys to their rest area to watch their Coke girl disassemble and reassemble an M16. The young girl appears to be about fourteen years old. I watch the proceeding holding my rifle just in case she has other motives. The troops know this girl because she regularly visits GIs in the field. She fieldstrips the weapon then quickly puts the rifle back together faster than most GIs. The guys laugh and applaud her accomplishment. She smiles when acknowledged for her weaponry skills.

I begin to wonder where she learned her dexterity and knowledge of the M16. Hopefully, her talent will never be used against an American soldier. I learn a valuable lesson by realizing these seemingly innocent children have been raised in a war-torn country and possess survival skills not apparent to the GI. I return my bottle to a smiling Vietnamese girl while the choppers appear for our departure from this location.

13

April 1969 (Bronze Star Effort?)

In the early afternoon on April Fools' Day, most of the Third Platoon is relaxing in the barracks. A heated card game is enjoyed by Tom Gabig, Ballard Curtis, Ray Cartiagno, Doc Struzik, and me. Usually I win at cards, but at the present time, my poker hands are all losers. Other guys are taking care of personal needs. Gabe just finished cleaning his machine gun before he sat in our poker game. Gabe's machine gun is probably the best-cleaned weapon in Vietnam. He takes pride in keeping his M60 in immaculate condition. Jim Pearson, Matthew Vaughn, Carl Williams, and Bobby Smith are bullshitting about everything in general. Clifford Reed and a few other guys go to our company barber, Bobby Holman, for a haircut. Gerry Sowder, Ivan Wilber, and Lonnie Ritter are writing letters back home, probably to their sweethearts. The grunts of the Third Herd are all together enjoying the peacefulness of the quiet afternoon. The men of this platoon get along well together and enjoy each other's company. We fight on the battlefield and not with one another. This creates a special brotherhood among us.

1SG Austin Hullette comes into our barracks, looking for men to assign to work details to make improvements in the company area. The mood of the men turns from a rare peaceful, happy moment to one of disappointment at the thought of performing details during a much-needed downtime period. Top starts to play base camp army with us, which robs the men of the bonding time we need to forget our plight when we engage in combat.

189

The guys bitch when Top proceeds to assign details to the men. I feel a need to speak up and challenge Sergeant Hullette about his actions. Being a pointman, I consider myself a take-charge unauthorized leader in the platoon. I approach the first sergeant and speak, "Top, the guys have been out in the field day and night under very stressful situations for the last six weeks. The men are exhausted and border on becoming a danger to themselves. We need more R&R in our base camp life to remain sharp in combat."

Everyone seemed to be waiting for someone to speak up because discontent begins. One of the guys yells out, "Milliken has a point, we're damn tired and need rest!" All the guys gang up on Top, voicing their concern about always having to work in the company area. Many of the guys state that base camp personnel don't help us fight the VC.

Sergeant Hullette looks me directly in the eye and calls me a poor excuse for a soldier. Apparently, Top has come to the quick decision that I'm a troublemaker and a shammer because of my dissenting opinion. That inference sends me in orbit. I pop back, "Top, when was the last time you were in the field? Do you realize what hardships and stress we cope with on a daily basis?" Everyone goes nuts yelling, "Yeah, Top, when are you coming out for some action?" With that remark, he turns around and leaves the barracks. I experience conflicting emotions of shame for turning the men against him but feel good about making my point about our need for more time off in base camp. My intention was not to embarrass or turn the men against him, but it happened. I think the men had inwardly been waiting for this occasion to express their concern about base camp politics as it pertains to their welfare. Maybe Top left without assigning details because he felt a twinge of guilt.

The next morning our platoon is on the roadside waiting for the choppers. Sergeant Hullette appears in full field gear carrying an M16. When I see him, an unbelievable feeling of guilt settles in my conscience. This old, respected, and decorated man has a need to prove to the troops he is capable of field duty. I rush over to him and apologize immediately for my insubordination the previous day. I tell him this is a young man's war. I emphasize the age factor, "Top, I am twenty-three years old and I find it difficult to compete with the eighteen- and nineteen-year-old men in the platoon." I beg him to stay in base camp where he belongs.

Sergeant Hullette tells me not to worry because the day is supposed to be an easy one. I wonder who fed him that bullshit or maybe he's just easing my conscience. I quickly reply, "There is no such thing as an easy day in the Mekong Delta. When you think the day will run smoothly, all hell breaks loose." At his age and physical condition, the heat and trekking through muddy rice paddies can give him a heart attack. Top will be a hinder and slow down the platoon. I do everything to convince him to remain in base camp. He insists on going with us, stating it will be enlightening to see the platoon in action.

Top gets on the lead chopper with me and the other pointmen, Clyde Poland and Carl Williams. We enjoy the flight and become familiar with each other on a more personal basis. The point team already knew Top was a good sergeant, but we begin to like him as a person too. Top is changing his opinion of me, especially when we brief him on what to expect on our first LZ.

As expected, the pilot tells us the choppers are heading into a hot LZ. On our approach to the landing area, we see the enemy running into the woodline bordering a nearby village. The gunships strafe the edge of the woodline with machine gunfire and rockets. The pointmen step on the landing skids of the helicopter, preparing to jump into the wet rice paddy about six feet below. We quickly maneuver to a dike that faces the village. I look back and see Sergeant Hullette in the rice paddy fumbling with his M16. He is a sorry sight with his muddy face. He looks afraid. I chuckle to myself because Top thrashes around in the muddy paddy but is going nowhere. He reminds me of myself the first day in the field.

The platoon positions itself in an L-shaped formation behind the paddy dikes. Pete gives the point team orders to secure the village while the gunships destroy enemy fortifications in the jungle. Clyde and Willy do a quick search of the village while I run directly through the village to secure the other side. I run full speed through the village, bypassing people scurrying into hootches. Some of these people are using delay tactics, trying to give the enemy valuable time to escape. My mission is to cut off fleeing troops on the other side of the village.

Within a short time, the platoon is on my side of the village. Pete gives me additional orders to enter the nipa palm to block the path the enemy might be using to escape. I move hurriedly with Clyde following through some low brush until we reach the nipa palm. Then we take a moment to assess the situation. We watch for enemy movement while listening to enemy gunfire on our right flank. Poland moves close to me. I tell Clyde to space his distance farther from me when we maneuver ourselves through the dense nipa. We proceed in a slow and cautious manner. Hopefully, the enemy will not spot us before we locate them. Instead of walking in the direction of the gunfire, we decide to shift course to our left flank. For safety reasons, we feel it best to remain in this area and let the VC run toward our site, instead of us trying to locate their position.

We approach a clearing in front of us with a view of the adjoining woodline that is on fire and full of smoke. The noise level is high from the continuous rocket explosions and automatic weapons fire from the gunships. We remain in crouched positions. I look to my right flank when a strange sensation comes over me. I feel as though I'm in the sights of an enemy weapon. I whirl around with my M16 blasting because I intuitively fear for my life. As I wheel around, I catch a Vietcong soldier aiming an RPG launcher at me. My automatic gunfire scores immediate hits on the soldier's legs. I can see in his eyes he is totally surprised by my quick reaction time. The soldier was trying to position himself for a clear shot at the Loach circling overhead but redirected his aim when he saw me. I beat him to the draw.

My initial hits seem to paralyze his body with pain. The man is helplessly pinned to the nipa palm in an upright stance with his RPG launcher still aimed in my direction. I can't comprehend why he gazes at me while not pulling the trigger on his weapon. He must be in unbearable pain, which makes him unable to pull the trigger on the RPG launcher. I take direct aim at him, scoring more hits to his lower body. Ejecting my empty magazine, I insert another and pump the soldier's body full of lead. I watch him hopelessly die while I continue firing. An hour's worth of thoughts pass through my mind in these last few seconds.

I imagine he is a soldier like me, caught up in a war over which neither of us has little control. He probably has a wonderful family who shares their love for each other. Even though the soldier is approximately thirty meters away, I can see the look of death in his eyes. I feel terrible ending his life and causing great pain to his family, but there is no choice.

The death of the soldier brings a comforting vision from God to me. The vision reveals I'll be seriously wounded in combat. My legs will be shot, and I'll feel the same pain and agony experienced by the man I just killed. God reassures me that my life will be spared without any preconditions, and eventually my body will recover from my wounds. Even though I killed this soldier, God will forgive me and not hold me personally responsible for his death; however, I'll bear this soldier's pain and suffering because of man's inhumanity to man. I ask myself, "Why? Why me? My life is no more precious than the one I just ended." I find it difficult to understand, but I do not question what I just experienced.

Seconds later, Clyde comes alongside of me. Clyde asks, "Where are the gooks?" I reply, "Keep loading the 16s. I know where they are." Clyde hands me his M16, and I begin to spray the nipa palm. Another VC is spotted about ten meters to the right of the dead soldier. I fire and register a hit to the right shoulder of this soldier. The soldier had an AK-47 rifle and appears to have long hair, indicating the wounded soldier may have been a woman. I keep firing and expend two more magazines of ammunition in the general area. I stop firing but grab another loaded 16 from Clyde, waiting for additional movement. Clyde and I pause for about five minutes until we decide to inform Pete of our situation. Clyde agrees to monitor this post and keep an eye out for the wounded soldier.

Clyde Poland reloads M16s for Jim Milliken during firefight.

I hurry back, retracing my path to the platoon. I come upon Pete, his RTO Doug Taylor, and Sergeant Hullette lying behind a dike. The men are briefed on what transpired. I glance over to Sergeant Hullette and notice by his facial expression that he's rather impressed by my cool, businesslike attitude about performing my duties as a combat infantryman. Pete gives me additional orders, asking if the team would check out the location of the possible second kill. I reaffirm his request, stating we will clear the area before we call up the platoon to our location. I ask Pete for his .45 pistol to use when I maneuver on the ground at close range. Pete gives me his handgun.

I return to Poland's site and find Larry Sandage talking with Clyde. They agree to cover me as I low crawl toward the clump of nipa palm to check for the wounded soldier. I start to crawl toward the dead soldier with the .45 in my right hand and my 16 slung over my left shoulder. I low crawl up to the dead soldier and fire one round into his head to make sure he's dead. I never turn my back on an enemy soldier unless I'm positive the person is dead. I continue to low crawl in the vegetation where I expect to find the other wounded or dead soldier. The suspected site is clean. There are no signs of a body, blood trails, or footprints in the mud. How could a wounded soldier cover his tracks in such a short period of time?

I signal Clyde and Larry to come forward. We look for signs of blood trails but don't find any traces. This really bothers me because there is no doubt in my mind about shooting another soldier. Supposedly, the VC can perform amazing acts of concealment. Maybe the body is stuffed in mud or possibly it was carried into the woodline. There is a high bank nearby that would allow for an easy escape without us seeing the enemy from our previous location.

Pete and Sergeant Hullette arrive at our position. Sergeant Hullette searches the dead soldier and finds documents and personal papers. I explain to them there is no sign of the other soldier I claim to have shot. Pete asks me to enter the woodline that is still on fire from the rocket attack. Pete assigns a few men to stretch out parallel to the woodline to provide cover for my entry. I give Pete his .45 pistol before moving on.

I run down a knoll through the mud to a small streambed. I move along the streambed with only a portion of my helmet exposed to draw fire. The elevation of the land protects my body from possible gunfire coming from the woodline directly in front of me. So far, my plan works. I follow the streambed, moving to my right flank, trying to draw fire before making my charge into the woodline. I choose a place to my right flank that is still on fire and emitting a lot of smoke. The VC should have left this section of the woodline due to the recent rocket attack. I enter the woods through this rocketed area. Nipa palm has been knocked down, creating a makeshift trail to follow. It's a good practice to follow bomb and rocket paths because there is no need to worry about booby traps. Usually, the booby traps become secondary explosions following the bomb or rocket blast.

Pointman Jim Milliken tries to draw enemy fire before entering nipa palm.

Jim Milliken enters an area rocketed by Cobra gunships.

Pointman Jim Milliken searches for enemy positions.

Directly in front of my location is a bombed-out building on fire. The woods are on fire to my right; therefore, if the enemy is still here, they should be located to my left flank. I move toward the burning building to check for bodies. Visibility is poor due to the smoke hanging in the thick nipa palm. My eyes are burning and watering from the smoke that's making it difficult to see. The sound of wood burning nearby and the choppers overhead impair my hearing. Directly behind me, a loud noise attracts my attention. I spin around and get ready to pull the trigger on my M16, when, to my surprise, Larry Sandage takes a picture of me. I halt my intention of shooting. He looks through his camera lens at me with a face frozen in fear, anticipating that I'll accidentally shoot him. Larry is shocked to see my immediate defensive reaction to a burning limb that just broke off a tree. Luckily for him, I aimed for a target instead of firing blindly on impulse. I probably reacted that way because the area behind me was already cleared.

My rifle is lowered as Larry gives a sigh of relief. I chew him out for sneaking up on me. Larry likes to quietly move about taking combat footage when the men are in tense situations. Larry agrees to follow me to the building and give me cover with his .45 pistol. Even though he is a combat photographer, Larry always helps out if an extra gun is required. We search the building but find nothing. Probably the Vietcong had use for this building in the past. We retrace our steps back to the edge of the nipa palm.

Pete enters the nipa with a small group of guys. Clyde, Willy, and Doug are with 3-6. Pete says command wants us to search the woodline, but he is satisfied with our success so far without incurring any losses. We decide to play along with command. We remain in the nipa following the path created by the Cobra rockets on the edge of the woodline. Pete agrees this is a good idea since the path should be free of booby traps. I take the lead with Clyde and Willy following.

As we travel down the rocketed path, we approach an intersection of VC trails. The path is very muddy, revealing footprints and a massive amount of blood splattered everywhere, which indicates someone is seriously wounded. I look to see where the footprints are coming from. To my surprise, this is the blood trail of the VC whom I wounded. Directly across from me is the knoll where I shot both Vietcong. It's difficult to comprehend how there are no footprints and blood from the site where I shot the VC to the edge of the nipa. As soon as the soldier entered the nipa, the footprints and blood trail are visible. I would like to know their method of concealment in such a short time.

I return to talk with 3-6 and the other pointmen. I tell them this is the blood trail of the soldier whom I shot in the shoulder. Pete says the VC can't be too far in the nipa based on the way the soldier is bleeding. We all agree. Pete asks me to follow the trail to hopefully find a dead body. I hate tracking wounded soldiers because they are more dangerous with their "John Wayne" attitude of survival. The blood trail leads to a newly constructed mud bunker. Footprints and blood are at the entrance to the bunker, denoting the Vietcong is inside the bunker. I low crawl up to the side of the bunker while checking my surroundings. To my left and directly in front of me are additional bunkers. Possibly there are many more soldiers holed up in these temporary bunkers.

My plan is to blow up this bunker and retreat to Pete's position, citing the individual has been killed. I don't want to engage entrenched enemy soldiers in fighting. There is a heavy concentration of nipa palm, making it difficult to see how the bunker complex is designed. If soldiers are holed up in this area, our platoon will definitely take casualties locating them.

I remove two grenades from my web gear. I take out the pin of one of the grenades and release the spindle while making my five-second count one thousand one, one thousand two, one thousand three, one thousand four, one thousand five. Then I throw the grenade inside the bunker. After the explosion, I immediately release the second grenade and toss it inside the bunker. The second explosion causes the new bunker to collapse in the middle. There is no doubt the grenades killed the soldier if the VC soldier was still alive. If the soldier was not already dead, the VC would have been buried alive.

I watch for enemy movement before I begin my retreat, low crawling from the area. When I'm at a safe distance, I rise and walk back to give my report. Pete is informed about the unconfirmed kill. He asks me to check the body. I tell him he will need a crew of men to dig the body out of the bunker. He calls in the kill giving the circumstances of the concealed body. Normally, when one calls in a body count, command gets off your ass because they're satisfied that the mission was successful. Pete tells the guys to take a break to hopefully wait for our exit from this LZ.

Pete, Clyde, Doug, Willy, and I sit among the nipa palm, waiting for the word about our next mission. All of us are silent and let our minds wander into the past, present, and future. My thoughts differ from those of my buddies. I dwell on the closeness of the major bunker complex where I suspect additional Vietcong are hiding. The complex is only twenty meters away as the crow flies in the nipa palm. Within ten minutes, we get orders for extraction to a new LZ.

Doug approaches me as we walk out of the nipa, saying, "Milkman, you should be put in for a Silver Star for today's activities. I look at Dougie with a smile, replying, "Taylor, I'm definitely not a hero. I was scared to death today." Later First Sergeant Hullette offers me items taken off the dead soldier. I decline his offer stating I don't take personal belongings from dead soldiers. Sergeant Hullette says, "Milliken, we decided to put you in for a Bronze Star for Valor for your bravery today." I look at him in an arrogant, unappreciative way, stating, "Top, please don't put me in for a medal. I will refuse it." I explain, "I don't want a medal for killing two people. It would be different if I were honored for saving a life." Then I repeat, "I don't kill for medals and souvenirs. I do it because it is my job, and the army is generous in giving me $65 per month combat pay." My sarcastic, nongrateful humor takes the sergeant by surprise. Top is trying to be good to me but is definitely pissed with my ungratefulness. Even though he is not pleased with my attitude, I feel he now respects me as a soldier, which is all I want from him. I truly meant what I said to him, except for the generosity of the military. I feel better not accepting a medal for the killing of the soldiers because it would be contrary with my vision from God.

On our next insertion, the point team gets orders to sweep toward a large blue. We walk for about five minutes before I spot someone coming out of a woodline into a grassy field. The person is approximately 150 meters away and isn't aware of our presence. As I get closer to him, I yell, "Dung lai! [Stop!] Lai dai! [Come here!] Lai dai! [Come here]." When he hears my call, he begins to run toward the river in front of him. His fleeing is a license to kill. I raise my M16 and fire at him, knowing I have little chance of scoring a hit at this distance. I miss as the suspect disappears in the river.

Clyde, Willy, and I run up to the blue with our weapons in the ready position. The river is very wide and swift. Even if the guy is an Olympic swimmer, he won't be able to navigate the current across this blue. We look for openings underwater into the banks of the river. The VC soldiers are noted for digging holes into sides of riverbeds to hide supplies and themselves if caught out in the open. We find no entrances. The water is too deep and swift to find possible entrances. We proceed to throw all our grenades in the water at the edge of the bank. Our efforts produce no results. Maybe we gave the VC a headache from all the underwater explosions. After searching for half an hour, we leave the area for base camp.

Tonight I'm off duty for the evening while the platoon goes out on night ambush. I enjoy the benefit of getting every fourth night off while walking point. My two months of walking point is scheduled to end on April 10. It will be a relief not to be exposed to the danger although I will miss my free time off for walking point.

I read in the *Daily Local News* that my good friend Don Risser was commissioned a second lieutenant in the Air Force. The article said he will be attending navigator school. I dropped out of Air Force ROTC at Grove City College because my poor vision would prevent me from being a pilot. I passed the navigator's test but elected to not spend five years in the service unless I could become a pilot. In Grove City's *Alumni News*, it was mentioned that a few of my Delta Iota Kappa fraternity brothers who became pilots fly jets in the northern part of South Vietnam. My Ellwood City neighbor and good friend Dave

Balazs should be coming to Vietnam soon. Dave was commissioned a second lieutenant in the Marine Corps.

An army propaganda magazine printed that Delta Company had more enemy kills last month than the 101st Airborne Division. Our battalion killed twice as many enemy as the marines did in the last month. I don't know how reliable these figures are, but I do know our company and battalion are gaining a reputation as outstanding units.

Today Larry Sandage comes to the field with the platoon. He is a wonderful esprit de corps for our group as he uses his photographic ingenuity of getting recognition for the platoon in military publications and hometown newspapers. Larry says he got several excellent photos of me yesterday, which he promises to copy for me when the film is developed. I'm curious to see the shots he took because I don't remember him taking any pictures except for the moment when I almost shot him. About a week ago, the machine gunner allowed Larry to fire the M60 at enemy positions. Larry really enjoys being a part of the platoon even if it's in a combat role.

The day is very quiet and uneventful until early afternoon. The platoon breaks into two groups to sweep separate areas. Pete and I lead one section of the platoon while Tom Gabig, who is acting platoon sergeant for the day, leads the other men of the platoon. The land is marked with *Tu Dia* signs and appears to be heavily booby-trapped. After sweeping for a half hour, our group hears minor explosions coming from the location of Gabe's men. The explosions continue until we receive word that Gabe hit a booby trap.

Pete gives me orders to link up with the other platoon members. When we arrive at their location, Gabe is still in the bush screaming not to come in because he fears the men will set off another explosion. He says his body is numb and in shock, but his legs seem to have enough strength to walk out of the woods. He asks for time to try and get out by himself. Pete calls for a dust-off as Gabe's men prepare to enter with flak jackets to protect him and themselves from further detonations. Just as the men enter the woods, Gabe appears walking in a slow, limping gait and collapses when he is clear of the bush area. Doc Struzik runs over to give Gabe medical attention. Doc bandages his bloody right leg, which is severely injured from the explosion. Gabe has wounds from his heel to his ass. Gabig's poncho and canteen protected him from further bodily injuries above his waist. Both pieces of equipment are torn apart from the force of the explosion.

Tom "Gabe" Gabig crosses a canal.

According to Gabe, Lt. Colonel Mahaffey, the battalion commander, was hovering above him in a Loach and ordered his men into the woods. Gabe informed the battalion commander about the many booby traps, but Mahaffey insisted on sweeping the area because CBS News was filming the sweep in another helicopter. Gabe decided to walk point because most of his men lacked the experience he had in the field. He entered the vegetation area filled with *Tu Dia* signs and proceeded to blow up six booby traps. He was detonating a seventh booby trap when he ran into another grenade booby trap. The dust-off helicopter arrives to take Gabe to the field hospital in Tan An where Ninth Division troops receive immediate attention before being transferred to a more permanent medical facility.

The platoon will greatly miss the experience and leadership Gabe gave the platoon. Today was supposed to be Gabe's last day in the field before taking his R&R in Hawaii. He planned to meet his wife in Hawaii for the Easter holiday. I hope the army gets in contact with her before she leaves for Hawaii. Since Gabe's home is a short distance from my parents' home in Ellwood City, I will make it a priority to visit him after we are discharged from the army.

Toward the end of the afternoon, I discover a recent burial of about fifteen enemy soldiers. All the graves have a communist star on the grave marker. I find this quite strange and think we should dig up the graves. This is the first time I ever saw marked enemy graves. I bet there are supplies buried in this fake graveyard. I mention my discovery, but since we have no shovels or bayonets with which to dig, we move on.

Jim Milliken is standing behind a
North Vietnamese tombstone.

We remain in the field this night to perform search-and-destroy missions. We do a lot of searching but hardly ever destroy anything other than enemy bunker fortifications or camping areas. Tonight we search hootches in a new location where we might find some signs of the Vietcong.

While taking a break, I think about the communist stars on the grave markings we discovered earlier in the day. All the graves had the same inscription on them. Could these recent graves be the NVA officers we killed over two weeks ago? We killed nineteen soldiers that day, but some were Vietcong and not NVA officers. I bet the graves are those of the officers. That would explain the communist star, number of graves, and the same inscription on the graves since their identification and personal papers were taken.

After the break, we walk the paddies for an hour before we arrive at a location of three hootches. I approach the nearest hootch around 2200 hours. A light flickers inside the hootch. Two mama-sans and a few children are visible. Platoon members surround the outside of the structure to protect my entering. The women are startled when I appear through the doorway with my M16 pointed in their direction. I question them about VC in the area. The younger mama-san knows what our intentions are but remains very quiet with a dumb look on her face. Whitey, Ralph, and a few other guys join me in the hootch to search the premises. They find nothing during the search. I tell the guys VC are in the area because these women and kids aren't inside their bunker sleeping. This is late for them to be awake. Normally at this time of night, I have to crawl inside the bunker to wake the occupants. The men are instructed to keep the women and kids quiet while I proceed to check out the next hootch. Halfway to the structure, the young mama-san starts to scream from the hootch I just departed. I dive to the ground for cover because she is alerting the VC of our presence. Then three armed VC hastily exit the next hootch in a direction from which I can't get a good shot at them.

I remain on the ground for about five minutes until I feel the VC have vacated the area. I approach the second home that is only a three-sided structure with no bunker. An old papa-san sits by a large fire cooking food. The three VC who ran are probably his sons coming home for an evening meal and some family time. The young mama-san is probably the wife of one of the three sons. There is no sense in harassing the old man, so I decide to return to the first hootch.

As I enter the hootch, the young mama-san is still mouthing off, giving the men a hard time. I tell them she almost got me killed when she alerted the VC in the next hootch about our presence. A minute in time can be the difference between having a point-blank shoot-out with three Vietcong and being killed. I tell the men to shut her up, and the guys look at me in a strange way as though they don't know how to do that. I lose my cool and hit her in the face with my fist. I knock her out with the punch and respond to the guys, "That is how you quiet her!" The guys are a little shocked at my behavior, but they don't risk their lives as often as I do on a daily basis. Also I feel a responsibility for the safety of each member of the platoon. When it comes to saving lives, I hide my feelings of compassion under nerves of steel so that nothing interferes with my job of protecting the lives of my platoon brothers.

We proceed to search the papa-san's shack and the third hootch. As we expected, the occupants were forewarned, and we didn't find anything. This happens every day when we know we are among enemy sympathizers and family, but we have little effect on them except inconveniencing them with a search. We do our best to make it known that we realize they are Vietcong.

Today is Easter Sunday. We have an early-morning briefing that CBS News will have a film crew joining us in the field to record our activities on Easter Day. I get the impression the crew is here to give a bright, positive outlook of how Ninth Division combat troops will spend their Easter. Two platoons move out to the main road to wait for the choppers. The CBS crew is already there and is instructed about the day's operation by our company commander, John Harrington. This crew gives the appearance they're going on a normal routine operation to the field that will be fun and exciting. Immediately I get a wary feeling that they are going to hinder our operations in the field.

We hear on the chopper radio that our first LZ is a hot one. Gunships have spotted fifteen VC and already have recorded a couple of kills. Now this camera crew is probably having second thoughts about spending the day in the field with us. The choppers approach our drop-off point. Cobras hammer the paddies and nearby high-grass areas for our insertion. We depart the choppers while we're fired upon from enemy positions. The Third Platoon moves into positions to return fire on the VC. The fighting continues for quite a while before we have the situation stabilized. During this time, I take two possible POWs or detainees. While we attend to the captured men, the CBS crew approaches us to film the proceedings. I get upset with this movie business, so I decide to mess up their film. On one of the prisoner's back I write HAPPY EASTER, and below the greeting I draw a picture of a hand displaying the middle finger. Pete Wood writes information on their backs pertaining to their capture. We march the prisoner past the film crew, and they get a shot of his back. Larry Sandage takes a photograph of the HAPPY EASTER greeting. I expect no one back in the States will view this section of the film or see Larry's photograph. Later I learn the language over the radios and that used by the troops during the fighting was so gross the film probably can't be edited into a televised production.

Lt. Wood writes on POW's back.

When we sweep the area, I notice the bullet holes in the ground from the Cobra helicopter miniguns. It seems like every square inch of a large area is peppered with bullet holes. I have heard that a Cobra has the equivalent firepower to cover every square inch of a football field in a minute. This claim may not be true, but I would definitely not want to be on the receiving end of that firepower. The sweep produces five enemy bodies and a number of POWs and detainees.

Today is April 6. I receive a letter from my parents in an Easter package. I share the jelly beans with my buddies. The guys are always sharing food and goodies they receive from home. Larry Sandage is making a run to Dong Tam today. I put in a request for four rolls of film. He does a great job shopping for members of the platoon.

I have been walking point since February 11. During this time, I have been very fortunate to have survived many dangerous situations. April 10 will be my last day to walk point because I fulfilled my two-month commitment on point duty. I probably will be assigned to squad leader in the platoon. I definitely feel the time has come to relinquish position in walking point because I am pushing my luck against the roll of the dice. I can't always be a winner.

In the late afternoon of April 7, the platoon is trucked to the Ben Luc Bridge to meet up with Tango boats that will take us to the field for the night. We get to the dock area in the early evening, which gives us about an hour to relax before the boats arrive. Tim, Clyde, and I sit at a small table to have a Coke when Dougie comes up to us laughing. Doug says, "You guys have to see this." Doug coaxes us to follow him back to a small building where an old mama-san awaits our arrival. The tiny old woman seems to have huge breasts. Dougie instructs the woman to take off her blouse, which she does. Underneath is what looks like a triple D white bra. This is the first time I ever saw a Vietnamese woman wear a bra. She proceeds to take off the bra, revealing breasts that are the size of small marbles. Dougie roars with laughter as the woman shows her pathetic boobs. We all laugh, including the woman. Out of pity, we give her some change for the big show. We go back to our seat while Doug plans to trick other guys in the platoon. What we will do for amusement!

The Tango boats arrive before dusk. The First and Third Platoons load on separate boats for our waterborne trip to the field. The boats move out from the dock area with the Third Platoon squeezed like sardines inside the one boat. I'm one of the lucky ones who found a spot to sit on the metal floor of the boat. Many of the guys remain standing for the two-hour trip. After a short time, a sore, raw spot forms on my back from a metal protrusion on the boat rubbing against me. Despite my wanting to sit down, I choose to get up and give my seat to someone else because I can't bear the metal rubbing on my back when the boat continually shifts in the water. I get up and someone takes my seat. It's so dark in the boat that I don't know who took my seat.

Only a few minutes pass when a gunshot goes off inside the boat. Everyone is silent after the blast, waiting for someone to say he is hit. No one says anything, but everyone knows one of us is shot. It's impossible for a bullet to miss a target when we're jammed shoulder to shoulder in the boat. Then Senical yells out to Dougie, who is sitting next to him. Senical feels Doug slumping over on him. Senical calls for some light. Guys light up their Bic lighters to see who is shot. Everyone seems fine until Senical checks out Dougie. Obviously, Dougie has been wounded, but there is no sign of a bullet wound, except for the expression on Doug's face. He remains speechless and appears to be badly wounded. Senical has the guys move back while he gets space to check Doug's body for a wound. Senical sees that Dougie is dying and starts mouth-to-mouth resuscitation. Everyone is stone silent, watching Bo trying to save Doug. Finally, Bo stops when he realizes Doug has died. I look into Doug's eyes and see he has a gleam in his eyes at death. Doug was always afraid of dying, but I believe he knew, at that instant, death is his fate, and God assures him a better place in heaven. Doug's face seems quite, peaceful, and relieved to leave this world. I will never forget his dying because he feared death in numerous combat situations, but when death came to this young man of nineteen years, he had no fear.

Senical announces that Dougie has died. In the background, one of the guys who accidentally fired the shot breaks down. Apparently, the guy was fooling with a .45 automatic pistol while on the boat. He knew better than to do that. Everyone's emotions run high trying to understand why this had to happen. Guys try to console the shooter while all of us pray for Doug and try to find answers to this madness. From the first day I got on the boats, I knew a tragedy would befall our platoon when we are transported at night. I expected something much more serious, which still may happen.

The Tango boat moves beside a large ship where Doug's body is removed from our boat. The platoon member who accidentally shot

Doug is taken aboard the ship to get psychiatric care and counseling. Our boat is now dead silent, mourning for Doug, whom we all loved very much.

I realize that bullet was meant for me. The person who took my seat was Doug. My life was saved by the metal rubbing my back. My life has been spared many times like this, by just being in the right place at the correct moment in time. Why was my life saved, and Doug's taken? Thinking about what transpired leaves me with a hollow, empty feeling in my heart. I just want to lay down my rifle and walk away from this insanity. Somehow in the next hour, I will need to muster the courage and fortitude from my grieving soul to walk point for the Third Platoon.

An hour passes when the platoon is notified to saddle up for our landing. I move forward to the front of the boat since I will be the first man to disembark. My body seems drained of all energy from my highly stressed emotional state brought on by Doug's death. The Tango boat ramp is lowered. The ramp is almost down when the enemy fires at our landing position. Without hesitation, I charge off the ramp and run over enemy bunkers, firing my M16. I keep running and firing until a parachute flare goes off above me. I hit the ground in a spread-eagle fashion because I'm vulnerable in the middle of a rice paddy. The enemy spots me in the light of the flare. They open up on me, firing from all directions. I play dead, even though I can hear bullets whistling by my ears and see bullets striking the dirt paddy within inches of my body. I remain motionless, praying these guys will eventually think they killed me. I must have had fifty to a hundred rounds fired at me.

I decide to make my move when the flare goes out and before another flare is sent up. The flare dies out, and I jump to my feet, running to the nearest paddy dike for cover. As soon as I get there, another flare lights up the sky. I wonder what the enemy thinks now when they see my body is missing from the paddy. Thank God they are lousy riflemen!

I lie still while the two platoons fan out in defensive positions. The enemy appears to have fled the ambush site. I look back in the direction of our troops and see a lit cigarette flashing in the darkness. I leave my position and follow the light until I come to a First Platoon soldier who has a cigarette in his mouth. I put my hand up to his face, grabbing the cigarette to extinguish it with my bare hand. We look directly into each other's eyes and say nothing. He knew this act of his was probably the most stupid thing an infantryman can do at night. Luckily for him, an enemy sniper is not around.

So far, this night has been a bust. I go back to Pete for instructions. Pete tells me what I want to hear. He tells me to move to my right flank and select an ambush site for the night. We call it a night because no one is up for additional contact.

The following day, we have off until early afternoon. Trucks transport us to Binh Phouc for a five-day mission to support a mechanized unit of tanks and armored personnel carriers. The $2^{nd}/47^{th}$ mechanized infantry unit has been clobbered in the last week. We heard reports they lost ninety men, mainly due to armored personnel carriers hitting mines. The casualties were mostly infantry troops who were riding on top of the APCs.

I just heard the weapon that killed Doug Taylor had a bad firing pin. Maybe company headquarters is saying that to ease tension about the tragedy or possibly that is a reason why the soldier was fooling with the weapon. In any case the soldier was negligent with the borrowed weapon. He normally carries an M16 to the field. Why he had a pistol is a mystery to me. Third Platoon has been told the soldier who accidentally killed Doug is on suicide watch. It will be a few days before he rejoins the platoon. We are alerted to keep our eye on him when he returns. I know it will be very difficult for him to adjust to his rejoining our unit. We will all do our best to include him in the platoon.

Weapons accidentally discharge frequently in combat zones. I have almost been shot three times by accident. The last time, five of us were in a circle in base camp. We were armed and talking when Clyde's weapon discharged among us. Luckily, the weapon was aimed straight in the air and did nothing other than scare the hell out of the group of guys. For some reason when I walk point, I sometimes get a desire to pull the trigger on my M16 for no reason at all. I have caught myself in this act a few times when my safety was off. Frequently I instinctively switch off my safety when I feel a presence of danger. I constantly check my safety because I'm unaware of my actions. Most of the men in the platoon have had lucky situations that could have turned into nightmares like that, which this soldier will have to live with for the rest of his life.

—

14

Binh Phuoc Mines and Booby Traps

Our trip to Binh Phuoc is an hour by truck. If we had traveled by helicopter, the trip would have been fifteen minutes. We arrive shortly before 1700 hours, just in time for a hot meal in the mess hall. The entrance to the base camp looks like a junkyard littered with blown-up armored personnel carriers. Apparently the 2nd Battalion/47th Infantry salvages the damaged equipment for spare parts. The appearance of this army equipment graveyard is not a welcome or friendly sight to our platoon. Rumors of high casualties the previous week take on a more credible meaning when we view the destroyed armored personnel carriers. I get the feeling our support here will be the platoon's suicide mission for the month. The Third Platoon is gaining a reputation of being very effective in the field. It's a Catch-22. The better a unit performs, the more dangerous the assignments become. It seems the army always takes advantage of the best.

We drop off our gear in a temporary barracks area used to house visiting support elements. After we secure our gear, the men inquire about the location of the mess hall. I thought the mess hall in our base camp was a catastrophe until I saw this mess hall. Everything is covered with a fine layer of dust caused by the mechanized traffic in the base camp. The mess hall is open to the outside light, which makes it hotter inside. The food is about the same, terrible but hot. I don't bitch about food because anything is better than eating C rations on a daily basis.

After dinner Tim, Big Lou, Leroy, Ralph, Whitey, and I ask for directions to the EM club. The club has a larger and better bar than the one in our base camp. The place is empty except for the bartender and one other patron. We order our beers and begin to ask the bartender questions about what is happening out in the field. His knowledge is not firsthand since he has always been a base camp soldier.

Two other men walk into the club. To Tim's and my amazement, one of our former buddies who entered Vietnam with us is one of the two men. We yell over to Dave Golwitzer and his friend to join our group. Dave updates us about many of the men who arrived in Vietnam and took in-country training with Tim and me. He tells us that Peter Bristol, John Failes, and Bob Hilfiker are doing fine. He heard that Tom Moreno has become an excellent soldier and leader. Sadly he says my good friend Lee Blank lost his foot when he hit a booby trap the first week out in the field. I always made fun of Lee's feet because they look like minesweepers. Lee is six feet six inches tall, which is almost the maximum height for an infantry soldier. I never thought he would have much of a chance to survive a year in Vietnam due to his size. His height makes him a trophy to the enemy.

I remember a time at Camp Bearcat when Lee and I walked by a massage parlor. Two Vietnamese women were outside trying to encourage customers. When they saw Lee coming, they ran inside the building, frightened that he might be the next customer. We laughed, and I encouraged Lee to enter the parlor to tease the women. He declined the opportunity, which would have been at his expense. Tim and I were sorry to receive the news about such a great, fun-loving guy. I hope Lee adjusts well to his new life. I believe he will because Lee is an upbeat person with a positive outlook on life.

Dave proceeds to tell the group about the 2nd/47th armored units getting their asses kicked the previous month. The casualties were high. Many GIs were killed and wounded. Numerous armored personnel carriers were lost. Almost all of the casualties occurred from mines and booby traps. The Vietcong bait the APCs to enter areas they have just mined. Dave said he heard our unit has a good reputation in the field. We were brought in to hopefully uplift the morale of the battalion. After a few beers, we thanked Dave for the information and news update on our old friends. He said he usually spends time in the club when he's off duty. He will visit the club more frequently this week to keep posted on our ventures in the field.

After breakfast, the Third Platoon faces the challenge of learning to ride APCs or "tracks." The platoon walks to the front gate of the base camp to board seven armored personnel carriers. The diesel engines make a hell of a racket as they spill out noxious fumes. I get on top of one of the APCs with Tim, Willy, and Clyde. Each APC has four to five troops mounted on top, while the driver and gunner ride inside. We leave Binh Phuoc base camp as the tracks kick up an unbelievable amount of dust on the dirt road. I ride on the fourth APC and can barely see the track in front of or in back of me. About a mile out of base camp, we enter the rice paddies.

When the APCs move through the paddies at twenty to thirty miles per hour, the troops try to ride these ponies. There is one iron handle grip to hold on to when the APC hits a paddy dike or rough terrain. Staying on the track is like riding a bull in the rodeo. The only difference is you may be on top of the APC for hours instead of a few minutes. You must relax your muscles and body when the terrain is smooth, then hold on tightly when you hit a paddy dike or uneven ground. The difficulty is to hold on with one hand and carry an M16 in the other. When the driver hits a paddy dike, the force of the APC going slightly airborne causes one's knuckles to slam against the metal shell of the track. My right knuckles bleed from the constant pounding of my hand against the shell. There must be a better way to ride this vehicle. By the end of the week, I might need a new hand if I don't figure out a better technique of riding this bull.

Our APCs move into position around other APCs that experienced the loss of one of their tracks from a mine explosion. The damaged APC had six men wounded from the mine explosion. Our tracks maintain security while the men are airlifted. I can see how easily these APCs are blown up. This armored carrier traveled through a narrow-level passage instead of taking the rough terrain through the field. The driver of these vehicles should think like a pointman when they operate the vehicle. Instead, they have a false sense of security when they are in an armored vehicle. My impression is these APCs are mobile time bombs. Due to their size, weight, and lack of maneuverability, the tracks are limited in their performance in most areas. The enemy soldiers must take great satisfaction in how easy it is to destroy them.

After half an hour, the tracks move to a new location in the paddies. We dismount the APCs to inspect the woodlines where the carriers can't enter. I lead our element on one side of the woodline while another unit operates in a woodline across the paddy. Willy and I walk in the paddy parallel to a dike, while the other unit walks on the dike next to the woodline. I look at Willy and say, "Willy, that pointman will be blown up in the next ten minutes." Just as I finish my sentence, we hear a loud explosion. Willy and I witness the pointman being hurled almost six feet in the air from the explosion. The force of the explosion indicates he stepped on a mine. From our vantage point, the man appears to have had a leg blown off. I feel bad predicting his fate, but one should never walk paddy dikes in a heavily booby-trapped or mined area.

We continue our mission as the other platoon dusts off their pointman. The area where I enter the woods has many bunkers. The impression I get about the terrain around Binh Phuoc is that the enemy is more visible than in other areas. This behavior indicates a cockiness that Vietcong are in control of this war zone. I approach a bunker in the clearing and get an uneasy feeling about its location in an open area. I stop for approximately five minutes to stare at the suspicious surroundings. When I'm ready to move forward, I look down directly in front of my feet and see a trip wire hooked to a grenade. My sixth sense told me to stop because the pieces didn't fit correctly for this puzzle. I show Willy my find so he can learn the thinking ways of the enemy. We blow up the booby trap and continue our search. The remainder of the day is uneventful, so we leave to return to the APCs for a ride back to base camp.

Jim Milliken checks a Vietcong bunker.

The next day events are more of the same except we travel now in an armored unit with tanks and APCs. I ride on one of the tanks. The armored unit enters a main village via a dirt road. The villagers come out of their homes to see what appears to be a parade of military vehicles. I get a good feeling sitting on the tank and being viewed as though the troops are liberators like the GIs who entered towns in Europe to free people from German occupation. The only difference is these Vietnamese civilians question our intentions. No one cheers as though GIs are the answer to their problems.

Later in the afternoon, the armored unit receives information on a suspected enemy gathering. The armored unit races through the paddies at forty miles per hour, hitting paddy dikes with a tremendous force. The APCs move in line toward a major jungle woodline. I sit on an APC since the tanks left our formation for another assignment. The APCs approach a large gaping ditch in the paddy. I hold on, expecting the driver to go down in the ditch and power up the opposite side. Instead, he makes a quick stop before entering the ditch, which catapults me and three other guys on top of the APC into the air to the other side of the ditch. The driver carefully drives the track down into the ditch and powers up the other side, throwing mud everywhere. We jump back on the track and continue our assault to the woodline. The tracks stop fifty meters from the woodline and open up with a massive firepower from the .50 caliber machine guns. The troops remain on top of the carriers until the firing ceases.

We dismount the tracks to search the woodline. I move out with Willy, who provides support to my flanks. The tracks did a lot of damage to the vegetation, but we find no traces of bodies or wounded soldiers. I search the enemy bunkers with caution because I found a booby trap near one yesterday. Depending on their location, the enemy develops patterns where they position booby traps and mines. Again I get an uneasy feeling about this location. Like yesterday, I scan the vegetation and ground, looking for something that does not fit the surroundings. Then my concern is justified. Directly at my side is another grenade booby trap near a bunker entrance. I hate Binh Phuoc because this location is loaded with mines and booby traps. The booby trap is detonated. We continue our sweep, finding nothing of importance.

Tonight the Third Platoon remains in the field with the APCs to set up an ambush site. I find this interesting because how do we conceal eight APCs in a rice paddy at night? The VC soldiers have to be idiots to not know the location of the ambush site. At dusk, seven APCs form a defensive circle like a wagon train protecting against Indian attacks. In the center is a track that has a mortar unit. We eat our chow before preparing a separate infantry ambush outside the perimeter of the tracks. This makes more sense to me when each unit has its own ambush site but serves as a support unit to both ambush locations.

Pete and Bo confer with Willy and me to outline the distance and direction in positioning our ambush site from the tracks. Willy and I walk half an hour before we check with Pete for a location to set up. Pete selects a dike leading to a group of hootches. We begin to prepare our routine L-shaped ambush at the junction of two dikes. Willy and I position ourselves at the far end of the L facing down a long paddy dike. Pete and Bo position on the short end of the ambush L. Both locations are equipped with starlight scopes for early warning of approaching soldiers.

I leave our position to place a Claymore mine about fifty feet down the paddy dike from our location. After setting up the Claymore, I return to our ambush position. I look through the starlight to view the Claymore mine. To my astonishment, I see two armed enemy soldiers walking in a hurried manner toward Willy and me on the dike. I quietly say to Willy, "Don't fire until I initiate the ambush by firing. I want them to walk on top of us before springing the ambush." Willy and I lie in a prone position on the left side of the dike. I put my M16 on semiautomatic because I know Willy has his 16 on automatic. I fear we might miss when we fire at night, so I want to have continuous firepower if we fail to kill them on the initial attack.

The soldiers walk ten feet from our position when Willy and I ambush them. Willy fires on automatic while I press off half the number of rounds he fires. Willy is out of ammunition, and I stop firing, listening for movement. The two of us are unable to see in front of us because of the smoke generated from firing our weapons. Then I hear one of the soldiers moaning on the right side of the dike. I place my rifle over the dike in line with the moaning and begin to fire until my clip empties. Willy reloads while I reach for a new magazine. Again both of us hold our fire, listening for movement. The moaning has stopped while the smoke clears. Now we're able to view the dead bodies. Willy and I keep our guard up in case more soldiers are near. I get the Claymore ready to explode.

Bo Senical runs over to our position and asks us why we waited so long to spring the ambush. Pete and Bo watched the proceedings through their starlight and were tempted to open up when the soldiers got close to us. I explain to Bo that I feared missing them from a distance. Without a starlight scope, it's very difficult to shoot someone at night, even at close range. I know from past experience as I have been on both the receiving and giving ends of shoot-outs at night.

Bo says he thinks some VC went into a hootch at the end of our dike. Bo and I move down the dike to open up on the hootch. We both fire a magazine of rounds at the hootch, setting it on fire. Pete requests the track mortar unit to set up parachute flares so we can better assess the situation. With the help of the illumination, Bo and I go over to the hootch to check for additional casualties. The hootch is completely burned except for some framework, which is smoking. Miraculously, an old man emerges from his bunker. He looks around in a confused state, probably wondering what happened to his home. I feel bad for the old papa-san, but the villagers will take care of him until his home is rebuilt. We find no signs of additional VC; therefore, we return to our ambush site. When I get back to our ambush site, I give Willy a high five for a good job in ambushing the VC. I can see Willy is quite upset with what has just transpired.

Pete reports the two enemy kills while we confiscate their AK-47 rifles. Pete has the platoon move to the other side of the village to locate a new ambush site near a woodline and a wet paddy. Now the platoon will be dinner for the mosquitoes breeding in the wet paddy. The remainder of the night is routine.

The next morning we do a brief check of the hootches. We pass by the two dead soldiers whose bodies have already started to bloat from the hot climate. The bodies are out of proportion and look fake. As soon as we leave the area, the VC will come to bury the soldiers. The tracks approach our location to transport us back to base camp. The driver of one of the APCs uses his vehicle to run over the dead bodies. Our platoon is disgusted with this needless action. I know this behavior will only incite the enemy to retaliate. Despicable acts in war only give the enemy additional motivation in their cause.

When we mount the tracks, the men treat us like celebrities because we scored a few kills last night. These guys are so used to getting their asses kicked that any positive action against the VC is a morale booster. I overhear Pete bragging about me to the officer in charge of the APC unit. That is the first time I ever heard anyone brag about my accomplishments. I guess all officers like to think they have the best men under them. I feel bad because when Pete gets a free moment, I must inform him this will be my last day walking point.

Pete finishes his discussion with the other brass. I approach Pete and say, "Yesterday was April 10, my last day to walk point. I request another assignment in the platoon." Pete knows my time is up but looks amazed at my request to be relieved. Pete's first remark is, "Really? Could you walk point for a few more days until I get a replacement?" I reply, "Pete, I've had four close calls in the last two days. I would be pushing my luck if I continue. What I promise to do is be a pointman when the platoon gets in a tough jam or there is an unusual circumstance." Pete says to me, "I think you will make a good RTO." That remark caught me off guard. I look at him and say, "I don't want to carry a radio. I'm a fighter, not a messenger." Pete says, "You will carry a radio tonight." I reply, "Okay," and leave.

I can't understand why Pete thinks I should be an RTO. I guess he is so used to having me up front with him that he wants to continue that relationship. After tonight, 3-6 will change his mind. I plan to purposely screw up all night long on the radio transmissions. The only way to get out of an assignment in the army is to get in trouble, which will be my goal tonight. Maybe then, Pete will change his mind and make me a squad leader.

The APCs take us back to base camp for a hot lunch. We have a few hours off before we'll return to the field for another ambush scheduled for tonight. After lunch, I go to the EM club for a cold beer. I'm surprised to see Dave Golwitzer sitting at the bar. Dave buys me a beer and starts our discussion by saying, "The rumor around base camp is that you guys kicked ass last night." I laugh saying, "I can't believe the word has gotten around base camp so fast." Dave asks me, "Did you see action?" I reply, "My pointman buddy Willy and I were the ones who killed the VC." Dave responds by saying, "I told my buddies you were probably the one who killed the gooks." I wonder to myself why he bragged to his friends without any knowledge of what happened. It is a little upsetting the way these men are treating us like saviors or heroes. I decide to leave the bar and keep my mouth shut about future operations.

Before dinner, we leave for the field to set up another nighttime ambush. When we arrive at our location, the APCs form a defensive circle. Tonight our infantry unit is going to remain in the circle for a short time before we leave for our outside ambush. I get on top of one of the APCs and grab a starlight scope to view the surrounding paddies for enemy activity. I don't expect to see anything because we just set up in this area and darkness settled in. I look through the starlight for only a short period of time before I locate three Vietcong soldiers moving in the paddies from our right to left flank. I jump off the APC to inform Pete and Bo of my sighting. When I reach their position, they already know about the VC. The lieutenant in charge of the APCs has ordered an APC to leave the formation and attack the Vietcong. Pete and Bo are bystanders to the activity.

I hurry back to my position in disbelief at the lieutenant's actions. I climb on top of another APC to have a front-row seat to view this fiasco. I watch as the driver of the armored personnel carrier revs its engine and turns on the headlights for the assault. The APC leaves the formation and charges the three Vietcong with the .50 caliber machine gun blazing. While watching this idiotic tactic, I notice that the gunfire becomes less effective the closer the carrier gets to the enemy. The Vietcong do exactly what any infantryman would do. They take cover behind the paddy dikes and wait for the APCs to get closer, which lessens its firepower and maneuverability.

When the APC gets closer to the hiding Vietcong, the driver changes tactics and tries to run over the Vietcong with the APC. The enemy soldiers rise up and shoot the driver of the track. Many of us can hear the driver screaming over the radio that he has been shot in the side of the face. The gunner is fearful the Vietcong will jump on the APC and throw grenades inside to kill them. What should have been an easy enemy kill has turned into a horrible nightmare. The messages coming over the radio are confusing, frantic, and disheartening. It sounds like the driver is still alive but has lost both eyes when a bullet ripped his face apart. From his moaning and cries, he sounds like he has only minutes to live. I pray for God to be merciful and take his life.

I get down off the APC to join Pete and Bo, expecting to be part of a rescue force. To my surprise, Bo and Doc Brothers have already left the perimeter to save the men in peril. We hear a firefight commence, and within a short time, the three enemy soldiers are killed. The track is brought back in formation. Because of the huge screwup, we remain silent about questioning the commanding officer on the status of their casualty. If Pete and Bo had been allowed to do their job, our platoon would have been successful in killing the enemy with no casualties.

When Bo returns from the rescue, he gives his version of what happened. Bo said he heard cries for a medic and yelled to David Brothers, "Doc, let's go!" Doc grabbed his medical bag and ran out to the APC unarmed. Bo followed behind Doc to provide cover. When they approached the APC, Bo got into a firefight with the VC while Doc administered aid to the wounded soldier. Bo killed one of the Vietcong, but erratic small arms fire persisted from the right flank. Bo got low behind a paddy dike and crawled toward the firing, hoping to get a good angle from which to shoot. A flare popped, illuminating the firefight scene. The other two VC spotted Bo and commenced firing. Bo hugged the ground until men from the perimeter of the APCs fired at the VC. Bo returned fire at the VC soldiers, who were then trapped in a cross fire. With the enemy pinned down, two soldiers approached the VC, killing them.

An hour later, the Third Platoon leaves the formation for the nightly ambush. The rest of the night is uneventful. I became an RTO for the night at Pete's request. I did my best to screw up call signs and to not use the proper radio military jargon. The next morning Pete tells me he received numerous complaints about my radio performance. He relieves me of my RTO assignment and honors my request to be a fighter. Pete says he will find a suitable job in the platoon for me. I have found out the best way to get want I want in the army is to screw up on what they want me to do.

For last night's brave response, Bo Senical and Doc Brothers are awarded the Bronze Star for Valor. Both of them are very deserving of the medal because of their efforts trying to save comrades. Lately I have been trying to get David Brothers, who is a conscientious objector, to carry a weapon. I have the greatest respect for his ideals and commitment to not place himself in the situation where he may be tempted to use the weapon on another human being. I mention to him that troops may not be around to protect him while he is administering aid to a fallen soldier. He may need a rifle to protect himself and the wounded he is trying to save. I say to him, "What if an enemy soldier points a weapon at you and you have no other recourse but to die?" Also I try to make him feel guilty by shaming him that he is risking other platoon members' lives, such as mine, to protect him while they should be fighting the enemy. I really like David. Hopefully, God will protect him because of his religious and moral principles.

Today will be our last day assigned to the Second/Forty-seventh mechanized unit. Currently the tracks are traveling down a dirt road on our way to our next mission. There is so much dust kicked up by the tracks that I use my fingers as windshield wipers to wipe the dust off my glasses. The dust is so thick that every few minutes I have to make passes across my glasses to clear the dust in order to see. I have dust caked almost an inch thick on my face. I don't disturb the dirt because the result will be an irritating rash. The APCs get off the road and enter the rice paddies. I take off my glasses and have a huge rim of dirt caked around my eyes. Carefully I remove the encrusted dirt. My skin is very irritated, but at least my pores are getting oxygen again.

We leave the tracks to sweep an area that has a strange aura. The pointmen take us through a woodline that opens up to a small cluster of hootches. While we walk, there is a quiet, deathly silence about this place. Finally, I realize there is no sign of life in the area. The platoon walks by a multitude of dead rats lying everywhere. Our medic enters one of the hootches to figure out the problem. He exits and announces this village is suffering from the bubonic plague. That explains the dead rats and the haunting eeriness of this location. Fortunately for us, the army has soldiers inoculated for bubonic plague. Besides having three shots for bubonic plague, all troops had shots for smallpox, yellow fever, cholera, polio, flu, typhoid fever, and tetanus. When I received these shots, I thought the army was being overly cautious about the prospect of getting these diseases. However, in the past six months, I have been exposed to many of these diseases that I believed to be a part of past medical history.

The tracks arrive to transport us back to base camp. Before jumping on the APC, I check my M16 and notice my weapon's safety has been in the off position. This has been a problem when I ride the APCs. The constant vibration of the weapon against the shell of the track causes the safety to release. Many times when I check the safety after riding the tracks, I find my weapon ready to fire. Extreme care and alertness are required when we ride these beasts. After we arrive at Binh Phuoc, the platoon wastes no time in packing up for our departure back to Tan Tru.

Showers are a welcome sight at company headquarters. The stay at Binh Phuoc did a job on my pathetic-looking skin. Besides sores, scratches, ringworm, and scars, I now have an irritating facial rash from being so dirty. My feet have developed small holes from trench foot. After a long shower using almost a cake of soap, I emerge from the shower stall a new man. Mail call brings letters from my mother, Mrs. Baumhauer, Jimmy Giancola, and Larry Boneck.

My mother talks about watching the news channels on the Vietnam War. She mentions that Ellwood City had a parade for a local man who was on the USS Pueblo. Mrs. Baumhauer writes a lengthy letter updating me on her family and local happenings in Oak Hill, the development in which I grew up near West Chester. She is pleased I wear the St. Patrick's medal she sent me, even though I'm not Catholic. I wear it with my dog tags. I figure I can't get enough religion in a war zone. I would wear a symbol from every religion if it would secure my existence. I wear the medal because it reminds me of those who care about me, especially the Baumhauer family and my many Catholic friends.

I open Larry's much-anticipated letter last. He seems to be doing fine except for the pain in his legs. He has the Red Cross looking for Billy West to get an update on his condition. Boneck says he's hospitalized in Camp Zama, Japan. After reading his letter, I immediately go to company headquarters to change my R&R date to visit Larry in Japan. When Larry was blown up, the next day I received permission for an early R&R to visit him. I promised Larry I would come visit him in the hospital. Command was very gracious in cancelling my May date for R&R and issuing me a new date of April 23. To give me that date, they changed the date of another GI. After reading Boneck's letter, I spread the news to the Third Platoon about his recovery and his address at Camp Zama. The guys always want to hear good things about those wounded men who have departed from our ranks.

Larry Sandage brings a large assortment of photographs to give to the guys. He gives me some great combat action photos of the day I almost shot him. He says two of my pictures have already been released for publication. He is still waiting for the pictures he took on Easter Day. I think most of the guys have a few pictures of themselves taken by him. Larry tries to include all the members of the platoon in his photographs. The platoon appreciates his work and his efforts to make our lives more fun and interesting.

The next day I assume a rifleman's duty in the platoon. The day provides no contact with the enemy, so as a reward, we get to remain in the field for the night. At night we set up our ambush site, yielding a kill for our sniper accompanying us to the field. I kind of miss not being directly involved with the combat proceedings. During guard on the ambush site, the three men at my location all had nightmares. Before, I spent most of my time with the point team; now I get a glimpse of how the fighting is affecting the other men in our group. I find it strange that I don't experience nightmares or bad dreams. Probably, due to my inability to go into a deep sleep. I seem to be always aware of my surroundings even when I sleep.

The next week is a welcomed change for me. I will be a new squad leader with the platoon's rear security. The platoon continues to see action, but I'm not directly involved in the firefights because of my new assignment.

15

Rest and Relaxation, Tokyo, Japan

Today, April 20, is an exciting day, which I have been anxiously awaiting since my arrival in Vietnam. I am leaving early for R&R to Tokyo, Japan, to allow for sufficient travel time. Before leaving the company area, each soldier must pass an inspection given by our first sergeant on his appearance and grooming. I trimmed my Fu Manchu mustache to regulation military length and got a haircut. My dress summer khaki uniform was cleaned and pressed with the proper medals displayed of three Vietnamese unit citations, two Vietnamese campaign ribbons, a National Defense ribbon, and the Combat Infantryman Badge. My brass and shoes are polished to an impressive, sleek look. I feel like a new person making my way to company headquarters for inspection. Top takes one look at me and gives me my orders. He cautions me to arrive back on duty as stated in the orders and reminds me that I represent our battalion when on R&R. Top wishes me a good time while I thank him for pulling strings for my early R&R.

I hitch a ride in front of the base camp to Dong Tam. I feel weird in dress khakis while in a combat zone. I miss my M16 already but borrow an M16 from the jeep driver to serve as a security guard even though I give the appearance of a greenhorn. Thank God the trip to Dong Tam is uneventful. I could not imagine being in a firefight dressed in my khaki uniform.

I spend the late afternoon walking around the Dong Tam to familiarize myself with the layout of the base camp. During my walk, I notice two pretty civilian women and a man approaching me. As we near each other, I recognize the man to be Skip Young, a.k.a. Wally Plumstead, of *The Adventures of Ozzie and Harriet* television show. Skip is accompanied by Sharon Mullikin and Susan Glicksman. They are on a USO tour of Vietnam. I enjoy a short chat with them and give thanks for their efforts in visiting the troops.

USO tour group, LToR Sharon Mullikin, Skip Young, a.k.a. Wally Plumstead, Susan Glicksman.

The next day I get a ride on a military air transport to Tan Son Nhut Air Base. The plane is full of men going on R&R. The trip to Tan Son Nhut is a short one. I marvel how easy it is for military men to catch flights anywhere in Vietnam.

At Tan Son Nhut there are long lines of soldiers waiting their turn to display their orders to get the proper airline reservations to their destinations of their choice. Many men take R&R in Hawaii, Australia, Thailand, Japan, and the Philippines. When I'm summoned with my orders, I learn that the next available flight to Tokyo is tomorrow. To my disappointment, the army has a limit on the amount of cash a soldier is allowed to take on R&R. Three men in the platoon gave me money to buy camera equipment in Japan. Their money plus extra funds I brought put me over the allowable limit, and I will have to leave six hundred

—

dollars in an airport army safe. After my paperwork is completed, I look for something to do to pass the long wait for my flight.

I grab a bite to eat and sit down with a group of Australian soldiers. These guys are a riot to watch. The soldiers are very fun loving, who seem to enjoy every moment of life. One of the older men invites me to join them in a bit of frivolity and drinking. Their flight also departs tomorrow. I leave the establishment with about twenty Australian soldiers for a night of drinking. These guys love to drink and pull pranks on each other. We get wasted from a heavy night of drinking. Every one of these Australian soldiers is hatless after a night of partying. They gave their bush hats away to admiring girls and other bar patrons. I never saw so many guys who didn't give a shit about anything. I talk to one soldier who has been in the Australian Army for about twenty years and his rank is private. He says he has been busted so many times that he lost count. Many of the other men are just like he is. All I can say is that they treated me great and showed me a fabulous time.

As the sun rises, we decide a few winks of sleep are in order before our flights later in the day. Now I understand why so many Americans love to travel to Australia on R&R or leave. The Australians love Americans and have always been a faithful ally to the United States. When my ten-day leave is authorized, Australia will be my destination.

Late in the evening, my flight to Tokyo is announced. I board with a small duffel bag containing underwear and personal-care items. It takes a long time to fill the large plane with a few hundred GIs. While in flight for about five hours, I talk with the men sitting near me. Eight of us decide to cast our fate together. The army recommends traveling in groups for protection against the GI predators about whom we have been warned. GIs are suckers for a good time, so there is always someone ready to relieve you of your cash.

The plane arrives around 0200 hours Tokyo time. The eight of us depart the plane together with our hand-carried luggage. It's early in the morning, and we anticipate having difficulty selecting a hotel for the week. When we exit the plane corridor into a main hallway, our group is surprised to see many R&R hotel locations represented by pretty Japanese females. Naturally, we listened to the most beautiful girl's sales pitch. This hotel advertising campaign seems very unusual to me. It appears as though the US government is doing its best to keep the soldiers from the mainstream Japanese people. This arrival site is essentially only for military personnel.

Our first question for the young woman is, "Is this hotel GI friendly where we can party all night long and raise as much hell as we want?" She smiles and replies in good English, "The hotel is secluded and is very accommodating to GI pleasures." The guys go wild when they hear the answer they hope for. We ask about the cost and details of the package the hotel offers.

The woman explains the total package cost is $125 American money for a week's stay at the hotel. The hotel offers Japanese- and American-style rooms. The basic difference is the décor. The American rooms have beds while the Japanese rooms provide sleeping arrangements on the floor. I have been sleeping on the ground for the last six months, so a comfortable bed will be a treat. The package provides each GI with two meals of his choice per day. Everyone gets forty free-drink tickets at the bar. All the guys' mouths open in awe when that number is mentioned. Two tours are provided to many of the local sites, including a dinner prepared in one of Tokyo's finest restaurants. A "Saki Party" is given at the hotel for all the GIs. She also mentions the hotel is girl friendly.

This deal is to our liking, so we don't check what the competition offers. We pay our $125, and a driver is summoned to escort us to a van for transportation to the hotel. The transportation to and from the hotel is included in the package. When we get in the oversized van, the driver tells us the ride to the hotel will be about two hours. We all look at each other in amazement, wondering what we bargained for. The driver explains the hotel is in the suburbs of Yokohama. We begin to have second thoughts about our hotel selection because we thought the hotel was near Tokyo. We load into the van while the driver opens two cases of cold beer for our trip. Another unexpected treat! I bet Uncle Sam is subsidizing these hotels for what we pay.

The trip takes a little less than two hours. I can't wait to get some sleep. I have been up for two days drinking a good part of the time. We enter the hotel and find many call girls waiting our arrival at 0400 hours. To their disappointment, we all head for our rooms to get some rest. We agree to meet in the dining room around 1200 hours. Then the party will begin.

At noon we have a big lunch that includes hamburgers and french fries. The first thing we need is civilian clothes. GIs aren't permitted to wear military clothing while on R&R in Japan. The hotel has a guide at our disposal who arranges free transportation to the local military post exchange. The PX has a spacious men's clothing section. The prices are unbelievably low. I purchase three sport coats at fifteen dollars each, three pairs of slacks, and five shirts. The total cost for all these items is ninety-four dollars. We return to the hotel to change into our new purchases.

I ask our guide for directions to Camp Zama to see Larry Boneck. He explains that I must take the train to Tokyo and then get on another line to Camp Zama. I thank him for the directions and give him a tip, hoping that the directions are good. After two hours, I arrive at Camp Zama; and to my dismay, the staff informs me that Larry had left for the states the previous day. I feel disheartened about missing my chance to see him because the R&R to Japan was all about my promise to visit him. After walking through a few wards and viewing the many wounded GIs, I decide to leave this depressing hospital environment for some fun.

In the evening, five of us hire a cab to tour Yokohama. The side street the hotel is located on is extremely narrow, as are most of the residential streets in Yokohama. We encourage the driver to drive fast down these narrow hilly streets. The driver laughs while we yell to go faster. Our group is jammed in this small cab traveling at a fast clip down a winding, hilly, narrow street. It feels as though we are on a roller coaster. This cabbie is a good driver not to have an accident under these conditions. At the bottom of the hill, the Yokohama police pull the cabdriver over for speeding. Collectively we give him money to pay the fine. The cabbie thanks us before he begins our tour. The last stop on the tour is a large GI night club for military personnel and their dates. We stay only a short time because we realize the local GIs stationed in Japan don't like the Vietnam GIs moving in on their women. Most of the girls in the club are Japanese.

When we arrive back at the hotel, a party is in progress. We enjoy ourselves all night long until 0500 hours when we call it quits for the night. We plan to meet at 1100 hours for lunch, then organize the day's activities. At lunch we decide to take the tour to Tokyo. A bus with a tour guide picks us up at the hotel. The young Japanese girl who is our tour guide speaks perfect English. The first stop on the tour is Olympic Stadium before we go to the Ginza District, which is the major shopping section of Tokyo. In the evening the bus pulls up in front of a beautiful hotel in downtown Tokyo. Our group is escorted into a special dining room prepared for our arrival. There are fifteen of us who have a headwaiter and his ten assistants serving us. The waiters are dressed in tuxedos and serve each course with amazing skill and grace. We enjoy a seven-course meal with filled wineglasses. We ask our guide what is an appropriate tip. She responds by saying the tip is included with the free meal. The staff would be embarrassed if we tipped them. All I can say is that we just had a $125 dinner. What a deal!

We arrive back at the hotel around 2200 hours to join the party in progress. There are about forty GIs lodged in this small but nice hotel. I have been looking for the name of the hotel and can't locate its name on anything. The hotel name doesn't even appear on a sign outside. Surely the nearby residents are aware of this establishment as a haven for Vietnam GIs.

The next day, five of us decide to return to Tokyo for the nightlife. The train ride takes an hour from Yokohama to Tokyo. The people at the hotel think our group is crazy making such a long trip for a few hours of enjoyment. They have ulterior motives, trying to get us to spend our money in the local area. Many of the people we talk to have a difficult life with very little money available for luxuries. Our guide saved money for four months to buy a cheap transistor radio he's very proud of. The Japanese riding the train keep their eyes on us. The people are curious about the verbose and colorfully dressed Americans. Americans are quite a contrast to their reserved demeanor and conservative dress. The Japanese are nicely dressed, but everyone wears the same boring grey and dark-colored suits with white shirts. There is no color in their wardrobe.

I strike up a conversation with an older Japanese fellow who asks me what Louisiana is like now. I tell him I have never been in that state. He finds that amusing since he spent time training in submarine warfare in Louisiana prior to World War II. I think it's ironic that we train our future enemies. We have a nice conversation but do not mention World War II or my involvement in Vietnam. As we get closer to Tokyo, the trains become very crowded and standing room is at a premium. Pushers are at each stop to shove as many people on the train as possible. These practices would not be tolerated in the States.

We enjoy our stay in Tokyo and agree we'll make this a part of our nightly ritual while on R&R. Another part of our nightly ritual is the hotel

---

party that commences around 2400 hours to 0500 hours in the morning. We get five to six hours' sleep before we repeat our schedule of touring and partying. I learn that one of the guys is from a different company in my battalion. His first name is Jack, and he is quite a swinger. The men I have teamed up with are a great bunch of guys. I would love to have them as members of the Third Platoon.

The next day the men are warned by the hotel staff to avoid traveling to downtown Tokyo because the city is expecting anti-American riots. Apparently, the Japanese want the island of Okinawa back. The United States uses the island as a strategic military base in the Pacific. I understand Japan's concern about our presence. The main island has many large air bases and naval stations. The American military presence is everywhere. The Japanese people are losing their culture by adopting Western ways in every facet of life. I'm disappointed to see their traditions disappear in such a short period of time after World War II.

Despite the warnings of possible conflict in Tokyo, we agree that our R&R will not be interrupted by a few Japanese misfits. Our train ride to Tokyo is pleasant but feels like a commuter ride to work. Now the ride is part of a daily routine. In Tokyo we walk down a crowded street where there is little room to maneuver because of the masses of people walking to their jobs. Many of the stores remain closed until 1400 hours, even though they stay open to 0200 hours the next morning. A car backfires, causing the five of us to hit the pavement in a prone position. The Japanese people stare at us lying on the pavement, but no one laughs or mocks us. I know most of them are aware what effects a war has on us.

Later in the afternoon, we turn a corner and see a huge demonstration in front of us. The demonstrators immediately notice us and race toward us. The five of us don't say anything to each other but continue to walk directly at the charging crowd. The demonstrators surround us and begin to shove us and shout anti-American slogans and obscenities. They realize by our looks and demeanor we're Vietnam combat veterans. We continue walking while they push and jostle us. I look directly into the eyes of many of the demonstrators, displaying a cold-steel look that shows no fear of them. My buddies do the same. To our surprise, the Japanese, who wear white bandanas with red Japanese lettering, part and let us pass by them. I find it difficult to believe that this large crowd of approximately two hundred people is fearful of the "Magnificent Five." I can see fear in their body language and doubt in their eyes. They know the American resolve in peril. When we're out of sight of the crowd, we acknowledge each other's courage for our performance under pressure.

In the evening, our group is confronted again by some men whom we refer to as pimps. These guys try to get us to enter the girlie clubs they sponsor. The only way we get them to leave us alone is to get a camera and take their picture. We find it funny to see them run in all directions. Our first night in Tokyo, we fell into their trap and entered one of the clubs. The army warned us about these gyp joints, but we wanted to have a firsthand experience of what the girlie clubs are like. When we entered, we were immediately given a table with girls joining us as we sat down. The girls asked for a drink. We inquired about the cost, and reluctantly the waitress said fifty American dollars per drink per girl. That is all we had to hear, and immediately we departed the scene. We heard horror stories of GIs blowing three hundred dollars in an hour to socialize with these bar girls.

The next day we go on a shopping spree in a market section of Yokohama. The guys find it amusing that my shopping list includes war supplies that are difficult to get in Vietnam. I buy a set of binoculars to use when I get back to Vietnam. I look for a large jungle knife but have no luck. My funds are dwindling; so in order to buy the camera equipment, tape recorder, watch, and family gifts, I must call home for money. I return to the hotel and order two scotch and sodas to take to my room while I call home. I anticipate a long wait getting connected to the States but wait only ten minutes before I talk to my mother. She is very surprised to hear my voice. I tell her to wire money from my account in Ellwood City to a major bank in Tokyo. She is upset about doing this, but I assure her everything will work out. I inform Mom the money is for an Akai tape recorder and gifts for the family. I tell her I have a limited amount of cash due to the cap on funds the military allows GIs to carry while on R&R. She says she will wire the money immediately.

I go downstairs to the "Saki Party" the hotel has for their patrons. The dining area is decorated in Japanese paper figurines and lanterns and is furnished with small tables that seat only two GIs. A girl is assigned to each table to serve Japanese food and saki. Each table has a large bottle of saki that is warmed under a Sterno heating implement. I taste the warm saki and say "number 1" in jest to the server. After a little saki, I feel as though a fireworks display is igniting in my head. I imagine lightning bolts traveling in my brain. This is a powerful drink, especially when it's heated. The alcohol has really impaired my brain. I stop drinking to fill up on food in order to avoid developing a major headache. After dinner I call it a night because of the thunderstorm raging in my head.

The next day our group goes on our second tour, which includes Japanese historical shrines, pagodas, and temples. We watch an elaborate Japanese wedding at a famous temple. We take a group picture in a department store with a pretty young girl who is an employee of the store. Our guide argues with us when one of the guys chooses this girl to join us in the picture. He explains she is of a low class in Japanese society, and it is offensive to have her in the group photograph. The argument embarrasses the young lady. We disagree with our guide and have the picture taken. Jack and I select a cosmetic package as a gift for her being polite to our group. While we're in the store, we tease the personnel who stand by the escalators to warn shoppers of the moving stairsteps. We pretend to not see the moving stair and fall. After we do this a couple of times, we realize this is serious business to them and not a joke.

I mention to the hotel guide that I'm going to Tokyo to shop after I receive my wire transfer money. He politely tells me that today is a national holiday celebrating the emperor's birthday. All the banks are closed for the holiday. That news is very disappointing to me because the following day, my R&R is over. I won't be able to make the purchases because tomorrow is a travel day. My main reasons for taking R&R to Japan was to visit Larry Boneck and to shop for cameras and electronic equipment. What a bummer! On the plus side of the trip, I met some great guys and thoroughly enjoyed myself. We stay in the hotel, play cards, drink, and socialize because the national holiday put a damper on our routine.

The next day the guys say their good-byes. Jack says he is going to stay a while longer, even though his R&R is up. I wish him good luck in not getting punished for being AWOL. I know my unit will miss me if I don't show up on time. The trip back to Vietnam is depressing. I understand how Jack wants a few more days of freedom to enjoy the civilian life. The transition from civilian life to a combat situation is difficult.

I can see I'll have trouble returning to life in the States, especially with the anti-Vietnam veteran perception of soldiers as drug addicts and baby killers. Even though we dress as civilians in Japan, we socialize as soldiers because of the fear and apprehension the Japanese people have of Vietnam veterans. The R&R gives me some insight of how much I have changed emotionally and what I perceive as my new values in life. My values are not those of the average American, but I realize change will be required to adjust to what I believe is society's insane way of life. When a soldier is in combat, he is forced to inflict pain and suffering on the enemy, and indirectly the civilian population is hurt in the process. I have become an understanding person and am sympathetic to the needy, oppressed, and those less fortunate than I am. Now I find it quite difficult to understand why people who are blessed with a good life can be so cruel and heartless to family, friends, and neighbors. The more one has in life, the greedier that individual becomes at the expense of others. War has given me a perspective of what is important in life. I know I will be a happy and content person when I have the opportunity to change. Somehow I have to conform to society yet keep the strong feelings of compassion and love for my fellow man.

When returning to my base camp, I decide to make an effort to get a job in division headquarters in Dong Tam, Vietnam. I enjoyed the civilian life in Japan so much that I would love to get a permanent job off the line. I make several inquiries to the administrative office of the Ninth Division In-Country Training Program. I walk in the office and immediately meet with an officer in charge. I explain my qualifications as an infantryman and pointman. I emphasize my extensive experience with booby traps and explosives. I find it rather easy to sell myself to this base camp officer. He states they will take me as a trainer but I will need approval from my company headquarters to change my assignment. I ask him to give me a letter I can take to my company commander requesting my much-needed skills and experience for in-country training at the battalion base camp. The officer says the division has a policy to not interfere with battalion procedures and staffing requirements. Again he states if I get approval of reassignment from my company headquarters, they will slot me in a training position. I thank the officer and leave, knowing this will never happen. Delta Company is short on men. If I request reassignment, it will land on deaf ears.

On May 1, I arrive back in my company area around 1700 hours. The guys and I converse about my trip to Japan. Big Lou and a few of the other Begoni Clan gave me money to buy camera lenses in Japan. They are disappointed to find out I wasn't permitted to take a large sum of cash on R&R. None of us was aware of this policy. I tell them that luck was on my side when I returned to retrieve the money from the airport

---

safe. I asked for my envelope and was given an envelope with the name Milliken. I opened the envelope, which contained only a small amount of money. I started to complain to the officer in charge when another GI approached me. The guy stated, "I believe I was given your envelope by mistake." I looked at the envelope with the name Milliken inscribed. What a coincidence: two Millikens put cash in the same safe while on R&R. He introduced himself as Bill Milliken. I thanked him for being so honest and told him this cash was given to me by platoon members. I would have had to repay them. Thank God Bill returned the cash because no one would have believed me about the loss.

The guys are pleased to learn I stopped in Tan An to make a liquor run before returning to base camp. I purchased two bottles of Chivas Regal and two bottles of other liquors. Since Larry Sandage is our only source for hard liquor, we have a policy for those returning on R&R to make a purchase for the guys. Our drinking will be postponed for another night since we are leaving for the field at 1900 hours. I tell the guys I saw our former platoon member, Curtis Dix, pulling road security on an armed jeep at the intersection of Route 4 to Saigon and the main road to Tan Tru. Dixie sends his best to everyone.

It is now 2100 hours and our platoon is in a small firefight. Damn! I have been back only four hours and shit hits the fan like I never left. Even though I experienced the soft, comfortable life for a few days, I find it easy to switch gears and be a combat soldier again. The guys inform me that Delta Company registered fifty-eight enemy kills in the month of April. Hopefully, the monsoon season is approaching and the fighting will subside.

We sweep the area the next morning but do not find any signs of casualties from last night's encounter. The day is spent in the field doing routine search-and-destroy maneuvers. The platoon is rewarded with an early return to base camp.

On our return to the company area, Specialist Hicks delivers the mail to the Third Platoon. I have a week's worth of mail and newspapers to read. I get a bottle of Chivas out of my locker to pass around while I read the mail. I have six letters from family and friends. My mother states she enjoys her new color television as she did in a previous letter. She says the color is very vivid, which is much different from my parents' old black-and-white TV. I'm pleased she has something to enjoy that might take her mind off my being in Vietnam.

While reading the *Daily Local News*, I come across a picture of me taken by Larry Sandage. Larry is outside the barracks with Bo having a beer. I summon him to show him the picture and thank him for making me a hometown legend. He laughs and says, "You're far from being a legend." I ask for the Chivas Regal to give Larry a glass of his favorite liquor. I tell him to stop back tomorrow night when the platoon will share another bottle.

Jim Milliken takes a rest break. (Photo appeared in Daily Local News, West Chester, PA)

Tonight our company club is offering a case of soda for the highest rat body count for the month of May. This is a takeoff on how command sometimes rewards GIs for enemy body and weapons count. Many guys stay up to participate in the first rat hunt. The next morning I view a small pile of rats near our barracks from last night's outing. I hear a few guys got serious about the hunt and were up to 0400 hours trying to bag a kill. Times must be boring when one resorts to killing rats as a source of entertainment.

Today rumors spread throughout the battalion that the Ninth Division may be a part of a massive plan to try to liberate prisoners of war who are held in many locations by the North Vietnamese Army. I hope these rumors are true because I would love to be a part of this mission. Supposedly, the army plans to attack all known or suspected locations at the same time. The attacks will utilize airborne troops with Cobra attack helicopter and jet support. Since we fly on a daily basis, our unit will probably be involved.

Everyone in base camp has heard the rumors. I learn that even cooks and support personnel want to be included in the raids. This is a mission that should be approved, regardless of the casualties that might occur. The services owe it to the captured men to make a supreme effort to release them from their bondage and suffering. This would be the best morale booster for all the troops in the Vietnam Theater. I hope higher command has the balls to execute this innovative plan, which has never been done on such a large scale. If it comes to flying into downtown Hanoi on such a mission, I will volunteer.

Today we receive our Vietnam yearbooks, which are published by a Japanese company. The yearbooks are much better than I expected. The yearbook begins with the battalion headquarters group and its support staff. The five companies are represented, followed by the recon platoon. The yearbook has almost everyone's individual picture, with many group photographs taken in base camp or out in the field. The best part of the yearbook is a listing of names and addresses of those photographed. Someday this yearbook will be a prized possession of mine.

SSG Gary Abrams takes over the position as platoon sergeant from Bo Senical. No one is more deserving than Bo to get a good job when off the line. He has been taking too many risks lately for a man who has done more than his share for the platoon. Since Doug Taylor's death, Bo hasn't been the same. Fortunately, the Third Platoon has incurred very few deaths; however, Bo gets depressed with the loss of a good man.

Sergeant Abrams reminds me a lot of Bo. In physical appearance they are both good-looking tall men who are in great shape. Mentally they both exude confidence and are skillful performing their jobs. As leaders they are open to suggestions and comments from their men. So far, Gary Abrams has performed well as a newcomer filling the shoes of Bo, whom I consider the best soldier in the Third Platoon. I like working with Gary because he asks for my input and respects my opinion. He seems to gather information before making decisions. Bo has tutored Gary about the Third Platoon because he already has a sense of trust that the men are well qualified in their fighting skills. Gary doesn't tell us how to do a task but merely gives the order to execute. Usually, new leaders want to monitor every detail of an assignment. My fear of losing a good leader like Bo has been tempered with the addition of Gary in command.

LToR Demolition expert Tim Firestone, Platoon Sergeant Gary Abrams and RTO Richard Coons.

16

Monsoon Season Begins

Today the Third Platoon has joint operations with the First Platoon. The platoons will be performing the same search-and-destroy mission but with a larger number of men working as a team. Soon after being airborne, a spotter plane locates a suspected enemy target. A gunship fires at the Vietcong as we enter for a landing. The landing zone where the lead chopper approaches near the target area appears too small to accommodate eight choppers. Confusion occurs when the pilots realize the size of the LZ. A safe insertion by all these choppers is questionable. A few choppers land while others begin to hover. Immediately command makes the decision for four of the Hueys to land and engage the VC while the other four look for another suitable landing area. Our chopper is hovering before departing the hot LZ with three other Hueys. The Hueys fly over a small group of hootches and land in a nearby field.

After we disembark the choppers, there is more confusion because the choppers land out of order, which creates a breakup of both platoons. Pete and the leadership of the Third Platoon land on the other side of the village, while remnants of the Third Platoon land in the second LZ. The First Platoon leader is missing his pointmen, who are with Pete's group. I volunteer to walk point with their tiger scout of the First Platoon. The leaders of both platoons radio back and forth to form a plan of action. The platoon leaders decide Pete's group will sweep toward the village and try to flush the VC out of hiding positions, while our group will act as a blocking force.

I get my orders to move toward the small village to create a blocking force near a tiny stream on our side of the village. As I move out, sporadic gunfire is heard from the advancing troops. When I get close to the village, I tell the first lieutenant of our group to hold the men on line in concealment while his tiger scout and I get closer for a better assessment of the situation. The tiger scout and I move closer in a crouched stance; then we begin to low crawl to a natural rise in the ground for a good view of the village. We lie in the position for about five minutes, listening to our forces getting closer.

Then I see a Vietcong run out of a hootch about thirty meters directly in front of us. The VC is carrying an AK-47 and is running in our direction. I wait a short time to see if any more Vietcong expose themselves before I begin firing. I rise to a crouched position and take aim at the fleeing soldier. Just as I'm about to pull the trigger, the soldier sees me aiming at him and throws his AK-47 about six feet in the air, holding his arms in an upright-stretch position to surrender. He surrenders so fast that I ease off the trigger and motion for him to advance toward our position. While the VC wades across the small stream toward us, we take cover lying in a prone position. The soldier keeps his arms in a raised position while walking in our direction. We continue to look for other signs of enemy that may try to fire on our position while we're taking this prisoner.

The Vietcong soldier arrives at our position. I grab him and throw him to the ground next to us, keeping my M16 aimed at him while the tiger scout frisks him for additional weapons. I shake my head in disbelief because this soldier is no more than fourteen to fifteen years old. The poor kid is shaking uncontrollably and probably believes we plan to kill or torture him. I pat him on the back and try to assure him in a low, calm voice that he is safe. He continues shaking, so I get some candy from my web gear pouch as an offering of peace and friendship. The candy brings a smile to his face, and I see he begins to trust me. I motion for the tiger scout to hold this position while I escort the prisoner back to the First Platoon leader for questioning. I wait while Francis Wolford of the First Platoon questions the prisoner. Wolford is a native of Guam and speaks a little Vietnamese. To my surprise, the young man is very cooperative and gives Wolford valuable information.

Wolford tells us the boy was forced by a Vietcong soldier to join the VC ranks after repeated threats to his and his family's lives. The boy says a person is in a bunker awaiting the arrival of the sweeping American force. He is planning an ambush; then he will exit the area after a few kills. The boy is emphatic that the man will never be taken alive. He says the Vietcong soldier has been a hard-core soldier for many years. The prisoner told Wolford where a machine gun is buried with military supplies.

The First Platoon leader calls Pete to inform him of the potential problem with the hiding Vietcong soldier. He requests Pete's men to make a lot of noise when they approach the village. Hopefully, the noise will alert and expose the concealed soldier. They continue to debrief the prisoner while I move to my original position, which is manned by the tiger scout.

I low crawl to the tiger scout and decide we should low crawl to our left flank where both of us will have a better view of someone hiding in the vegetation. Another reason I decide to change our location is because the soldier may have seen us take the young boy prisoner, which would give him a general knowledge of our bearings. I try to communicate with the tiger scout using hand signals to let him know of my plan of action. Many of our tiger scouts understand English, but this scout seems to understand only hand gestures. I hate to play pantomime in a war situation. At least he is reacting in the correct way by intensely looking ahead for movement while keeping quiet.

Ten minutes pass as the troops enter the other side of the village. They make a lot of noise. Normally, the men move in a fast, quiet manner. In a thick dark green foliated area, I notice what appears to be a small patch of skin. The skin looks like a part of someone's leg. I get the attention of the tiger scout and point to my observation in the undergrowth. I ask him, "VC? VC?" He responds by nodding his head before he says, "VC." I find it difficult to understand the scout. Is he just agreeing with me for the sake of agreement, or does he actually believe this is a Vietcong target? I hate to shoot at something when I'm not certain about my target. I have no choice but to shoot before I lose my chance. Too much is riding on my killing this VC before he kills one of our men. I take careful aim where I believe the trunk of the body to be. I fire one shot and see the flesh appear to go limp. I commence firing more rounds at the target area. I can still see the flesh, but there is no movement. Hopefully, I shot the Vietcong soldier and not another GI out of position.

I move back to the Platoon leader to inform him of the possible kill and location of the body. He calls Pete and gives the location of the suspected enemy kill. The advancing troops search for the body while our men provide cover. I return to my position and await the arrival of the troops. I see guys move near the body and hear the good word. Someone yells out, "The dead gook is over here."

Our groups have linked up, so we rise from our blocking-force positions and join the sweeping team of men. I refrain from viewing the dead soldier, but one of the First Platoon guys tells me the Vietcong was armed with an AK-47 and had a few other weapons in his bunker. He made one fatal mistake of exposing his skin in the jungle vegetation. If he would have had black pajamas on or wore camouflaged pants, I would have never noticed him.

The information from the prisoner turned out to be very valuable in possibly saving a life. The machine gun and supplies are dug up in the location pinpointed by the prisoner. The POW is transported back to command for further interrogation. Hopefully, the intelligence personnel will be easy on him because of his age and because he has been very cooperative during our questioning of him for pertinent information. If the intelligence people are smart, they should offer the kid a piece of candy. The men regroup into their original platoons before the choppers pick us up for our next LZ.

In the evening we return to base camp for dinner and the night off. Larry Sandage drops by for our party, and I get the remaining liquor out of my locker for our nightly celebration. Big Lou is already strumming his guitar, and the guys wait for their nightly treat of booze. Most of us can now drink quite a few beers without being impaired to a great degree. I know my alcohol consumption has increased considerably, which could be a concern in civilian life. Unfortunately, drinking is a way of life for a combat soldier. I actually look forward to two or three beers when we get back from the field.

Gary Abrams stops by to talk with me. He says I have been recommended for promotion to sergeant. That good news catches me off guard because only three months ago, I was promoted to a specialist four. The extra money will finance my military leave to Australia later in the year. Gary says it will take four to six weeks before the promotion is finalized, but the pay will be retroactive to the date of the recommendation. He says I will be a team leader and will get more assignments in a leadership role. I welcome the change in my platoon status and appreciate his confidence in me. Gary asks me if I would be willing to take a platoon out in combat operations. He states our company is in need of officers and qualified men in leadership roles.

I'm very surprised he asks me if I'll consider being an acting platoon sergeant. Gary must have already talked to higher command about this possibility. Gary explains that I will be required to serve only an additional month on the line in the leadership role before command will reward me with a cushy job around base camp for the remainder of my tour. I reply by saying, "The possibility of my taking a platoon out is remote because I will take on the responsibility only if I were promoted to staff sergeant. I will not take on the responsibility of a staff sergeant and be paid at a lesser job of sergeant." Gary says, "I understand how you feel. What we can do is put you in for staff sergeant the day your orders come in for sergeant." I say, "Okay, that sounds great to me. If I'm put in for staff sergeant, I will take on those responsibilities immediately."

I inform Gary the only part of the job I feel unskilled at is calling in artillery and communicating with command. I express the need for additional instruction and practice to feel confident in performing these functions. He assures me that I'll receive the necessary training for the position because he is mentored by Bo Senical even though he graduated from the Army NCO School. Gary shakes my hand and leaves. I feel honored that he considers me a worthy candidate for platoon sergeant. When the time comes, hopefully, Gary will recommend me for the position.

The monsoon season has begun. It now rains on a daily basis but only for short periods. I have been told when the season gets into full swing, the weather becomes unbearable. Already the troops are bitching about the increase in the mosquito population. Later in the season, the mud becomes an infantryman's nightmare. Presently it is showering and providing a cool, refreshing breeze. Our platoon should experience more downtime in the future because of bad weather conditions. The platoon will probably spend more time walking and taking boats to the field instead of relying on the Hueys for transportation.

Today is May 8, and the Third Platoon enjoys another no-contact day in the field. The company body count is posted periodically. The last time I stopped by company headquarters on May 5, the enemy body count was ten. Since that date, Delta Company has had little contact with the enemy. When one feels the situation is getting better, all hell breaks loose. I expect a major confrontation in the near future because of the

—

recent inactivity in the field. I try to be optimistic about the future days ahead, but the reality of war gives me a pessimistic attitude. I have been in the country almost six months and expect better days ahead; however, I find the need to bear down with resolve and get tougher to cope with the continuing stress of combat and the harsh life.

We return to base camp for chow. At 2000 hours we hook up with a Tango boat that transports us to our nighttime mission. Thank God I am no longer the first one to depart the boat at night. All the other members of the platoon leave the boat before I exit as part of rear security for the platoon. After we disembark the craft, a gentle rain begins. We spend an hour tromping through wet paddies until the pointmen find a suitable place to set up for the night. I am prepared for tonight because I brought a poncho to shield my body against the rain and damp, chilly air.

I lie on the ground with the poncho pulled over my head, which serves as a makeshift blanket. I doze off and waken to rain dancing on my face. My poncho has been taken off me by my buddy Gary Reitan. I try to grab the poncho from him, but he has it wrapped around him. While I push and shove Gary to retrieve my poncho, he moans with displeasure. Finally, I get his attention by saying, "Piggy, you took my poncho!" He responds to his nickname and gives the poncho back to me. I don't have the heart to leave him exposed to the elements, so I ask Piggy if he wants to get underneath the poncho with me. It turns out to be a smart move on our part because our bodies keep us warm under the protective poncho liner.

The next day I go for my scheduled dental visit with the battalion dentist. He cleans my teeth and then gives me the bad news about my teeth after a thorough examination. I know my teeth need repair work because I had sections of three teeth broken off from being hit in the face. He informs me I have many cavities in addition to my chipped teeth. The dentist schedules me for work to begin the following week. This is the first dental appointment I've had in over two years. My mouth is a mess, which is no surprise to me because of the abuse I have given my teeth in the last six months. I have enjoyed a daily sugar habit of candy, soda, and beer. Rarely do I brush my teeth because our platoon spends so much time in the field. When the platoon went on Bush Masters, I went for days without brushing. I developed an attitude to be more concerned about my life than my teeth. I feel my teeth can always be replaced but

—

my life is a onetime deal. It seems I rationalize not performing everyday cleanliness chores because the next day may be my last.

On May 10, the entire battalion is awarded a down day from the field. The battalion doctors have treated many soldiers for trench foot problems. The men are ordered by their company headquarters to air their feet during the day by wearing sandals. There are five to ten men in our company who are not fit for duty because of severe foot infections. All of us have some degree of foot-immersion problems. My feet have developed small porous holes from constant wet exposure.

May 11 is another rainy day. The monsoon season is definitely beginning. The temperature remains hot, so my fatigues dry out quickly after a downpour. My clothing dries completely in fifteen minutes, but my canvas boots are another story. The boots dry fast, but we are constantly wading in wet paddies and fording blues. The grunts find it impossible for boots and socks to dry completely because of our unrelenting movement in and out of water. The army should devise a better boot and sock for jungle warfare.

On May 12, 1969, the Daily Staff Journal opens for S3 Section, Headquarters, Second/Sixtieth Infantry:

Time In   Incidents, Messages, Orders, Etc.

0001   Journal Opened:

0005   TOC to Bde: Co A in night locations. (JDM)

0013   ALANTIC ISLAND to TOC: Boats confirmed for insertion
            tonight.
            Pick up at 1306H for extraction. (JDS)

0245   TOC to Bde: At 0240H received 12 incoming 82MM mortar
            rounds, counter mortar fired 0243H. At 0248H incoming
            stopped. Negative casualties. All hit inside base camp.
            XS674618 tube location.

0320   TOC to Bde: D-26 leaving berm to Tan Tru. D-26 helped
            sweep area where VC were spotted.

0430	Bde to TOC: CH-47 cancelled for 1700H. (JDM)
0435	TOC to Bde: At 0430H received 3 incoming rockets (unknown size), counter mortar fired 0433H.
0455	Bde to TOC: ARVN's were going into AO BEAGLE, they have been diverted to grid XS6071.
0520	TOC to Bde: AO OHIO is clear. (JDM)
0530	COIC to TOC: Thu Thua just about overrun, gunships on station, I VC company (GRAVETT).
0530	Bde to TOC: Where Co A is located, ARVN's are moving into the area XS5071.
0635	TOC to Bde: 5 VC (BC) for SAF team XS593666.
0640	COIC to TOC: SAF team XS593666 credited with 5 VC (BC), (ROSARIO).
0705	TOC to Bde: D-26 RRF closed base camp. (JDM)
0730	COIC to TOC: Targets 3, 4, 8, 10, 11 are clear.
0830	TOC to Co B, C, D, Recon: Informed of TG Ting.
0937	TOC to Bde: Jayhawk 223 C&C on station. (JDM)
0945	Bde to TOC: AO MOUSE XS528585 road to XS517564 to XS583546 prov boundary to start. AO PYTHON XS625500 to XS627493 to north blue to start.
0950	TOC to Bde: Damage report, Co B latrine destroyed, S3 Jeep heavily damaged, shower heavily damaged, 9 flat tires, ½ of one wall in Officers club destroyed.

1000	TOC to Bde: C-16 up 1035H down 1043H XS669580, C-36 up 1050H down 1055H XS554563, Recon up 1100H down 1105H XS713563, D-36 up 1253H down 1305H XS488710, A-26 up 1302H down 1320H Tan Tru.
1000	Bde to TOC: Gunships will be delayed until 1030H. If insertions are required we may use Stogie team.
1000	Co E to TOC: Road is open.
1020	TOC to Bde: AHC on station this time. (JDM)
1135	Bde to TOC: 1 man Co A hurt leg getting off boat. Taken to 9th C Medical Tan An.
1145	TOC to Bde: 0430H attack was not rockets, it was 3 75-RR rounds.
1145	TOC to Bde: Damage report, 1 latrine destroyed, 1 shower torn up, 1 supply room for S4 destroyed, roof & TA equipment, 1 Jeep heavily damaged, 1 Jeep lightly damaged, 12 flat tires, Officers club hit corner of club (75RR) damaged wall, roof, some furniture & TV.
1210	OUTLAW to TOC: Co A, 1 VC (BC), Stogie 2 KB.
1230	TOC to S4: Trucks take 1 platoon Co C to Ben Luc at 1216H, 3 trucks to pick up Co C at Ben Luc Bridge at 1308H.
1305	TOC to Bde: Stoggie 22 picked up heat casualty and 1 wounded from Co A element.
1310	TOC to Bde: U.S. dustoff, urgent litter, XS488710, A-6, gunshot, 2 personnel, names Young, Marsh, taken to Tan An 1325H. (JDM)

1315   TOC to Bde: SAF Team got a 3 VC (BC) and 1 MG, 1 RPG 7 launcher, & 1 AK-47, XS593666, Counter parts got 2 VC (BC), 3 AK-47, 110 Chi Com grenades, 10 B-40 rockets, (Lieutenant Hunder).

1330   TOC to Bde: D-26 up 1503H down 1520H XS488710, A-36 up 1520H down 1535H Tan Tru, B-26 up 1535H down 1600H XS488710, A-16 up 1605H down 1730H XS488710.

1330   TOC to Bde: 1 urgent dustoff, gunshot wound XS488710, A-6 taken to Tan An, complete 1435H.

1350   TOC to Bde: D-26 dusted off by AHC slick. Taken to Tan An, lightly hit, XS488710, Lieutenant Patrick Tiessonniere.

1620   TOC to Bde: Co A has 7 personnel wounded or by heat, A-36, A-26, Co D has 1 person wounded. (MW)

1630   Bde to TOC: Will receive 1 AHC from Greyhound by 1730H will also receive guns. (MW)

1710   TOC to Bde: Greyhound on station. 1710 TOC to Bde: Vultures on station.

1715   TOC to Bde: C-16 up 1740H down 1744H Tan Tru, C-36 up 1747H down 1752H Tan Tru, Recon up 1750H down 1758H Tan Tru.

1830   TOC to Bde: Stogie 11, 1 VC KBA XS488710.

1830   Bde to TOC: Bn on yellow alert tonight, 2/3 on berm all night.

1855   TOC to Bde: D-6 XS488710 urgent dustoff, 2 ambulatory gunshot, LN 93, 110, taken to Tan An. Complete 1943H. The two men wounded are Daniel Driscoll and Sheridan Schwark.

1900   TOC to Bde: LOH requested 1209H to 1000H VR for R-6. (Sp4 Scaggs)

1910   Bde to TOC: Shadow 76 will be on station at 1945H. Moonshine will replace. (Lieutenant H)

1935   TOC to Bde: Dustoff urgent litter, B-6, 2 U.S. gunshot wounds, XS490705, LN 109, 124, taken to Tan An. Complete 2100H.

1940   TOC to Bde: Stogie released at 1935H. 1945 TOC to Bde: Stogie 16, 2 VC KBA XS488710.

2000   TOC to Bde: Shadow flare ship on station.

2015   TOC to Bde: Co B, 1 VC (BC), XS488710.

2020   TOC to Bde: Stogie slicks released.

2045   TOC to Bde: 2 U.S. litter gunshot wound XS488710, D-6 urgent dustoff, LN 85 taken to Tan An. Complete 2140H. *The urgent dust-off is James Milliken*[italics mine].

2100   TOC to Bde: 2045H Received 3 75RR rifle rounds, 2046H incoming ceased, negative casualties, negative damage, suspected position of RR XS671612.

2245   Bde to TOC: Target clear, AO CUB XS6371 to XS6571 north to boundary west and south to start. AO KID XS7074 to XS7274 to XS7276 to XS7076, AO FOX XS655730 to XS6963 to XS6975 to XS655750.

2250   TOC to Bde: Stingray gunship developed mechanical trouble, departing this station.

2330   TOC to Bde: Request gunships for 55 in contact area, Stingray 26, ETA 15 min.

2340   TOC to Bde: Shadow 62 on station this time.

2350   TOC to Bde: Stingray 26 on station, released at 0025H. Summary: Co A terminated 24H checkerboard operations vicinity CM XS4768 and conducted AM RIF, Co B provided local LPs and conducted AM RIF, Co C provided local APs and conducted AM RIF, Co D provided Bn & Bde AM RIF, Projected Operations: Co A will conduct training, Co B will conduct training, Co C will terminate 24 H checkerboard operations, Co D will terminate 24H checkerboard operations and commence 24H checkerboard operations.

2400   Journal Closed.

EPILOGUE

Delta Company had its first reunion in the Wisconsin Dells in 1970. The reunion was attended by about twenty veterans who were in various stages of adjusting to civilian life. Many of the men, like me, were suffering from post-traumatic stress syndrome. At that time we realized we were experiencing difficulties but were unaware of the severity or cause of our condition because there was little information about and proper treatment of post-traumatic stress disorder. I suffered for two years before I made changes to cope with my stress problems, which I still have to some degree today. Unlike many veterans, I never had bad dreams or nightmares. I was a disabled, aggressive veteran who had little fear of anyone, and that presented problems for me. I spent nine months in hospitals recovering from wounds, which provided time for my body to cope with my stress disorder. I wonder what the consequences would have been if I didn't have this crucial time to adjust to a new life.

In August of 1972, I met Linda, the love of my life. She was a beautiful, shapely blonde with flowing hair who had a contagious, enthusiastic smile. In contrast to other women I dated, she was proud of dating a Vietnam veteran. She took an interest in me by cooking for me on a regular basis and encouraging me to widen my horizons through continued education, music, sports, theater, and travel. We married in July of 1973 and purchased our first home, where we lived for ten years. In the late 1970s, Linda and I became proud parents of two daughters, Susan and Christine. During this time, I attended Widener University Graduate School to obtain my master's degree in finance, while I worked as an accountant at Sun Olin Chemical Company. Linda was a wonderful mother to our children. She left her job as a reading specialist and devoted the next seven years to nurturing and teaching our daughters. Linda returned to her teaching profession when both girls entered school and continued mentoring the girls to help them develop into well-rounded individuals, who became good musicians, athletes, and students.

Susan studied at the University of Salamanca in Spain and graduated with a bachelor's degree in English secondary education from Millersville University. She received her master's degree in TESL from West Chester University. She married Michael Lord Jr. in 2002. They currently reside in Colorado and are both teachers.

Christine received her bachelor's degree in psychology, double major in sociology, and a master's degree in social work at the University of Pittsburgh. She is a licensed clinical social worker, LCSW, who practices in Pennsylvania.

Ed Sanicki of the First Platoon organized a company reunion in St. Louis, which was attended primarily by members of the First and Second platoons. In April of 2002, I attended a Delta Company reunion in Atlanta, Georgia. Before the Atlanta reunion, Pete Wood contacted me and challenged me to locate and invite members of the Third Platoon to the reunion. The Atlanta reunion was a success! Sixty men from Delta Company attended, of which eighteen men were from the Third Platoon. In 2005, Delta Company had its third reunion in Washington, D.C. Over sixty veterans were at this reunion, with a total attendance of 115 people, including family and friends. Delta Company is forever grateful to Ed Sanicki for reuniting the men.

Since we didn't have a company reunion in 2007, Pete Wood offered his summer home in Canada for a Third Platoon reunion. All the reunions have become a bonding experience for the members of Delta Company. I write and call my brothers on a frequent basis. How fortunate I am to have such a wonderful group of men as brothers!

I retired from Sun Company in 2005 with almost thirty-eight years of service. During retirement I have pursued interests in family genealogy, writing this book, and traveling. Linda continues to work as a reading specialist and looks forward to retirement.

I have enjoyed a fulfilling life, despite major adjustments I have made because of my wounds. I would not alter anything in my life because happiness is only obtained by having a positive and optimistic outlook, even in adversity. God has blessed me and my family.

—

GLOSSARY

AC-47 gunship	A heavily armed plane with side-firing weapons primarily used on nighttime operations.
AK-47	A fully automatic 7.62 mm assault rifle used by NVA and VC.
AO	Area of operations.
APC	Track vehicle used to transport troops and supplies. Armored personnel carrier.
Article 15	A nonjudicial punishment that can be awarded for minor disciplinary offenses.
ARVN	Army of the Republic of Vietnam (South Vietnam).
AWOL	Absent without official leave, meaning to leave a post or position permission.
B-52	A long-range high-altitude US strategic jet bomber.
Barney Fife	Deputy sheriff on the Andy Griffith television show.

BC	Body count.
Bde	Abbreviation for *brigade*.
berm	A low earthen wall constructed as a defensive position on the perimeter line.
birds	Slang for helicopters.
Bobbsey Twins	Principal characters in a series of children's novels.
blade time	Flying in a Huey helicopter as logistical support.
bush hat	Australian infantry soldier's dress hat.
blue	Pertains to any moving body of water.
C&C	Command and control.
C4	A one-pound white block of plastic explosive carried by military personnel.
cache	Hiding place for enemy supplies and weapons.
Camp Zama	Location of the Army Military Hospital twenty-five miles south Tokyo, Japan.
Catch-22	A satirical historical fiction novel set during World War II. The phrase means "a no-win situation."
Charlie	Short for Victor Charlie, meaning the Vietcong.
Chi-Com	Abbreviation for Chinese Communist.
chopper	Slang for helicopter.

cluster fuck — Slang for soldiers who gather closely together in small groups.

Cobra — The AH-1G small Bell attack helicopter.

commo — Short for *communications*.

Confederate money — Paper money issued during the American Civil War by the Confederate States of America.

court-martialed — One who has been found guilty of an offense under military law by a court of military officers.

C rations — The standard packaged meals eaten in the bush.

DEROS — Date expected return from overseas.

Didi mau — Vietnamese for "go quickly," "get lost."

Donut Dollies — Nickname for American Red Cross women who entertain and give supplies to the troops.

dust-off — Medical evacuation by helicopter.

elephantiasis — Extreme enlargement and hardening of tissue especially of the legs.

EM — Abbreviation for *enlisted men*.

fire in the hole — Standard warning that an explosive detonation in a confined area is imminent.

fleshettes — Beehive-type round composed of thousands steel darts around an explosive charge.

foxhole — A shallow pit dug by a soldier for immediate refuge against fire.

Fu Manchu	A mustache with ends that hang downward toward the chin.
GCC	Grove City College.
gook	Derogatory term for a Vietcong or NVA soldier.
grenadier	Operator who fires a grenade launcher.
Grovers	Students, professors, and alumni of Grove City College.
grunt	Term used for any fighting soldier in Vietnam.
Ho Chi Minh	Vietnamese leader and first president of North Vietnam.
Ho Chi Minh Trail	Complex maze of truck routes, footpaths, and river transportation system from North to South Vietnam.
hootch	Vietnamese thatched hut or simple dwelling.
howitzer	A short cannon used to fire shells at medium velocity and with relatively high trajectories.
Huey	Nickname for the Bell UH (utility helicopter).
IG	Inspector general (inspection).
KBA	Killed by air.
KP	Kitchen police work assigned in the military dining facility.
Lai dai	Vietnamese for "come here."

Life of Riley	Popular 1950s television series. Term suggests an ideal life of prosperity and contentment.
listening post	Security detail that provides early warning to enemy in the area.
Loach	Abbreviation for Hughes OH-6 light observation helicopter.
Long An Province	Located in the lower Mekong Delta Basin south of Saigon. Area of operations for Delta Company.
Long Binh Jail	Primary military incarceration center in Vietnam.
LZ	Abbreviation for *landing zone.*
M16	Automatic 5.56 mm assault rifle used by American and ARVN forces.
M60	Light machine gun that fires one hundred rounds per minute of 7.62 mm cartridges.
M79	Single-shot grenade launcher (40 mm shell).
mad minute	Troops open fire for a short duration on a suspected enemy target (harassing fire).
mama-san	Slang for an Oriental female or elderly woman.
Medcap	Medical Civil Action Program in which US medical personnel ministered to the local population.
MEDEVAC	Abbreviation for *medical evacuation.*

Mekong Delta	Rice-producing region of South Vietnam known for the many miles of crisscrossing waterways.
moped	Low-powered motorized vehicle.
Mosquito chopper	Chopper with an aerial crane attachment used to lift disabled vehicles and move supplies.
MPC	Military payment certificate.
Nam	Slang for Vietnam.
napalm	An incendiary mixture of fatty acids and gasoline used in bombs.
NCO	A noncommissioned officer, usually a squad leader or platoon sergeant.
nipa palm	A large palm tree having long leaves often used for thatching.
no *bic*	From the Vietnamese word *biet*, meaning "to understand." "I don't understand."
NVA	North Vietnamese Army.
OCS	Officer Candidate School.
papa-san	Slang for Oriental father or elderly man.
piaster	Monetary unit of South Vietnam.
Plain of Reeds	Low flatland region subject to flooding July through December. The plain dries out January through May.
punji pit	Camouflaged hole filled with sharpened bamboo sticks smeared with excrement intended to maim the victim.

PX	Post exchange, a retail military store.
Quonset	Prefabricated portable hut having a semicircular roof of corrugated metal.
recoilless rifle	An antitank weapon that fires a 90 mm shell.
RIF	Reconnaissance in force patrol.
ringworm	Contagious skin disease characterized by a ring-shaped scaly red patch of skin.
ROK	Republic of Korea (South Korea).
RPG launcher	Enemy antitank weapon, rocket-propelled grenade.
R&R	Rest and recreation. Normally a seven-day vacation during a one-year tour.
RRF	Ready reaction force.
RTO	Radio telephone operator. The man assigned to carry the PRC-25 radio.
saki	Japanese wine made from fermented rice.
sampan	A flat-bottomed boat propelled by oars or a small motor.
shammer	Someone shirking their duty by feigning illness or incapacity.
skid	Helicopter's landing wheel.
SKS rifle	A Russian semiautomatic bolt action 7.62 mm carbine.

slicks	A Huey used primarily to transport troops.
SP package	Abbreviation for special purpose package, a box containing an assortment of candies, cigarettes, writing supplies, and other sundries.
stand-down	A unit withdrawn from action for a rest period.
striker	Hand-held instrument used to detonate claymore mines.
Tan Son Nhut	The large US air base on the outskirts of Saigon.
Tango boat	Armored troop carrier boat used by the Mobile Riverine Force.
Tet	The lunar New Year celebrated in Vietnam as a national holiday.
Third Herd	Nickname for the Third Platoon.
tiger scout	Vietcong soldiers who had defected and were integrated into American units as scouts.
TOC	Tactical Operations Center, a command ship.
tracks	Slang for armored personnel carriers. Any vehicle that moved on treads instead of wheels.
trench foot	A foot condition caused by prolonged exposure to dampness.
Tu Dia	Pronounced "too die," a booby trap sign reference to death.
USO	United Service Organizations.

VC	Vietcong.
Vietcong	An insurgent organization fighting against the Republic of South Vietnam.
Yokohama	Leading port and industrial center located in southeastern Japan.

INDEX

C

Camp Bearcat, 21–22, 75, 211
Camp Scott, 1, 24–25, 29, 37, 45,
    57–59, 67, 94, 101, 125
Camp Zama, 13, 14, 221, 227, 252
Cantrell, Keith, 94
Carson, Johnny, 77, 119
Cartigiano, Ray, 27, 51
CBS News, 201, 204
C4 (explosive), 73, 89, 98, 252
Charlie Company, 25, 29, 186
Chico (backup soldier), 129
Chieu Hoi, 105–6
Christine (author's daughter), 249–50
circle jerk, 87, 89
Cobra (helicopter), 2–3, 9, 12, 89–
    91, 120–21, 141, 146, 150, 154,
    197, 205, 235, 253
Combat Infantryman Badge, 110, 223
Connie (author's sister), 153
Cotter, Mike, 143
C rations, 56, 73, 89, 117, 168, 210, 253
Curtis, Ballard, 32, 189

D

Daily Local News, 32, 66, 77, 82,
    182, 199, 234
Daily Staff Journal, 243
Delta 3-5. *See* Senical, Bo
Delta 3-6. *See* Wood, Pete
Delta Company, vii, 2, 20, 24–26,
    29–30, 32, 34, 36, 46, 49, 53,
    56–57, 61, 72, 75–76, 94–95,
    110, 118, 125, 140, 142, 145–46,
    155, 157–58, 179, 185–86, 200,
    232–33, 241, 249–50, 255

Delta Iota Kappa, 199
Deutschlander, Tom, 27, 41–43, 62
Dinky Dau (tiger scout), 141–42
Dinsmore, John, 39–41, 44, 56, 184
Dix, Curtis, 60, 233
Dixie. *See* Dix, Curtis
Doc Brothers. *See* Brothers, David
Doc Burry (medic), 9
Doc Struzik. *See* Struzik, Joe
Dong Tam, 22–24, 66, 117, 165, 205,
    223, 232
Doobie. *See* Stancill, Delbert
Dougie. *See* Taylor, Doug
Driscoll, Dan, 11
Dulin, John, 43, 52, 94–95, 142
Dulin, Kathy, 52, 142

E

eagle flights, 28, 40, 83, 98–99, 104, 113,
    116, 120, 125, 129, 135, 141, 166
Edinger, DeWayne, 14
Ellwood City, Pa, 14, 31–32, 52,
    199, 202, 221, 230
Enlisted Men's Club, 29
Etherton, Larry, 111

F

Failes, John, 21, 211
Falkum, Bruce, x, 8–9, 49, 73, 84,
    86, 89, 119, 122, 133–34, 141,
    188, 203, 210
Field, Larry, 4
Firestone, Tim, 17, 50, 78, 99, 140, 165,
    178
First Platoon, 62–63, 65, 77, 147,
    162, 208, 237–40, 250

77–78, 81, 86–89, 94–95, 100,
107, 110, 118, 125, 135–36,
139–40, 145, 147, 149–50,
155, 157–58, 161–62, 169–70,
182–84, 186, 189, 205–8, 210–
11, 214, 219, 221, 229, 233,
235–37, 241, 250, 258
Thomas, Charles, 75
3-6. *See* Wood, Pete
Thunder Alley, 24–25
Thu Thua (outpost), 78–80, 93, 244
Tiessonniere, Patrick, 246
Timm, Barry, 25
Tinari, Phil, 111
Tonight Show, The, 119
Top. *See* Laughead, Robert
Twigg, Joe, 9–10, 63–65, 84, 149
Twiggy. *See* Twigg, Joe

V

Vance (backup soldier), 129
Vaughn, Matthew, 63, 189
VC, 35, 41, 47–48, 63, 66, 97,
120–21, 123, 125–27, 129–30,
132–34, 136–39, 144–48, 152,
156, 162–63, 167–68, 170, 172,
174–75, 180–82, 184–87, 190,
192–94, 197–99, 203–5, 215–
19, 237–39, 243–47, 251, 259
VC (dog), 145
Vietcong, 22–23, 28, 41, 47, 53,
59–61, 68, 75, 77–78, 84, 95,
97, 105, 107–8, 112–14, 116–
17, 120–23, 125–26, 132–33,
136–38, 142, 146, 148, 154–58,
160–62, 167, 170–71, 173–75,
179–82, 184, 187, 192, 196–98,

203–4, 211, 213, 218–19, 237–
40, 252, 254, 259
Vietnamese Armed Forces, 41
Vietnamese Navy, 107, 136–37
Vietnam War, x, 158, 221

W

Washington, Carl, 75
Wayne, John, 95, 197
West, Billy, 42, 46, 48, 70, 90, 92,
175, 221
Westmoreland (general), 21
Whitby (battalion sergeant major),
118
Whitey. *See* Falkum, Bruce
Widener University Graduate
School, 249
Wilber, Ivan, 187, 189
Williams, Carl, 67, 160, 189, 191
Wolfe, Leroy, 32, 39
Wolford, Francis, 238
Wood, Pete, 1, 4, 6, 10, 77, 80, 84,
89–90, 96, 126, 129, 146, 172,
174, 178, 180, 197, 205, 217, 250
Woods, Patrick, 57

Y

Youhan, Jim, 67
Young, Skip, 224. *See also*
Plumstead, Wally

266